EAST END PARADISE

Jojo Tulloh is food editor of *The Week*, and lives
in London with her family.

JOJO TULLOH

East End Paradise

kitchen garden cooking in the city

PHOTOGRAPHS BY
Jason Lowe

ENGRAVINGS BY
Andy English

VINTAGE BOOKS
London

Published by Vintage 2011

2 4 6 8 10 9 7 5 3 1

First published in Great Britain in 2009 as *Freshly Picked* by Chatto & Windus

Vintage
Random House, 20 Vauxhall Bridge Road,
London SW1V 2SA

www.vintage-books.co.uk

Addresses for companies within The Random House Group Limited can be found at: www.randomhouse.co.uk/offices.htm

The Random House Group Limited Reg. No. 954009

A CIP catalogue record for this book is available from the British Library

ISBN 9780099523598

The Random House Group Limited supports The Forest Stewardship Council (FSC), the leading international forest certification organisation. All our titles that are printed on Greenpeace approved FSC certified paper carry the FSC logo. Our paper procurement policy can be found at: www.rbooks.co.uk/environment

Printed and bound in Great Britain by
Butler Tanner and Dennis Ltd, Frome, Somerset

For Stephen with love

What wondrous life is this I lead!
Ripe apples drop about my head;
The luscious clusters of the vine
Upon my mouth do crush their wine;
The nectarine and curious peach
Into my hands themselves do reach;
Stumbling on melons, as I pass,
Ensnared with flowers, I fall on grass.

Meanwhile the mind from pleasures less
Withdraws into its happiness;
The mind, that Ocean where each kind
Does straight its own resemblance find;
Yet it creates, transcending these,
Far other worlds, and other seas;
Annihilating all that's made
To a green thought in a green shade.

Andrew Marvell – 'The Garden'

INTRODUCTION

I hear the clink of the bottles being carried to the well from
which they will be pulled up, cooled, for dinner tonight. One
of them, red-currant pink, will accompany the green melon; the other
a sand-grown wine, amber-coloured and over-generous,
goes with the salad of tomatoes, pimentos and onions soaked
in oil, and with the ripe fruit.   Colette – *Break of Day*

Everything I hope this book will be is contained within these few lines from Colette, such simple words yet so purposeful; they feed all five senses and transport you immediately to the warm South. They hold the dream of a better life, a life most city dwellers would think beyond their reach.

Most of us crave a simpler existence. A life lived in harmony with nature. A life connected to the earth and to the seasons. You can call it an earthly paradise or a bee loud glade, it's simply the pre-industrial dream we hold on to when our feet are pounding the pavements grey. Whether it's a lakeside cabin, a cottage tucked under a wooded hill or a shack on the edge of the sea, it's a place where peace drifts slowly down. A place where there would be time to pick wild berries and gather mushrooms, sow salad, dig potatoes, grow flowers, catch fish or maybe even keep bees. For almost all of us it will stay just that, a fantasy, an impracticable dream, but before we give up on it entirely there are small things we can do to weave that vision into our day-to-day life and start making pieces of the dream into reality.

Eight years ago on a grey and forbidding day in East London, I dropped my first seed potato into the sticky, wet March soil and changed the way I cook for ever. The bare, muddy strip of earth I inherited as a novice vegetable grower is almost covered now, with plum trees and artichokes, raspberry canes and rhubarb patches. Flowers self-seed and return each year, breaking up any symmetry I try to impose. The plot slides back and forth, from order to chaos and back again, the only constant the wicker basket that comes home filled to the brim with vegetables and flowers, over and over again.

With each season that has passed, kitchen and allotment have grown closer together. I cannot imagine one without the other and a look at my kitchen bears this out. During spring and summer the blue glass jug on my kitchen windowsill is full of home-grown flowers: borage and marigolds to start with, dahlias and sunflowers later on. Above the sink, sieves, whisks, saucepans and colanders hang from a rack alongside short plaits of garlic and strings of shiny red onions, bunches of dried lemon verbena and sunflower heads waiting to be broken up. Secateurs sit next to a weighing scales and a large ball of twine teeters on top of the Kenwood mixer.

When I come in and lift my heavy basket up onto the kitchen counter I feel a deep sense of satisfaction. As the dirt is washed off and the produce piles up, the cold wet mornings are forgotten. Soon small bowls of cherry tomatoes and squash blossoms sit next to a colander full of beetroot and courgettes waiting to be cleaned, there is a great jumble of knobbly potatoes next to bunches of herbs packed into brown paper bags. It may sound back to front, but growing things has made cooking easier. Fresh produce doesn't need much preparation to raise a meal above the ordinary. An omelette served with a salad of ribbed Italian tomatoes and mustard and rocket flowers can become a supper to remember; a rushed lunchtime sandwich of peppery rocket leaves, tomato, cheese and freshly picked cucumber provides a moment of pure pleasure in a busy day.

In my kitchen cupboards I store up high summer with jars of pickled cucumbers and spring onions, jellies, chutneys, cordials and marmalades; blackcurrants sleep steeping in vodka, waiting for the day they will be turned into cassis. Underneath a 1950s kitchen unit stacked high with spices, tins, noodles, pasta and rice is an old scratched Huntley and Palmer biscuit tin, filled with seeds enough for three allotments.

Cooking from the allotment means I can't help but cook seasonally. Now I pick first

and then decide what to make with it. The pressure of trying to plan what to cook is gone; the garden does it for me. Thinning spinach seedlings gives me a handful of baby spinach just enough to add to a dish of chana dhal with mint and lime. There may be only a few late broad beans left but they can be mixed with pesto and spaghetti to make lunch for two and at the other end of the scale, a glut forces me into invention as we face several meals featuring the same vegetable. This year a bumper crop of globe artichokes gave us the luxury of a frittata made entirely with their hearts. Gluts account for the large number of courgette and sorrel recipes in this book, two crops that never let me down. At other times the failure of a crop means I have much less than I expected and must come up with a way to make the most of my precious harvest.

I have to fit my garden in around my husband and three children, they eat whatever I grow and my cooking is very much uncomplicated, everyday family food. Almost every day in summer I make a simple salad of fresh herbs, peppery flowers and lettuce, eaten, as often as possible, outdoors in our postage-stamp sized garden, in high summer a jungle of bamboo and banana. For my daughters I cook clear Asian broths with greens, slices of chicken and fresh coriander, fried courgette flowers and pizzas spotted with capers. I try and revive my hard-working husband with romantic tapas and piri piri squid on the barbecue, and I make celebration dinners of chicken marinaded with preserved lemons and olives and covered in a smoky-sweet honey, tomato and paprika-heavy sauce for my friends.

My grandmother was a skilled if frugal cook with a distinctive culinary style much influenced by wartime privation. The care she took over food, and her dog-eared copy of Elizabeth David's *French Country Cooking*, first showed me what cooking and writing about food could be. These days poetry, travel books, novels and films all give me ideas. Lately, I've been inspired by the picnic Sybille Bedford packs as she sets off on a journey to Mexico and the breakfast Anaïs Nin in her diaries describes making for Henry Miller. Long before I ever knew what *affugato* was I watched Juliette Binoche tip her black coffee over a small bowl of ice cream in Kieslowski's *Three Colours: Blue*. Grief had whittled her down to the tiniest of pleasures, sipping bitter black coffee, sweetened with a teaspoon of vanilla ice cream. It soon became a favourite of my own.

Living in the heart of a city means I have access to an unprecedented number of ingredients from around the world and these provide the accents to the vegetables I grow. Behind the bright blue walls of an Athenian grocer in Queensway, near to where I work, I buy packets of pickled vine leaves, smoked cod roe and wedges of hard Greek cheeses. Back home in Hackney, I buy stiff, crackling rice papers from Vietnamese markets, loops of sausage, jars of horseradish and beetroot pickle from the Polish deli, and from the local Turkish corner shop, green almonds and sweet melons, huge bunches of herbs, big blocks of feta and crusty flat breads dotted with nigella. On Brick Lane I can breakfast on spicy sweet chai, a chilli spiked omelette and a chapatti greasy with butter. At lunchtime I walk up to the Turkish bakery on the corner for *pide*, a flatbread pizza rolled up in paper. In this way I can travel the world without ever leaving home.

To begin at the beginning

My first home in London was in a tower-block shaped like a cereal box. Each flat had a sitting room with a balcony just deep enough for a chair and a narrow window box. There was no greenery – concrete and glass stretched to the horizon, a sea of grey punctuated by four upturned chair legs, the chimneys of Battersea power station. Beneath me the traffic kept up a constant, steady roar. In desperate need of something natural, I planted the window box with leggy flowers and tall grasses and soon, as the sun went down, their graceful silhouette was all I saw. I travelled within the pages of my books, I wandered through Venetian vegetable markets at dawn with Elizabeth David. I walked beside the Pacific Ocean through endless fields of green with chef Deborah Madison. It was her atmospheric description of the farm that supplied the San Francisco restaurant, Greens, that inspired me to seek out a little plot of my own with which to feed my family and my soul.

I moved east, replaced my narrow window box with a minute garden and went in search of an allotment. The waiting list for allotments in Hackney was five years so I went looking in the neighbouring borough. The two sites in Leyton that are nearest to our home are in the shadow of Leyton Orient's football ground. On paper they are highly insalubrious – a municipal dump and waste disposal centre on one side, pylons looming on the other. On our first visit the allotments looked shabby, the sloping site seemed windy and exposed. It was February and not much was growing, apart from a few cabbages. The sheds looked tatty, cars queued up on a slip road at the end of the plot and the whole place felt neglected. It was a long way from the pastoral escape I had dreamed of. I hid my misgivings and took the tour.

The first site I saw was full of old men, rose bushes and brussels sprouts: it was traditional and pleasing in its own way but nothing compared to its neighbour. This jumble of plots had a more lawless feel; vines sprawled higgledy-piggledy over open-sided rooms complete with daybeds (and the odd sink) and barbecues rusted in the rain. Happily for me, one of the Turkish lady gardeners took a shine to me and a plot miraculously came free.

That first summer, I was rewarded with a place where I felt far away from the city without ever leaving it. Poppies self-seeded and covered my garden in a carpet of red and pink petals, globe artichokes produced head after tightly-furled green head. A small packet of meadow seeds, bought on a whim at a supermarket checkout, painted a square of wild flowers onto the first bed I sowed, an unlooked for triumph that sustained me through the blighted beans and dried-up corn. I learnt that our site is an inspiring mix of Turkish, Portuguese, West Indian and English gardeners, each with their own approach and their own vegetables. My plot may be sandwiched between a busy road, a sewage works and a dump, but its fertile soil is dark and alluvial with the texture of very rich chocolate cake.

I was given a patch next to a formidable Turkish woman called Makbala, dressed in headscarf, ankle-length dress and sandals. She was a skilled and inspiring neighbour. In her sixties but enormously strong, she worked on four plots (600 square metres of soil) as well as on mine, keeping it up for a friend until I took it on. I was lucky – bar a few weeds, my 150 square metres were in fairly good condition. All that I needed was a shed. This my husband built for me out of timber scrupulously salvaged from skips. But by the time he'd bought the clear plastic corrugated sheeting that I'd decided I had to have for a lean-to greenhouse, it ended up costing nearly as much as a ready-made shed. My sister decorated the door with a pattern of parrots and the children painted a scribble of owls and numbers on one side.

On the day I began digging, Makbala watched me for a few minutes before snatching the spade from my hand – she quickly dug more in thirty seconds than I had in five minutes. When she was satisfied that she had set me straight, she let me carry on unmolested.

One day she beckoned to me. I followed and found her crouched behind her shed. In a shallow hole she had built a fire over which she was making flatbreads. She heated a curved disc of metal over the fire pit, rolled out the dough paper-thin and then flung it across the metal for a minute or so. When the bread had coloured, she smeared it with one end of a pack of butter, crumbled over some feta from a large tin, rolled it up and gave it to me.

She was generous with her plants, too, giving me dark-leaved mints, bitter seedlings

of dandelion and chicory and chilli peppers ready for planting out. She mocked my planting schemes and raised her eyebrows at my haphazard watering, but on cold spring mornings she would sometimes bring me a small glass of hot, dark red tea and a big bag of sugar to sweeten it.

I had very little knowledge of vegetable gardening when I began. I looked across at Makbala's garden and watched how she worked and what she grew. Makbala worked in her garden every day and it showed: row after fruitful row bore witness to her husbandry and experience. She grew Sweet Williams and long green peppers, potatoes, curly bitter endives, pumpkins, purslane, sorrel and giant lines of red beans; against her vast shed she had planted vines, irises and great sheaves of gladioli. I copied what Makbala did each spring, digging the entire plot over, spreading it with muck and replanting it, starting with potatoes. I pored over complicated *potager* schemes in glossy gardening books but in the end settled for slicing my plot into five beds, divided by paths, and got on with turning the soil. It was as simple as picking up a spade and starting to dig.

I have learnt to garden in the same way I learnt to cook, with curiosity and delight standing in for experience. I am very much an enthusiastic amateur rather an expert. My battles against weeds, slugs, droughts and floods are often unsuccessful but beside the wonder and satisfaction of planting and harvesting your own food none of these trials matter and it's a wonder worth sharing. Alice B. Toklas describes it perfectly in her eponymous cookbook:

> *The first gathering in the garden in May of salads, radishes and herbs made me feel like a mother about her baby – how could anything so beautiful be mine? And this emotion of wonder filled me for each vegetable as it was gathered every year. There is nothing that is comparable to it, as satisfactory or as thrilling, as gathering the vegetables one has grown.*

BASIC INGREDIENTS

Salt is always Maldon sea salt, with flakes that grind to a fine powder pressed between finger and thumb.

Pepper is black peppercorns freshly ground. A decent pepper grinder is a good investment.

Eggs are medium sized and the best I can find. By best I mean direct from a farmer if possible. Above all they must be free-range. The same goes for chickens.

Butter is always unsalted.

Lemon juice is always freshly squeezed.

Spices are bought whole and then ground on the day of cooking. I use a dedicated electric coffee grinder but a pestle and mortar will do. I buy small amounts of whole spices and renew them yearly at the very least.

Ginger is always root, bought with a pinky blush and smooth shiny skin (not wizened). It must be kept in the fridge, peeled and grated to order.

A bunch of greens is always an approximate handful but I have small hands so very roughly 150g in weight.

Parmesan is always a block, grated as fine as you can, minutes before use.

Olive oil for cooking is just olive oil. Keep the extra virgin for salad dressings and for thin threads zigzagged over tomatoes.

Onions are shallots whenever possible, especially if the recipe requires raw onions, as they have a milder more interesting flavour, or I use bunches of spring onions with plenty of greens.

Pizza flour is OO pasta flour if you can get it but strong white bread flour will do (don't skip the semolina in the pizza recipes as the texture makes the pizzas taste like the real thing).

Meat is the best I can afford. I keep meaty meals down to three times a week and buy meat from a good independent butcher.

Chick peas can be tinned but use dried chick peas if they are to be the main attraction (they have a nuttier subtler taste and a superlative texture). In less polluted times cooks soaked their chick peas in wood ash and rain water. Using mineral water with a low calcium content makes a huge difference when cooking chick peas. Soak and cook them in Volvic and you will end up with a chick pea that cooks quicker. It will retain its shape but bursts into the smoothest purée against your palate.

Apples are always English.

HERBS AND EDIBLE FLOWERS

There is one wild, delicious corner where things grow at their own
sweet will. Flowering shrubs jostle poppies and roses, and sweet-
scented flowers tangle themselves among the grasses. It is left so at
the will of the master of the garden, whose hut stands opposite it...
For some years he has lived in it, looking on his wild patch by day
and sleeping amid its scents at night.

Minnie Pallister - *A Cabbage For a Year*

If you can grow only one thing, let it be herbs. Using fresh herbs is the single most important thing you can do to transform the quality of the food you prepare at home. Their smell alone makes them worth growing – crushed in the fingertips, the volatile oils present in the leaves release an aromatic blast that never fails to cheer and invigorate.My ideal house would have an entrance thickly overhung with scented herbs and flowers; returning home would always be uplifting no matter how bad the day had been.

A small patch of herbs mingled with night-scented flowers, planted a few yards from your back door, will please both cook and guests; the former has just a few short steps to take to snip what she needs for the evening meal, while those waiting to be fed can delight in the transporting smells. Scent is a powerful trigger for long-buried memories. The smell of crushed mint leaves recalls my grandmother and the fresh herbs we cut for her perennial lunch of salad and cold meats. Her herb garden was minimal (one marjoram bush, a few chives, a rosemary bush, some winter savory and a bit of mint) and poorly tended as she much preferred wild flowers, yet it served her well and she cut a little from it each day.

But unfortunately, however much we might long for a little patch of sunny, south-facing earth, most of us living in cities will have to make do with a few small pots on a doorstep or a window-ledge. Don't feel hard done by as even something this modest can have a powerful effect; no matter how humble your herb garden, it will make an enormous difference to the way you cook. Fresh herbs never fail to bring other ingredients to life both with appearance and taste. The pungency of freshly cut herbs teaches you so much more about which flavours work well together. Adding a little at a time will ensure you're never overwhelmed.

At its most basic your herb garden might contain a few pots containing parsley, marjoram and thyme, with chives, mint and basil in the summer. If you have the space you might aspire to a gloriously overgrown bed of herbs and flowers, lettuces and lavender, with hot-orange pot marigolds straggling through a haze of blue borage and the sharp cut-out leaves of lovage. On top of this you can add night-scented stocks and nicotiana for evening fragrance, and for contrast chives grown alongside old-fashioned pinks, and parsley with striped marigolds. If you really have nowhere to grow anything then you are probably living in the heart of the city and might be lucky enough to live near a Turkish, Greek, Indian or Middle Eastern grocery shop that will sell you huge bunches of dill, parsley, coriander and sorrel for a very reasonable sum.

Herbs can be highly decorative too. Every time my family comes with me to the allotment my elder daughter picks a beautiful bouquet of herbs, which quite often ends up in a jug on the table. This I found out recently was once a common practice when big, aromatic bouquets of marjoram, thyme, fennel, lemon balm and rue were used to sweeten the air. They make a delightful alternative or addition to cut flowers.

Once upon a time, herb women were found in every village, walking human pharmacopoeia, they sold herbs in the street and collected them for apothecaries. My own knowledge of herbs is limited to culinary uses but whether I am pounding basil to make pesto, arranging a highly scented bunch of flowers and herbs to sweeten the supper table or picking mint leaves for tea, herbs are the one part of the garden that is completely indispensable.

Essential herbs for the garden

Bay

If you don't have a bay tree, or room to grow one, keep your eyes open for one growing locally. I discovered a bay hedge on the edge of a nearby car park so whenever I need a leaf for flavouring stock or stew I just go out and pick one. There really is no comparison between fresh and dried bay leaves, and I use them most frequently in a simple *bouquet garni* tied together with a few sprigs of thyme and some parsley stalks to flavour home made chicken stock, vegetable soups or meat stews.

Basil

Fresh basil's natural partner is a wonderfully ripe tomato anointed with salt and good olive oil on a piece of soft crusty bread. Basil comes in many different forms, from large, floppy, shiny green leaves to tiny bush basil. The large kind is probably best for everyday cooking. Basil likes a sunny corner and you really need to wait for the ground to heat up before sowing direct. Otherwise it's best to start in a seed tray on a windowsill or in a greenhouse and then either pot out or keep it going on the windowsill. Before the first frosts come you can use up your crop by making a good supply of homemade pesto which can be eaten with green beans and tiny potatoes or stirred into minestrone when it's ready to serve.

Chervil

The frondlike leaves of this subtly aniseed flavoured herb are nearly as attractive as the taste. Chervil is a component part of the *fines herbes* used to flavour salads, omelettes and scrambled eggs. It does well in custards for tarts and in soups (like basil and chives it should only be added at the last moment to preserve its fresh, green appearance).

Chives

I can never have enough chives. Snipped into soups swirled with yoghurt, sprinkled over salads of beetroot and goat's cheese, or chopped into a batter with shredded courgettes for fritters, their light oniony flavour is always complementary and never insistent. Whenever you leave your garden for a week or two cut the chives right down to the ground and you will be rewarded with a lush and tender crop on your return.

Coriander

The delicate white flowers of coriander that has run to seed are a welcome sight in my garden, but I use so much that I usually have to buy it. It is essential for Indian cooking (from chick peas to curries to fresh green chutneys) but also to flavour fresh tomato salsas and salads of chilli-spiked crab, or rich dishes of black bean salsa and Spanish influenced dishes of chorizo, tomato and pumpkin.

Dill

The light aniseedy flavour of dill complements boiled potatoes for a Scandinavian inspired lunch. It can be mixed with cream and mustard to make a sauce for cured salmon, or layered with cucumbers soaked in a sweet vinegar for a salad that brims with taste and crunch. I buy huge bunches to make gravadlax (home-cured salmon) or mix it with fish and potato to make fish cakes, and crab for a fresh tasting crab cake. Layer the flowery crowns of fresh dill between brined cucumbers to make your own crunchy green dill pickles.

Fennel

A few fronds of young fennel leaf go well with crab. Fennel can also be used as an alternative to dill. Fennel bulbs can be sliced thinly with radishes to make a very good salad when dressed with lemon and oil. If fennel is braised in the same way as chicory it makes a fine partner for grilled fish or chicken.

Parsley

My kitchen counter is hardly ever without an earthenware jug full of parsley and a large bowl of lemons. I grow or buy flat-leaf parsley as I find it much tastier and less tough than the curly-leaf variety. I use the stalk to flavour stock or as part of a *bouquet garni*, while the leaves add colour to the custard in a tart and can be sprinkled into soups and over salads (tomato and sherry vinegar is particularly good) or used as the chief component in a tabbouleh. I often make a large batch of garlic and parsley butter which can be moulded into a cylinder and wrapped in cling film; slices can be cut off as needed, used to stuff mushrooms for roasting, make garlic bread or on top of a steak.

Marjoram

Fresh marjoram goes well with squash and courgettes. You can tie it into your summer *bouquets garnis*, rub it into chicken breasts for a simple marinade, mix it with oil and lemon to make *salmoriglio* (an Italian green sauce) or snip a little into your salad. You can use both the leaves and the flowers. In his indispensable book, *Simple French Food*, the cookery writer Richard Olney makes an omelette with courgette and marjoram as part of an extraordinarily elaborate tower of five different kinds of omelette, stacked together and cooked in a bain-marie – it's the sort of recipe that brings you out in a cold sweat, but the marjoram and courgette tip is a good one.

Mint

Fresh mint is so useful it is hard to know where to start: it's delicious in homemade lemonade, in tabbouleh, steeped in boiling water as mint tea, with potatoes, broad beans and peas in a salad, as mint sauce, in a simple green salad, cut up and scattered over fried courgettes seasoned with chilli and garlic, or over oranges for a Middle Eastern fruit salad.

Oregano

Dried oregano is synonymous with pizza, but this herb can be used fresh as well, particularly in tomato-based sauces. It's worth picking a large bunch in summer and hanging it up to dry in the kitchen to use over the winter as it's one herb that only really releases its scent once dried.

Savory (winter and summer)

Winter savory comes back year on year (you make new plants by dividing the old), but summer savory must be sown each spring (and has the edge on flavour). They look very similar – small green leaves on tiny twiggy stalks. The young leaves can be chopped in salads, used to flavour tomato sauces or tied with other herbs as a *bouquet garni*.

Sage

With its soft, velvety grey-green leaves and impressive spikes of blue flowers, sage is a very attractive plant to have in the herb garden. The leaves have a strong taste and, when fried, go well with squash or pumpkin risotto or soup added at the last moment. Chopped sage is excellent combined with ricotta as a flavoursome stuffing for pasta or chicken. You can make yourself a very good breakfast of sage fried eggs by frying two or three sage leaves in butter and then cracking an egg into the pan.

Tarragon

Tarragon is delicious with roast chicken (forced under the skin with butter) or used to flavour egg custards for tarts. Put a few sprigs into a bottle of white wine vinegar to make your own tarragon vinegar.

Thyme

Thyme is an essential part of my herb garden. I use it constantly whether it is stuffed inside chickens with lemon and roasted, chopped up small to flavour vegetable tarts or sprinkled over roasted squash, root vegetables, grilled meats or in soups and stews. If you have room, it is worth growing both common and lemon thyme in your garden.

Herbs to buy as plants: chives, thyme, rosemary, mint, sage, winter savory, tarragon, marjoram, oregano.

Herbs to sow yourself: parsley, basil, chervil, coriander, dill.

Edible flowers

Flowers make an unusual and very tasty addition to salads. Rocket, nasturtium or squash flowers can be added at the last moment after you have dressed the leaves.

Borage
This plant is very easy to grow (seeds can be sown directly into the ground) and has the habit of self-seeding everywhere. I don't mind this as its flowers are first to arrive on the allotment, even before the poppies, and bunches of them decorate my kitchen window-sill from early May. The stems droop alarmingly when cut but recover after a day or two. If the bed is needed for other crops the borage plants can be chopped up and dug into the soil. They make a green manure that is, according to Patience Gray, as effective as comfrey. The star-shaped blue (and sometimes pink) flowers of this vigorous plant (and borage is supposed have invigorating properties) look beautiful in lemonade or in a salad as a contrast to the hot orange and reds of the peppery nasturtium flowers. I sometimes make borage flower ice cubes by freezing an individual flower in each block of ice. The leaves can be used to flavour cream cheese (*see page 24*) and in Italy are sometimes used as a stuffing for ravioli. In England borage is most commonly found flavouring jugs of Pimms.

Hyssop
Bees love hyssop and make very good honey from visiting the tiny, dark purply-blue flowers held on top of long stems with spike-shaped leaves. Hyssop blooms add a distinctive hot note to a salad. Its use in the herb garden dates back to pre-Christian times and it was often used in medieval cookery. Not quite so common in the kitchen today it is a plant very much worth reviving. It is wonderfully aromatic if boiled to make a syrup for fresh fruit such as apricots, peaches and plums. It has a strong flavour so use it sparingly.

Boraged goat's cheese
Serves 4 as part of a picnic lunch

*5 tender borage leaves
(if you have plants that have
self-seeded from the year
before, these leaves can
be picked right through
the winter)
a mild goat's cheese or cream
cheese (about 200g)
a few borage flowers to
decorate (if in bloom)
sea salt and pepper*

Borage leaves look tough and unappetising when growing but chopped up fine they lose their hairy texture and will fleck a creamy white goat's cheese with dark slivers of emerald green. The taste is both cool and tangy, the borage hinting at cucumbers. It's delicious in summer but helpful in winter for bringing a fresh, herby taste to the table. The mild cool taste makes it a good partner for smoked fish or, in cooler weather, bean and garlic soups.

Chop the leaves finely and use a fork to blend them with the goat's cheese. Season and press down into a suitably sized ceramic pot. Decorate the plate with a few flowers if it is summertime.

Variations
Goat's cheese looks very attractive rolled in chopped herbs. Try dill, tarragon, lemon thyme or rosemary, or experiment and come up with your own mixture.

Tisanes

Fresh mint or lemon verbena leaves steeped in boiling water make the best herb infusions but fresh leaves are not available all year round, so prepare for winter by making your own tisane (dried herb tea mixture). First cut a large bunch of fresh mint or verbena from your herb garden. Wash the herbs and shake them dry. Tie the stalks together with string and hang these bunches upside down in paper bags (this stops them getting dusty) from a hook or saucepan rack in the kitchen. When the herbs are dry (two weeks should do it) strip the leaves and store them in large jam jars. Use them in the same way you would use loose tea-leaves, allowing a tablespoon of dried leaves for a medium-sized teapot.

Nettle tea
Nettle leaves can be dried in the same way to make nettle tea. Nettle has strong anti-histamine qualities making it a good tea for people who suffer from itchy skin complaints or hayfever.

Camomile tea
Camomile leaves and flowers can be first washed and then hung up to dry. To make the tea, steep the dried leaves and flowers in boiling water and then strain.

Verbena or Vervain or Verveine (*verbena officinalis*)
Also known as the holy herb, wizard's herb or enchantment herb, this can be found in herb gardens and growing wild on waste ground in Britain and has from Roman times been thought to hold magical properties. These I can't vouch for but it is supposed to aid relaxation and help with insomnia.

Lemon Verbena (*aloysia citriodora*)
Fresh leaves can be used to flavour lemonade and jellies or for a refreshing lemony tea. In winter dried leaves can be used to make tea, as above. It should not be confused with the common hardy perennial Lemon Balm or with *verbena officinalis* (above).

Blackcurrant leaf tea
Dried blackcurrant leaves can be added to a pot of Indian tea. The taste is similar to that of green tea.

SPRING

I N SOME WAYS, the very end of winter and the beginning of spring is my favourite time of year in the vegetable garden. At first glance there is nothing much to see, but when you look a little closer you can spot tightly-furled green buds on fruit bushes, downy buds on apple trees, spikes of garlic and a few stubby wrinkled rhubarb shoots standing out crimson and green against the damp dark earth. The earth is slowly warming up but weeds are still dormant. Expectation is everywhere, possibilities seem limitless and so far nothing has happened to check my dreams of a garden more bounteous than any other year.

GROWING SALAD POTATOES

As potatoes are available in every supermarket, what is the point of growing them? To find out why, you must first find yourself a home-grown, freshly dug and boiled waxy potato and eat it with butter and salt. You'll never ask again – nothing can match its flavour.

For me, the pleasure of harvesting and then eating the first potatoes of the year is one of the high points of allotment life. As I push the fork beneath the plant and pull up to reveal golden or dark-pink tubers dusted with soil it is as if I am uncovering buried treasure. I usually manage to fork a fair number of potatoes as I go along the row. My record is one potato on each prong of the fork. Before I dug potatoes I had no idea that I could be as clumsy underground as I am overground.

I have had most return from growing waxy, thin-skinned salad potatoes such as the yellow Charlotte, the extraordinarily knobbly Pink Fir Apple (an old English variety) or the dark red-skinned French varieties Red Laure and Roseval, all of which have a very good flavour and can be eaten simply with butter and chives, peeling or not as you prefer. The skin of a freshly picked potato will rub away with only the slightest pressure from your thumb or when scraped with a sharp knife under running water. Later on when they are older, I peel off the papery skins after cooking.

Chitting
Gardening magazines and books will encourage you to 'chit' your potatoes. The instruction is to place them in a light, unheated room so that shoots form. There may be people living in cities with large, spare, unheated rooms in which to spread out kilos of potatoes, but I am not one of them. I noticed that the two Portuguese sisters to my

left at the allotment never bother to chit. They just cut their seed potatoes in half and plant them resting on cabbage leaves and peelings and they always pull in a monstrous harvest. Last year I didn't chit either and it made no difference at all.

Growing

I usually aim to plant my potatoes towards the second half of March, but you can do it up until the end of April. If you choose the right kind of day, when the earth is damp but not sticky, planting potatoes is an extremely satisfying job. Depending on how energetic you are feeling, you can either dig a trench about 10-15cm deep or simply make holes with your trowel at the same depth. I make a trench, first putting a plank on the ground to stand on so as not to compress the earth (it also helps to keep me digging in a straight line). The dark alluvial soil of the allotment is a joy to dig, the spade's blade slips in straight, compressing the earth behind and giving it a sheen. At the bottom of the trench each seed potato rests on a wet sticky blob of well-rotted manure (from the Hackney City Farm), the loose earth is then drawn back over like a crumbling coverlet. I leave roughly 40cm between each plant and 60cm between each row. The last few rows always feel like hard work but walking away leaving eight rows of sleeping tubers in the ground gives me the same feeling I used to get as a child, shaking a full piggy bank.

As the plants begin to grow, you should draw up the soil around them. This prevents too much exposure to light, which will turn the tubers green and poisonous, and supports the young plant. Potatoes like a lot of water – give them a really good drenching once a week rather than a desultory sprinkling several times a week.

Planting potatoes without a garden

Even if you don't have space to grow them directly in the earth, you can always try growing potatoes in bags of compost with holes poked into the bottom of the bag to allow drainage or by making a simple raised bed by stacking old car tyres, one on top of the other. The high-rise tyre method of planting is ideal for those with very limited space. Just plant a potato in the bottom of the middle tyre, fill it up with soil and when the shoots appear, add another tyre, some more soil and plant another potato on top. In this way potato plants can be grown one on top of each other in a stack of tyres. My daughter's primary school class successfully grew potatoes, using this method, on the concrete outside the door of their classroom.

Harvesting

By June you should be able to start harvesting your potatoes. Charlotte will be ready first (from June), Pink Fir a little later (end of August), as it's a main crop rather than an early. If you need to clear the space for follow-on crops, a variety classified as early (quick growing) or second early is probably best for you. To store my potatoes I buy very large surplus coffee sacks from the Monmouth Coffee Company (£1 each) that I air out in my shed ready for harvest. Potatoes that are kept somewhere cool and dark should last well into the winter. (Coffee sacks can also be laid on the ground in spring and used to warm up the ground, suppress weeds and keep in moisture. This year, I planted fruit trees and surrounded them with hemp mulch mats. Thinking along the same lines I cut some of my coffee sacks into squares to put round courgettes and squashes, both to act as a mulch and to help keep them slug free.)

Potato recipes

In this book, recipes for specific vegetables are given in the season in which they are harvested so potatoes are in the Summer section.

BOULESTIN'S GARDEN

The ways of cooking were very primitive; that is to say they were
perfect and gave results which I did not appreciate enough then, and
which we try now, often in vain, to imitate.

X. Marcel Boulestin – *My Two Countries*

The idea that eating food made with just a few home-grown or locally procured ingredients can be a very fine thing is nothing new. X. Marcel Boulestin (1878–1943) was promoting his own kind of pared down, seasonal cookery long before most of us were born. Boulestin was an entirely unpretentious French cookery writer who sought, in his witty, unpatronising way, to help English men and women achieve the 'excellence, simplicity and cheapness' of French bourgeois cookery. As a columnist in the *Evening Standard*, writing in the 1920s, Boulestin was able to reach everyone from society hostesses to those cooking on a one-ring burner in a bedsit. He championed straightforward, elegant cooking in a way that made everyone feel capable. The roots of his approach lie in his childhood. In his biography he describes his family's garden, a garden that for him 'symbolized more than anything else French country life and the threshold of summer itself'. It was a wild, unkempt, garden with 'fruit trees among the flowers, here a pear tree, there a currant bush, so that one could either smell a rose, crush a verbena leaf or eat a fruit'; it had borders of box, 'but also of sorrel and chibol; and the stiff battalion of leeks, shallots and garlic, the delicate pale green foliage of the carrot, the aggressive steel grey leaves of the artichokes, the rows of lettuce which always ran to seed all too quickly'.

Boulestin's recipes seldom run to more than four ingredients, often less. Whether he is writing about the suitability of pairing fresh watercress with roast chicken or describing a soup of peas flavoured with sorrel and chervil, his recipes have that rare and praiseworthy quality of being both immediately appealing and thoroughly achievable. Boulestin's recipes are a model of good cookery writing; he stands in a long line of writer-cooks who came into the kitchen through a shared delight in food and who learnt from experience rather than from professional training. It is from him and those illustrious writer-cooks Elizabeth David, Richard Olney, Patience Gray and Alice Waters that I learnt how to cook and whose path I aspire to follow.

SPRING FOOD FROM THE VEGETABLE GARDEN

The wrong kind of sorrel

With the bright taste of lemons caught in each of its tender green leaves, sorrel is the acid drop of the vegetable plot. Beautiful, tasty and resilient, it is a most versatile and prolific crop; I make sure that I never leave my garden without having first stooped to pick a small sheaf of its leaves and I am not alone in my love of sorrel. That most august of lettuce lovers, John Evelyn, notes in his *Discourse on Sallets* (written in 1699) that sorrel is 'never to be excluded' from his salad garden.

There are 'divers kinds' of sorrel according to Evelyn but the two most often grown are the common garden variety *rumex acetosa*, which has long spear-shaped leaves, and the tender southern European variety *rumex scutatus*, also known as French or buckler-leaved sorrel (a buckler was a small parrying shield). The more common kind, *rumex acetosa*, grows wild in England (ardent foragers take note) but as the leaves get bigger it can be a little tough and most vegetable books advise you to grow the smaller buckler-leaved variety. Although, intriguingly, Evelyn also singles out a Greenlandic sorrel for special praise:

> *… the best is of Green-land: by nature cold, abstersive, acid, sharpning appetite, asswages heat, cools the liver, strengthens the heart; is an antiscorbutic, resisting putrefecation and imparting so grateful a quickness to the rest, as supplies the want of orange, limon, and other omphacia.*

It doesn't really matter which kind you grow as even the supposedly inferior variety is a fine friend to have in the garden. So strive for *scutatus* but don't despair if you end up with *acetosa*.

Growing

When I got my 150 metre square plot in February 2002, I had the fiery enthusiasm of a new convert. Fierce winds and grey skies did not deter me and the entire plot was dug over and ready for sowing by March. A seductive description of 'ribbons of sorrel' in a vegetarian cookbook meant that sorrel was one of the very first things I planted. It was part of a patchwork bed of roots and greens. That first bed, I am not ashamed to admit, was inspired by a magazine spread of a vegetable plot split up into squares (winsomely divided by little wicker hurdles). Aside from the fact that it looked so pretty, always a good place to start, there are sound reasons for planting like this: the more diverse your planting, the less likely disease is to strike. In my 12 squares (each measuring 1m by 1m) I planted blocks of spinach, chard, parsley, beetroot, a mixture of meadow flowers and carrot (I had read somewhere that the latter was a good way of avoiding carrot fly – it also turned out to be a good way of growing very small carrots) and some sorrel.

This first sowing of large French sorrel has kept me going for six years. Sorrel grows almost in spite of me: it can be ignored, I can forget to water, it can withstand cold and heat. It likes sun but will tolerate shade and this makes it ideal for city gardeners with less than ideal plots. In summer the plant sends up tall spikes, each holding thousands of tiny flake-like pink and green petals, like bushels of confetti. You are supposed to cut down the flowering spikes to make the leaves grow but I can never bear to and usually I am rewarded with some self-sown seedlings. If no seedlings appear I just divide existing plants and replant in a different place – every three years is often enough.

In this way I have kept myself constantly supplied with sorrel, which is a good thing because as you will see I adore it. It is a most uncomplaining companion, growing abundantly throughout the summer, surviving attack by snails and slugs and growing on through most of the winter. Its long growing season encourages you to think of endless new ways to use it in the kitchen. Even in the dog days of winter when the ground is stony with cold and only the tiniest stubs of new rhubarb are showing, the sorrel patch is still productive; a welcome precursor of the fresh tasting salad leaves the summer months will bring. It is best to pick the leaves when they are young and tender; if they are the size of a dock leaf they are too tough.

Cooking

It amazes me that, although Evelyn made special note of it more than 300 years ago, sorrel is still a relatively obscure leaf. One reason for its lack of popularity could be the rather sludgy dirty green colour it turns when cooked. The best way to get round this is either to use it raw (I slice the sorrel into ribbons and add it to an everyday green salad with rocket and dandelion chicory also known as catalogna lettuce) or sprinkle them over a potato salad dressed with vinaigrette. To use it cooked, you can stir it into soups or dhals to conceal its colour or hide it in a gratin between layers of potato where only its flavour will stand out. By adding it to soups at the last minute you can preserve its bright colour.

Like rhubarb, sorrel contains oxalic acid, and should not be eaten by those suffering from kidney complaints or rheumatoid arthritis. If you can't eat sorrel or have trouble getting hold of it, there is a list of alternative greens for each recipe given at the end of this section.

Avgolemono soup with sorrel and orzo
Serves 4

1.5 litres homemade chicken stock (see Basics, page 276)
50g orzo (Greek grain-shaped pasta); use basmati rice if you can't get hold of orzo
3 egg yolks
juice of 1 lemon (taste and add more if lemon is small)
a handful of sorrel, destalked and cut into ribbons
a handful of chives or spring onion tops, sliced into thin slivers
sea salt and pepper

Avgolemono is a Greek sauce of stock thickened with egg yolks and flavoured with lemon juice. When thinned with chicken stock, it makes a very good soup with a clean, sharp sophisticated taste that entirely belies the ease of its preparation. Its powers of restoration make it especially excellent for anyone on the mend. Orzo is a small rice-shaped pasta sometimes called *krithiraki* and can be bought in Greek or Cypriot grocers. It takes a little longer to cook than you might like so if you're in a hurry to eat, leave it out and add a toasted sourdough crust to the bottom of each bowl instead. Green garlic, spring onions, onion tops or chives can be added, if available.

In a heavy-bottomed saucepan heat the chicken stock until it is just boiling and add the pasta or rice. Simmer gently until the pasta is cooked (approx. 12–13 minutes).

In a bowl, whisk together the egg yolks and the lemon juice. Take a cup of hot stock and whisk into the egg and lemon mixture. When it is well mixed, add to the pan and simmer for 5 minutes. Taste and adjust the seasoning. Remove from the heat and add the greens. Serve immediately.

Pizza with sorrel, Taleggio and an egg
Makes 2 medium-sized pizzas (enough for 2 people)

1 x quantity pizza dough (see
Basics, page 274)
a handful of semolina
(optional)

for the topping
150g Taleggio (if you can't
find this strong tasting
creamy white cheese
use Mozzarella)
25g Parmesan
olive oil
2 large free-range eggs
a bunch of baby sorrel
leaves, washed, dried and cut
into ribbons (and a few
rocket flowers if available)
a handful of chives, chopped
finely
sea salt and pepper

Pizzas made with super-fine OO pasta flour are very fine, very crispy and very thin affairs. Just make sure you get your oven as hot as you can. This recipe is a bastardisation of Pizza Fiorentina – pizza cooked with spinach and an egg – but with fresh sorrel standing in for the spinach. The lemony bite of the sorrel works well against the creaminess of the cheese but don't put it on until the last possible moment or the heat from the pizza will wilt the sorrel and make it go a revolting grey-green. If you don't have sorrel, tender young rocket or mustard leaves are a good alternative.

Make one quantity of pizza dough *(for instructions see Basics, page 274)*

While the dough is rising, grate the Parmesan and chop the Taleggio into slices about ½cm thick and 2cm wide. Preheat your oven to 250°C/gas mark 10, or its highest setting.

Get two large baking trays and cover them with baking parchment or sprinkle the trays with semolina.

Flour your work surface and, either using your hand or a rolling pin, flatten the dough out into 2 rectangles that will fit the baking trays. (If you want two circular pizzas use the detachable bottoms of quiche tins.) You are aiming to get the dough as thin as possible without tearing it. Gently flop the dough onto the tins instead, pinching together any small holes that might have appeared. Don't worry if your first attempt goes wrong. Simply scoop the dough up and try again, this time using a rolling pin and some extra flour.

Dot the pizzas with the Taleggio and sprinkle on the

Parmesan, leaving some space around the edge and leave a space in the centre for the egg. Season with sea salt and pepper and zigzag a thin stream of olive oil over the top. Just before you're about to put the pizzas in the oven, crack an egg onto the middle of each one. Put the pizzas on the top two highest shelves. The extreme heat will instantly start to cook the egg and stop them from spreading too far. The pizzas should take about 10 minutes, depending on how crispy you like it and how efficient your oven is. They are ready when the cheese is bubbling nicely and the crusts are showing artistic looking splashes of golden brown.

If you do not have a fan oven, turn the pizzas around halfway through. You will find the top pizza cooks quicker. Take it out and move the second pizza up to the top shelf for 3 more minutes. We always eat the first one together whilst the second one is crisping up.

When each pizza is ready, put the tray on top of the stove. Have a large wooden board ready beside the stove. Pick up the sides of the parchment paper, if using, and slide the pizza onto the board. If it sticks, then push a thin metal fish-slice underneath. Scatter over the ribbons of sorrel, the chopped chives (and rocket flowers if using), and a few more drops of olive oil. Cut into slices and serve immediately.

Sorrel gratin inspired by Richard Olney

Richard Olney was a food writer whose way of life was as inspiring to me as the food he describes in his cookbooks. He may have been born in Iowa but he ended up a highly respected authority on French gastronomy, living in a magical retreat high in the Provençal hills. The life glimpsed in the margins of Olney's recipes is a beguiling one. In summer meals were eaten under an arbour hung with vines and strung with coloured lights; when night fell an atmosphere of carnival prevailed. A large toad named Victor would regularly descend the stone steps of the terrace to watch the revellers before hopping away into Olney's garden, a tangle of herbs and flowers planted beneath ancient, neglected olive trees where flowers mingled with hyssop and basil and the terrace was paved with antique floor tiles. Here Olney served his friends informal meals such as lamb chops rolled up and skewered with a rosemary branch, rubbed with olive oil and salt and grilled over fruitwood embers. One of these friends was the English writer Sybille Bedford, a woman with whom he shared a 'passion for the table, for freshly plucked or dug vegetables and creatures pulled from the sea the moment before being eaten alive, grilled or sautéed'.

The lunch Olney devised for his friend Sybille began with scrambled eggs with truffles, followed by sorrel gratin, salad of garden lettuces spiced with fresh salted anchovies and chopped hyssop and finished up with cheeses. Here's my version of the gratin.

Sorrel gratin
Serves 4 (or 2 greedy people)

600g waxy yellow potatoes
3 shallots
2 tbsps of butter (40g), plus some for greasing
300g sorrel leaves
nutmeg
200ml crème fraiche
100ml milk
3 tbsps grated Parmesan
sea salt and pepper

The good thing about this recipe is that the initial boiling of the potatoes and onions cuts down the baking time. One of the hardest things about making a potato-based gratin is waiting for it to be ready: the smells are too enticing.

Peel and slice the potatoes into very thin discs (using a mandolin is quickest). Slice the shallots thinly and put them in a saucepan with the potatoes. Add a good pinch of salt and a small amount of water – the onion and potato mixture should be poking up out of the water so err on the side of scant. Mix them around and then put the lid on the pan and bring the water up to the boil. Keep a close eye on it and when it's boiling remove from the heat and drain.

In a separate pan, melt 1 tbsp of the butter and add the sorrel, stirring well until all the water from the leaves has evaporated and you are left with a fine purée. Remove from the heat and set aside.

Preheat your oven to 190°C/gas mark 5.

Butter a gratin dish, by that I mean a deep (8–10cm) ovenproof ceramic dish. Put a thick layer (at least 3 slices thick) of the onion and potato mixture into the bottom of the dish. If any of the potato slices are stuck together gently separate them out. Add just a few scrapes of nutmeg as a little goes a long way. Season lightly with sea salt and pepper.

Next spread over a good thick layer of the sorrel mixture and then add another thick layer of potato and onion. Season as before, then add more sorrel and more potato. Don't worry too much about how many layers of sorrel you do, just so long as you end up with enough potato to make a crust on top of the sorrel (a single layer is fine).

Heat the crème fraîche in a pan and whisk in the milk to thin it, bring up to a simmer then pour it over the potato and sorrel layers. Season, dot with 1 tbsp of butter and scatter the Parmesan over to form a nice thick layer. Bake for 45 minutes–1 hour, checking the oven after 30 minutes. If the gratin looks as if it is getting too brown then you can always put a little tin foil on top for the last 20 minutes or so.

The wonderful aroma of crisping up Parmesan should alert you to the fact that the dish is ready but slip a knife into the middle to make sure. There is nothing worse than eating a slightly hard gratin and trying to persuade yourself that the potatoes are cooked.

You can eat this dish on its own or serve it with roast chicken or a Dover sole fried in butter.

Sorrel omelette for one
Serves 1

2 eggs (good free-range ones)
1 tbsp milk
a dab of butter
a handful of sorrel leaves (no stalks) sliced into ribbons
2 tbsps freshly grated Parmesan
sea salt and pepper

Sorrel omelette is a favourite lunchtime standby of mine. There is something luxurious about it despite the simplicity of its ingredients.

Crack the eggs in a bowl and whisk well, then add the milk (omelette purists may add water instead if they wish). Heat a heavy frying pan over a medium to high heat and add the butter. Let it melt and swirl around the pan. When it is hot but not quite smoking add the egg.

Tip the pan so that the egg evenly covers the bottom, coating it thinly. Throw in the sorrel, season and add the Parmesan. After just over a minute give the pan a little tap on the cooker to dislodge the omelette and tip it out onto your plate. Eat up with a good slice of bread and butter and a few leaves from the salad garden (if in season) or a chive and tomato salad.

Note: this makes a pale fluffy omelette so you may wish to cook it a tiny bit longer than a minute if your taste is for a crisper golden bottom.

Sorrel tart with feta and yeasted dough

Serves 4

1 x quantity yeasted tart dough (see Basics, page 272) You need to make the yeasted dough 1 hour ahead of the other preparations

for the filling
a little butter, for frying
1 large bunch of sorrel, leaves only, washed and cut into ribbons
1 bunch of spring onions (approx. 6), finely chopped
3 eggs
100ml milk
150ml single cream or crème fraîche
1 tsp grated lemon zest
2 tbsps freshly grated Parmesan
100g feta

Once you've got the hang of this recipe you can adapt it. Alliums (leeks, wild garlic, onions) all make great tart fillings as do spinach, asparagus, chard and tomatoes. Use whatever is at its best in your garden or market.

Make one quantity of yeasted tart dough and put it in a 20cm tart tin (*for instructions see Basics, page 272*).

Preheat the oven to 180°C/gas mark 4. If you put a baking tray in the oven when you turn it on and later place your tart on top you will find it will crisp the bottom up very nicely, as well as catching stray drips.

In a heavy-bottomed saucepan melt a knob of butter and slowly cook the sorrel and spring onions until soft. Remove from the heat and place in a sieve so that any excess moisture can drip out.

In another bowl beat the eggs with the milk, the cream or crème fraîche and the lemon zest.

Sprinkle the Parmesan over the base of the tart and then spread over the sorrel and onion mixture. Crumble feta on top and then pour over the egg mixture, ladling in the last few spoonfuls to make sure it doesn't overflow (the custard mixture will be quite high in the tin). Carefully place the tin on the tray in the oven.

Bake for 40–45 minutes. The tart will look risen and golden brown and after you have cooked a few you should also be able to smell when it is ready.

Allow the tart to rest for a few minutes before serving with green salad.

Hot sorrel soup
Serves 4

1 tbsp butter (approx. 15g)
1 shallot, thinly sliced
1 celery stick, finely chopped
200g potato, peeled
and diced
1 litre good homemade
chicken stock
a bunch of sorrel leaves,
sliced into ribbons
plain yoghurt or crème
fraîche, to garnish
a few chives, to garnish
sea salt and pepper

Melt the butter in a medium-sized pan. Sweat the shallot in the butter until pale and translucent. Add the celery and then the potato and cook for a minute or two before adding the stock. Bring up to a simmer and cook until the potatoes are soft. Remove from the heat and add the sorrel leaves (no stalks), then blend with a wand or in a food processor. Taste and season. Serve each bowl of soup with a good swirl of yoghurt or crème fraîche on top and one or two chives, alongside some sourdough toast rubbed with garlic and olive oil. If you like, you can serve the soup in the French way, placing a sourdough crust rubbed with garlic and olive oil, in the bottom of the bowl before you pour in the soup.

Cold sorrel soup
Serves 2

12 very tender baby sorrel
leaves, shredded
240ml plain yoghurt
3–4 tbsps water
(nice and cold)
a pinch of sea salt
1 tsp freshly toasted and
ground cumin

This is more of a green lassi than a soup. It is cool, refreshing and cleansing. Best eaten on a hot day.

Using a blending wand or a food processor, mix the leaves with the yoghurt. Thin with a little water and add the salt. You can rub the mixture through a sieve if you don't like texture in drinks but it's not essential. Refrigerate. Just before serving, spoon into a bowl (or glass) and sprinkle the cumin on top.

Puy lentils with sorrel

Serves 4

1 tbsp olive oil, plus more for drizzling
1 clove garlic, crushed roughly with the flat side of your chopping knife
1 shallot, peeled and diced
1 carrot, peeled and diced
250g puy lentils
500ml hot chicken or vegetable stock
a small bunch of sorrel, leaves only, cut into thin ribbons
juice of 1 lemon
150g feta or goat's cheese (1 thin slice per serving), optional
extra virgin olive oil, to garnish
4 slices sourdough bread, to serve
sea salt and pepper

You can serve this as a side-dish with chicken or as a meal in itself by placing a thin slice of goat's cheese or feta on top of each serving.

Heat the olive oil in a medium-sized heavy-bottomed saucepan with the garlic. When the garlic is just beginning to colour, but before it becomes brown and bitter, add the shallot and carrot and sweat gently for about 5 minutes. Add the lentils and stir for 1 minute. Next add 400ml of the hot stock (or hot water from the kettle) and turn the heat down. Allow the lentils to simmer gently for about 20 minutes, keeping your eye on the pan to make sure it doesn't dry out. If it does, add a little more stock or water. When the lentils are tender but still have a bit of bite, remove from the heat and add the sorrel and the lemon juice. Season and add the cheese if you wish, swirl over a little olive oil and serve with a good slice of sourdough bread.

Sorrel risotto
Serves 4

*a knob of butter
(approx. 20g)
1 tbsp olive oil
2 shallots (or 1 onion),
chopped
300g risotto rice
1 litre chicken stock
(kept hot on the stove)
a large bunch of sorrel
leaves, sliced into ribbons
(approx. 100g once
prepared)
4 tbsps freshly grated
Parmesan, plus more
to serve
1 tbsp crème fraîche
a knob of butter, to finish
1 tbsp chopped chives
sea salt and pepper*

Melt the butter in a large pan with the olive oil. Add the shallot or onion and sweat over a low heat. When the onion is soft, add the rice and stir for a minute until every grain of rice is coated. Add a little of the hot stock (a ladleful at a time) stirring well each time and adding a little more as it is absorbed. After about 20 minutes the risotto rice will be ready (it should be tender but still have bite). If your stock runs out, just use a little hot water from the kettle.

Take the risotto off the heat and add the sorrel, Parmesan and crème fraîche, mix well and season. Add another knob of butter. Allow the risotto to sit for a minute or two. Taste again and adjust the seasoning if it needs it. Serve with the chives scattered over the top. Put a block of Parmesan and a grater on the table so anyone can help themselves if they need more cheese.

Sorrel dhal

Serves 4

450g chana dhal (split yellow lentils)
3 thick slices of ginger (unpeeled), smashed with the handle of a knife
½ tsp turmeric
½–1 tsp salt
a pinch of garam masala (see page 245 for homemade mix)
a knob of butter (approx. 20g)
2 cloves garlic, peeled and flattened with the flat side of your chopping knife
2 green chillies, deseeded and finely sliced
a bunch of sorrel leaves, sliced into ribbons

I often make spinach dhal but since I've discovered how beautifully cooked sorrel breaks down and blends with split yellow lentils I love this one too. This recipe produces a lemony dish of lentils flecked with dark green.

Put the chana dhal in a saucepan and cover with about a litre of water, bring to the boil and remove the scum with a wide spoon. Add the ginger and turmeric and cook for at least 1½ hours. Keep your eye on it during the last 30 minutes and add a little more water if it is too dry, stirring occasionally. You are aiming for a thick purée with the pulses very soft to the touch. Add the salt and garam masala (*see page 245*).

Just before you are about to serve the dhal, heat a knob of butter in a heavy frying pan. Add the garlic and the chillies, quickly followed by the sorrel. Cook the sorrel down gently for 5 minutes until it starts to disintegrate. Tip the whole mixture into the pan with the cooked dhal. Add a little hot water from the kettle if it looks too thick. Stir well and set aside until you are ready to eat it. This dish goes well with sour chick peas and chapattis (*see pages 243 and 244*) for a simple Indian supper.

Sorrel makes a wonderful everyday salad with rocket flowers, nasturtium flowers, rocket and catalagona lettuce, with a simple oil and vinegar dressing. Or you can use it as an alternative garnish over tarts and dishes of beans, pasta or lentils if chives or basil are not to hand.

Alternatives for sorrel

Sorrel cooks down in a most singular fashion, collapsing into a sludgy purée. No other green will do quite that but wilted spinach dressed with a little lemon juice (*see page 121*) makes a respectable alternative in tarts, soups, risottos, gratins, dhals and omelettes if no sorrel is to hand.

When sorrel is used raw, as in the pizza with Taleggio, tender young rocket and mustard leaves are a good alternative.

Puy lentils can be dressed with parsley instead of sorrel. Chop the parsley fine and mix with a spring onion also chopped fine, both well seasoned and tossed with freshly squeezed lemon juice and extra virgin olive oil.

Sorrel and new potato salad

See page 129. If no sorrel is available then use a tablespoon of finely chopped parsley.

Wild Greens

For centuries wild greens have relieved the monotonous diets of isolated communities as far apart as the Greek islands and Appalachia. In the past, it was common for island and mountain folk to suffer physically from the limitations of their diet, especially during the winter months when bad weather sealed them off from the outside world. Necessity forced them to exploit any way of supplementing that diet. It's no coincidence that in those hard-to-reach places locals saw the coming of spring as a chance to supplement their diet with the first lush green growth of wild plants. In Greece, the ones gathered with the root are called *rakikia* and the leafy greens are called *horta* (in parts of America they gather 'creasy greens').

In her book *Honey from A Weed*, Patience Gray records the terrible liver pains suffered by the islanders of Naxos towards the end of winter. For them, the iron-rich leaves and roots of plants were a necessity; for us, their astringent flavour is more of a delicacy – although we, too, can benefit from eating the vitamin and mineral rich leaves of wild plants, which run rings round anaemic supermarket vegetables.

City dwelling foragers need to be careful where they pick, as weed-rich verges may be intermittently sprayed with weed killer or polluted by dogs. As natural habitats in parks and reserves may have rules about picking, wild gardens and the edges of allotments are especially good places to look. You can make *horta* (*see page 48*) from wild plants or a mixture of weeds and young vegetable leaves that you might find in your garden. Mix twice as many of the blander tasting leaves (chard, spinach, beet) with more peppery and bitter options (rocket, dandelion, mustard). Here are a few of the options:

young beet or chard leaves	parsley
mustard leaves	sorrel
poppy tops	mallow
nettle tops	rocket
baby spinach	dandelion

Horta

Serves 4

for the dressing
5 tbsps olive oil
2 tbsps lemon juice
sea salt and pepper

In Greece, they serve *Horta* as separate dish at the start of the meal but you could serve it alongside grilled or roasted meat or as part of a mixed meze-style lunch with fava (split pea purée).

for the greens
400g mixed greens (spinach or chard leaves)
200g mixed herbs or wild leaves

Whisk the oil and lemon juice together, season and set aside. Wash the greens and the herbs or wild leaves well and remove any tough stalks. Bring a large pan of salted water to the boil and add the leaves. Cook until tender for no more than 5 minutes. Drain, then use a wooden spoon to squeeze out the excess water. Place the greens in a bowl and pour over the dressing. Adjust the seasoning if necessary and serve.

Nettle quiche
Serves 4

1 x quantity yeasted tart dough (see Basics, page 272) You need to make the yeasted dough 1 hour ahead of the other preparations.

for the filling
a bunch of nettle tips and leaves (approx. 150g)
a knob of butter (approx. 20g)
4 green garlics (about the size of spring onions) white and green part cleaned and finely chopped)
3 eggs
100ml milk
150ml crème fraîche
1 tsp finely grated lemon zest
1 tbsp thyme leaves, very finely chopped
3 tbsps freshly grated Parmesan
a handful of freshly cut chives, roughly chopped
sea salt and pepper

In springtime, or before they get too tough, nettles make an excellent filling for quiche. Their taste is unique, somewhere between spinach and asparagus. You can sometimes get them in farmers' markets but with a small amount of effort you should be able to find your own supply growing wild. I have an abundant supply growing behind my shed at my helpfully weedy allotment. Remember to harvest only the tender tips and be sure to wear rubber gloves. As with other wild greens, do use common sense when choosing where to pick them. If you can't find young garlic, use spring onions and a peeled and crushed clove of garlic instead.

Make one quantity of yeasted tart dough (*see Basics, page 272*). Grease a 20cm tart tin with butter and put it in the fridge until you are ready to use it.

Preheat the oven to 180°C/gas mark 4. Place an upturned baking tray in the oven (this will ensure your tart has a lovely crispy bottom).

Bring a large pan of salted water to the boil and blanch the nettles, in batches, for 1 minute. Spread the nettles out on a clean tea towel to drain.

In a heavy-bottomed saucepan melt a knob of butter and slowly cook the finely chopped garlic. When it starts to soften, put the lid on and sweat for 5 minutes. Add the blanched nettles and stir to coat with a little of the buttery juices, then remove from the heat and reserve. Taste and season.

In another bowl, beat the eggs with the milk and crème fraîche and add the lemon zest, thyme and seasoning.

(cont.)

After an hour's rising, take the pastry ball (you may have to scrape it out of the bowl with a spatula) and put it in the centre of the greased tart tin. Start pushing it down with the heel of your hand using a little extra flour if it gets a bit sticky. It might look as if there isn't going to be enough but gradually the dough will thin out from the centre and you will be able to push it well up the sides of the tin.

Sprinkle the Parmesan over the base of the tart. Spread the nettles and garlic mixture over the top and pour over the custard. Carefully place the tin in the oven. Bake for 40–45 minutes until the tart will looks well risen and golden brown. Allow it to rest for a few minutes then sprinkle over the chopped chives just before serving.

Another use for nettles

Tender nettle tips can be tossed with olive oil and a little fresh chilli and used as a topping for pizza, as in the next recipe. You don't need to blanch them first as the intense heat of the oven will put paid to any stings, just use tongs when handling them before they are cooked.

Nettle pizza

Makes 2 medium-sized pizzas (enough for 2 people)

1 x quantity pizza dough (see Basics, page 274)
1 tbsp of semolina (optional – but it makes the bottom very crispy)

for the tomato sauce
1 tbsp olive oil
1 clove garlic
1 x 400g tin whole plum tomatoes
½ tsp oregano leaves
a pinch of sugar

for the rest of the topping
25g Parmesan
150g mozzarella (goat's cheese would make a nice alternative here)
a bunch of nettle tips and leaves (approx. 100g), tossed with olive oil and sea salt
1 small red chilli, finely chopped
olive oil
sea salt and pepper
a handful of chives, chopped

Follow the instructions for pizza dough *(see Basics, page 274)*. While the dough is rising, make a quick tomato sauce by heating the olive oil in a small pan with a peeled and crushed clove of garlic. Add the tomatoes and the oregano and a pinch of sugar. Put the lid on and cook hard for 5 minutes, stirring occasionally and using your wooden spoon to break up the tomatoes a little. Remove the lid and simmer to a thickish paste (about 10 minutes).

Also whilst the dough is rising, grate the Parmesan and chop the mozzarella into slices about ½cm thick and 2cm wide. Preheat the oven to 250°C/gas mark 10, or its highest setting.

Get two large baking trays and cover them with baking parchment or sprinkle the trays with semolina.

Flour your work surface and, either using your hand or a rolling pin, flatten the dough out into two rectangles that will fit the baking trays. (If you want two circular pizzas use the detachable bottoms of quiche tins.) You are aiming to get the dough as thin as possible without tearing it. Gently flop the dough onto the tins, pinching together any small holes that might have appeared. If it tears, scoop the dough up and try again, this time using a rolling pin and more flour.

Take a couple of tablespoons of tomato sauce and spread them out over the surface of the dough (not too thick or it will be soggy). Dot the dough with the mozzarella, spread the nettle tips and chilli over the pizza and sprinkle on the Parmesan. Season with sea salt and pepper and zigzag a thin stream of olive oil over the surface of the pizza. The pizza should take about

10 minutes depending on how crispy you like it and how efficient your oven is.

If you do not have a fan oven, turn the pizzas around halfway through. You will find the top pizza cooks quicker. Take it out and move the second pizza up to the top shelf for 3 more minutes. We always eat the first one together whilst the second one is crisping up.

When each pizza is ready, put the tray on top of the stove. Have a large wooden board ready beside the stove top. Pick up the sides of the parchment paper or slide a spatula under the pizza and lift it onto the board. Scatter over some chopped chives and a few more drops of olive oil. Cut into slices and serve immediately.

Green garlic and potato soup
Serves 4

8 bulbs green garlic (home-grown they will be about the size of spring onions)
50g butter
400g potatoes, peeled and roughly chopped
4 x slices sourdough bread
olive oil
chives for garnishing
2 tbsps crème fraîche or Greek yoghurt (optional)
sea salt and pepper

This is a gently-flavoured soup for springtime which makes good use of the first green growth of garlic. If you want to, and have access to woodland, you could use ransomes (wild garlic leaves) instead of young garlic.

Clean the garlic, removing the tough outer skin and the withered tops. You should be left looking at something that resembles a very juvenile leek with equal parts of white and green. Chop into thin rings.

Melt the butter in a heavy-bottomed saucepan and sweat the garlic very gently. It should soften but not colour. Salt, cover and steam for 5 minutes. Add the potatoes and cook for another minute. Cover with about 2 fingers-depth of boiling water from the kettle and cook very gently until the potatoes begin to break apart. Using a fork or a potato masher, break the potatoes down a little more. Season. In the bottom of each bowl place a lightly toasted piece of sourdough bread, sprinkled with oil and salt (but not in this case rubbed with garlic: you don't want to overwhelm the delicate taste of the new season garlic). Pour over the soup, sprinkle with chopped chives. If you like your soups creamy you may also like to add a spoonful of greek yoghurt or crème fraîche to each bowl.

Variation
Use 200g of good quality tinned Spanish white beans in place of 200g of the potatoes.

Green garlic tart with potatoes and cheese
Serves 4

1 x quantity yeasted tart dough (see Basics, page 272) You need to make the yeasted dough 1 hour ahead.

for the filling
a small bunch of green garlics, bulb and greens (6 earlier in the season, when they look like spring onions, 4 when they get fatter) a knob of butter (20g) 1 leek, white part only, cleaned and finely chopped 1 medium potato, peeled and cubed 100g creamy white cheese, cubed (a soft British cheese such as Wigmore or Waterloo would be perfect but dolcelatte will do) 3 eggs 150ml crème fraîche 100ml milk 1 tsp lemon zest a handful of flat-leaf parsley leaves, roughly chopped sea salt and pepper

Make one quantity of yeasted tart dough and leave to rise for an hour (*for instructions see Basics, page 272*). Grease a 20cm tart tin with butter and put it in the fridge until you are ready to use it.

Preheat the oven to 180°C/gas mark 4. Place an upturned baking tray in the oven (this will ensure your tart has a lovely crispy bottom).

Remove the outer skin of the garlic plants and trim. Wash well. Chop them finely, making sure you use a decent amount of the green part too. In a heavy-bottomed saucepan, melt a knob of butter and slowly cook the finely chopped garlic and leek. When they start to soften, put the lid on and sweat them for 5 minutes. Remove from the heat and reserve. Bring a small pan of salted, boiling water to the boil and cook the potato cubes until just soft. Drain in a colander and add to the garlic and leek mixture. Season, to taste.

Cut the cheese into small cubes. In another bowl beat the eggs and whisk in the crème fraîche and the milk and add the lemon zest.

After 1 hour's rising, take the pastry ball (you may have to scrape it out with a spatula) and put it in the centre of the tart tin. Start pushing it down into the tin with the heel of your hand using a little extra flour if it gets a bit sticky. It might look as if there isn't going to be enough but gradually the dough will thin out from the centre and you will have enough to push it well up the sides of the tin.

Scatter the cheese over the base of the tart and then spread over the garlic and potato mixture. Pour over the egg mixture. Carefully place the tin in the oven on the baking tray and bake for 40–45 minutes until the tart looks well-risen and golden brown.

Allow the tart to rest for a few minutes. Sprinkle over the parsley before serving.

Chicory

Chicory has a reputation for bitterness that puts many people off. Confusion is piled on by the huge number of different salad plants that are lumped under the name chicory: frizzy mops of pale curly frisée, tight dark red hearts of radicchio, torpedoes of creamy Belgian witloof and the forager's version, dandelion. Chicory itself gets called different names (endive and escarole) and people can't seem to agree on how to pronounce endive. All this has perhaps held chicory back as a winter green and it does need a bit of forethought but don't let that deter you.

The bitter, crunchy leaves of raw chicory need strong balancing flavours – rich and creamy cheeses such as goat's cheese or Roquefort are perfect. The latter is particularly good in the bistro salad mainstay of walnut, chicory and apple. Chicory also stands up well to strong tasting, oily chunks of smoked eel or fish. Salty and crispy ingredients are another good foil for chicory – crisp squares of bacon and the soft yolk of a poached egg and frisée form another classic salad combination. Sweet sharp juices, such as lemon, pomegranate or blood orange, combined with creamy nuts such as hazel or walnut work well, as do the tart sour-sweet tastes of balsamic or sherry vinegars and capers. The peppery leaves of rocket and watercress contrast very successfully both in colour and taste. To make the most of chicory's rigid form you can use the individual leaves of pale Belgian chicory as an alternative to toasts for holding dips such as Swedish prawn skagen with dill in a creamy dressing.

Growing your own

When it comes to green vegetables that grow over winter, there seems to me no contest between cabbage and chicory: cabbage is much trickier (it's far more susceptible to pests) and, when compared to a cream and red-flecked heart of radicchio, far less alluring.

As previously noted, chicory comes in a staggering number of varieties, some of which can be grown as salad while others are more suitable for forcing – this means you have to dig them up and bring them inside.

When and how to sow

Chicory is sown in summer, dug up in late autumn to be forced, and may not finish cropping until well into spring, depending on when you bring it indoors. Although it can start cropping in winter I have placed it here as it crosses the seasons. If you don't grow your own then the last days of winter and the beginning of spring are the time when you are going to see the largest range of chicory available in shops and markets.

If you are growing outdoor hearting varieties, expert saladier Charles Dowding recommends you sow them after the longest day (June 21st), as longer days make plants shoot up and flower whilst less daylight encourages lots of leafy growth and sweeter hearts. If you don't have much space in your plot, you can sow seeds indoors in a seed tray in June and plant them out in July as space becomes available. This makes chicory a good follow-on crop for broad beans, peas and early potatoes (slug damage may be limited this way too). You could try leaving the plants in the ground and covering them with flowerpots but they may rot. The best way to guarantee a reliable source of chicory is to force it indoors. This is surprisingly easy and provides you with the freshest chicory you'll find without you ever having to leave the house. The individual bulbs of chicory are known as chicons.

Sowing outside

If planting direct, sow in shallow drills and plant out 3 to 4 seeds per station, about 25cm apart in rows 30cm apart. About a month after sowing, thin them out to one plant per station. Apart from a little watering and weeding you can now forget about your chicory until November. You can use chicory purely as a salad component, sowing it and harvesting it as a cut-and-come-again leaf but the adventurous should really try forcing their own.

How to force chicory

To force a plant is to make it grow in unnatural conditions (deprived of light) in order to produce faster growth (and paler vegetables). Rhubarb and chicory are both commonly forced vegetables. The chicory that probably first comes to mind is the pale yellow-tipped bulb known in Belgium as witloof, and this is the most reliable forcing chicory. But the red-flecked Italian varieties, such as Rossa di Treviso, are worth a try too. When salad is scarce, home-grown chicory is a great resource. Because it is grown indoors it is an ideal winter crop for fair-weather gardeners who don't like going out in the cold. Plants are sown in the summer, then dug up and trimmed in November ready for forcing.

The main difficulty in forcing chicory is persuading other members of your household that bringing large pots of soil into the house is a good idea. For some people (my husband is one of them) opening a cupboard that usually contains coats and finding a big tub of damp black earth is deeply disturbing and, in his case, enraging. Serving up lots of different delicious chicory salads should help them overcome this response.

In November, dig the plants up carefully and trim the leaves down to the roots. Shorten the roots to about 8–10cm. Stand them upright in a flowerpot and fill in with old potting compost (the chicory will get its food from its root not the compost). Cover with an old sack. (Coffee bean sellers will usually sell you their old coffee sacks very cheaply, if you buy lots ahead of time you can air them out ready for storing potatoes and covering chicory).

You need to store the chicory somewhere dark and cold, such as a shed or garage. As you need it, bring the pots indoors and place them in a warm cupboard – the heat will cause the chicons to swell and bulb up in about 2–3 weeks. The chicories in the cold will take much longer. By gradually bringing your crop in from the cold you stay in charge of growth. If you have limited space, lay the roots down in damp sand and pot them up as you need them.

Cooking chicory

Chicory is a most versatile vegetable, being as good cooked as it is raw. The main thing to remember when cooking chicory is that it exudes quite a lot of water so long slow cooking or grilling is a better option than boiling.

Grilling chicory

The easiest way to cook chicory is to grill it. Wash but don't dry the chicons (the water stops them burning), then split the red or creamy heads in half, brush either with butter or with a vinaigrette made with balsamic or sherry vinegar and a teaspoon of thyme leaves and grill (either over coals or in the oven). Turn the chicory frequently, brushing it with the vinaigrette as you do so, until it is brown on the outside. Roast it in a hot oven for 15 minutes to get the heart really tender.

Grilled chicory can be added to risotto, sliced and put on top of pizza or served with meat as a side vegetable.

Braised chicory

Serve any number

1 chicory per person
butter
1 tsp of sugar (optional)
lemon juice
sea salt

Cooking chicory well so that it ends up soft and tender with caremelised juices, tasting sweet not bitter, takes care and patience. You will need an hour or so to get the chicories perfectly cooked through. Depending on what kind of vessel you use you may also need to add a very small amount of water. If you find the chicories too bitter, you might want to add a little sugar.

Remove any tired looking outer leaves and give the chicory a quick wipe with a clean tea towel. Thickly butter a heavy pan or any nice bit of earthenware that can go on the stove top. The chicory should fit snugly into the pan. Dot a little more butter (1 teaspoon per chicory head) on top and add the sugar if you prefer things a little less bitter. Cover with a piece of buttered parchment paper and the lid. Cook over a low heat, turning the chicories every 15 minutes until they are tender and a good golden colour. If they look as if they are catching, add a very small amount of water. After about an hour test the chicories with the point of a knife to make sure they are tender all the way through. Squeeze over some lemon juice and season with salt.

Blanched dandelion, caper and rocket salad

Serves 4 as a side-dish

for the dressing
3 tbsps single cream
1 tbsp lemon juice
1 tsp finely grated lemon zest
sea salt and pepper

With the bitter taste of dandelion and the peppery taste of rocket, this salad is a good match for smoked mackerel or hot-smoked salmon fillets. If you want to get fancy try growing the striking looking red-ribbed dandelion, with its dark-red spine edged by green foliage.

for the salad
2 blanched heads of dandelion (make your own by putting a flowerpot over some dandelions for a week)
a small bunch of rocket (approx. 100g), flowers too, if possible
1 tbsp capers

Whisk the salad dressing ingredients together and set aside. Wash the salad leaves carefully and dry them. Leave them wrapped in a napkin or paper towel in the fridge until you are ready to assemble the salad.

Arrange the rocket, dandelion and capers in a bowl. Pour over the creamy dressing. Sprinkle with rocket flowers if you have them.

Witloof, Roquefort, slices of pear (or apple) and toasted walnuts.
Crisp green apples cut into thin slices, chicory, watercress and Stilton.
Raddichio, blood orange segments, goat's cheese and toasted walnuts.
Slivers of smoked eel, baby beetroot or slices of larger beets,
    chicory and watercress.
Raddichio, toasted walnuts, goat's cheese and pomegranate seeds.
Dandelion and sorrel.
Frisée, crispy bacon, poached egg and chives.
Chicory, beetroot, orange segments and walnuts.
Beetroot, chopped *fine herbes* (ideally parsley, chives, chervil and
tarragon, but just parsley and chives will do too) and endive.
Chicory, boiled waxy potatoes, shallots and parsley.
Or try *Salade Carmen*, a recipe of X. M. Boulestin, the early twentieth century
food writer: chicory, celery and beetroot in a French dressing made with cream
and lemon juice instead of vinegar.

The following makes a Mustardy vinaigrette that goes very well with
chicory-based salads.

Whisk together 1 tablespoon Dijon mustard, 1 tablespoon lemon juice,
3 tablespoons olive oil and season with sea salt and pepper.

Rosemary, radicchio, Taleggio, Parmesan and caper pizza
Makes 2 medium-sized pizzas (enough for 2 people)

1 x quantity of pizza dough (see Basics, page 274)
1 tbsp semolina (optional but it makes the bottom very crunchy)

for the topping
25g Parmesan
150g Taleggio (if you can't find this strong tasting creamy white cheese use mozzarella)
a few leaves of raddichio
1 tbsp capers
½ tbsp finely chopped fresh rosemary leaves
1 tsp finely grated lemon zest
olive oil
sea salt and pepper

Make one quantity of pizza dough (*for instructions see Basics, page 274*). Whilst the dough is rising, grate the Parmesan and chop the Taleggio into slices about ½cm thick and 2cm wide. Heat the oven to 250°C/gas mark 10, or the highest setting you have.

Get 2 large baking trays and cover them with baking parchment. Scatter 1 tablespoon of semolina over the bottom of each tray.

Flour your work surface and use either your hands or a rolling pin to flatten the dough out into rectangles that will fit the baking trays. (If you want circular pizzas use the detachable bottoms of two quiche tins.) You are aiming to get the dough as thin as possible without tearing it. Gently flop the dough onto the tins, pinching together any small holes that might have appeared. Don't worry if your first attempt goes wrong. Scoop the dough up and try again, this time using a rolling pin and more flour.

Dot the dough with the Taleggio. Place the raddichio leaves on top. Scatter over the capers, rosemary and lemon zest, sprinkle on the Parmesan. Season, and then zigzag a thin stream of olive oil over the surface of the pizza. The pizza should take about 10 minutes depending on how crispy you like it and how efficient your oven is. The cheese should be melted and bubbling.

Slide the pizza onto a large wooden board, cut into slices and serve immediately.

Variation
If you wish, replace the capers with Parma ham.

Growing rhubarb

Rhubarb plants stay productive for many years and are very hard to kill. If you have room, they look good in a flowerbed. If you haven't inherited rhubarb on your plot, you can start yours off by buying a crown (a bit of rooted stalk with leaf) potted up at a nursery or garden centre. I planted one the first year I had the allotment and we have had more rhubarb than we can eat ever since. Plant your crown when dormant (midwinter) and give it a good feed of horse manure once a year. Restrict yourself to pulling just a few stalks in the first couple of years. Once it is well established, rhubarb can be picked from the end of winter or very early spring to midsummer. If your rhubarb flowers in May (mine never has for some reason) don't worry about trimming it back, just relax and enjoy the mass of creamy inflorescence. If you want to force rhubarb, you can buy terracotta forcing pots or a chimneypot. I was given an old terracotta chimneypot this year so I put it over part of my rhubarb patch. I topped the pot with a tile to shut out all the light and weighted it down with a brick. I was rewarded with my most beautiful crop yet: slender sparkly stalks of pale pink rhubarb. They were so good that I was too mean to share them with the kind chimneypot-giver. Be warned, forcing weakens the plant so you might want to have two patches and force them on alternate years.

Pulling rhubarb is a very satisfying job. If you hold the stalk right down at the bottom and tug, the whole pink and white base comes out in one. Once you've trimmed off the base and the elephant ear leaves you're left with a pearlescent pink stalk with a sheen on it like a stick of seaside rock.

Rhubarb and pomegranate compote
Serves 4

500g rhubarb cut into
3cm chunks
150ml pomegranate juice
(remove the seeds from a
pomegranate and crush
through a sieve until you
have enough juice)
1 tbsp grated orange zest
3 tbsps granulated sugar

This compote can be served warm with a swirl of rich, yellow, Jersey cream or with muesli and Greek yoghurt for breakfast.

Put the rhubarb, pomegranate juice and orange zest in a heavy-bottomed pan and stir in the sugar. Over a medium to low heat, simmer very gently until the rhubarb is just done (about 6–8 minutes). Turn off the heat and leave in the saucepan. The rhubarb will continue cooking for a while. Try not to over-stir as you want to try and avoid turning the whole thing to mush (but don't worry if you do; it will still taste nice but just won't look as appealing). Taste the compote; rhubarb varieties vary in sweetness and you may need to add a little more sugar.

Roasted rhubarb with star anise and pomegranate juice
(*see Winter page 218*)

Rhubarb-and-custard tart
Serves 4

1 x tart case, made with
flaky pastry
(see Basics, page 271)
icing sugar, to decorate

for the filling
300g rhubarb stalks (cut in
half lengthways and sliced
into 5cm batons)
1 tbsp caster sugar
1 tsp finely grated ginger

for the custard
1 egg
1 egg yolk
3 tbsps caster sugar
(preferably vanilla scented)
2 tbsps plain flour
4 tbsps crème fraîche

Make the tart case and bake blind (*for instructions see Basics, page 271*). Reserve the pastry trimmings.

Put the rhubarb in a bowl and sprinkle over the sugar and grated ginger. Leave for at least 30 minutes to macerate. Meanwhile, whisk the egg, egg yolk and sugar together then add the flour and the crème fraîche, whisking them all together well to get a very smooth custard. Drain the rhubarb in a sieve.

When the pastry is a pale golden colour, take the tart tin out of the oven. If any small holes have appeared make a paste out of the remaining pastry with a little water and glue them up. Spread the rhubarb mixture over the bottom of the tart, turning the rhubarb flat-side down. Bake for 15 minutes and then take the tart out of the oven and pour the custard over the mixture. Then bake at 180°C/gas mark 4 for another 30 minutes, or until the custard has just set.

Allow the tart to cool and sieve a little icing sugar over the top.

Variation

A simpler, custardless rhubarb tart that requires no pre-baking can be made by rolling the pastry out onto a rectangular baking sheet (lined with baking parchment). Fold over the edges of the pastry a little (about 1cm) to form a raised edge. Brush the edges with an egg wash (an egg beaten with 1 tablespoon milk) and sprinkle over a little sugar. Cut the rhubarb and prepare it as above (macerating it in sugar and ginger) and spread the drained lengths out over the pastry. Sprinkle a little more sugar over the top. Bake the tart for 30–40 minutes, pushing

down the rhubarb with the back of a spatula halfway through to release some of its juices. Serve with plenty of thick cream. If the top looks like it's going to brown too much before the bottom is cooked, cover the tart with tin foil, but if you don't notice in time you can always cover up the dark parts by scattering over a few mint leaves once you've taken it out of the oven.

Rhubarb jelly
Serves 4

1kg of rhubarb
2 tbsps granulated sugar
1–2 tbsps caster sugar
4 leaves gelatine (9g in total)

Preheat the oven to 180°C/gas mark 4.

Wash, trim and cut the rhubarb into 4cm chunks. Put in the bottom of an ovenproof dish (an oval Le Creuset is perfect). Scatter over the granulated sugar (you can always add more later if it is not sweet enough) and leave to let the juices draw out for 20 minutes. Pour a little cold water over the rhubarb (it should come about halfway up).

Cover and bake the rhubarb in the preheated oven for 45 minutes (the rhubarb should be soft). Allow to cool. Line a sieve with muslin or an unused J-cloth and drain the rhubarb. Collect the juice (the roasted rhubarb can be used to make fool, chutney or just eaten as a compote).

Measure the juice. You should have about 200ml. Dilute with water to bring it up to 450ml. Taste it. If it needs more sugar add at the heating stage (see below).

When you have obtained 450ml of juice, pour 100ml of it into a pan and heat (but do not let it boil as this will impair the flavour). Now is the time to add the caster sugar should you need to, stirring to dissolve. In another bowl, soften the gelatine in cold water for 2–3 minutes, squeeze it and then add to the warmed liquid. Stir well until it is dissolved. Pour this mixture into the jug with the rest of the juice and whisk in. Pour into a 450ml jelly mould, a small bowl or 4 small wine glasses.

Leave to set, preferably overnight. If you are turning out your jelly, dip the moulds or bowl in a bowl of just-boiled water very briefly and then run a knife around the top before tipping out onto a serving plate.

Rhubarb cordial
Makes 1 x 75cl wine bottle

1kg rhubarb, cut into chunks
2 tbsps granulated sugar
caster sugar (200g for every 250ml of juice)

Preheat the oven to 180°C/gas mark 4. Wash, trim and cut the rhubarb into 4cm chunks. Put in the bottom of an ovenproof dish or a deep roasting tray.

Scatter over the granulated sugar. Leave for 30 minutes to let the juices draw out of the rhubarb a little. Sprinkle over 2 or 3 tablespoons water. Cover and bake for 30 minutes.

Have ready a scalded jelly bag suspended over a bowl (I hang mine off my plate rack but an upturned stool will do). Leave the mixture to drip through for several hours. This is one time when squeezing your jelly bag is absolutely allowed so give it a good squeeze after an hour or so and then leave it for another hour. Pour the juice through a clean muslin (an unused J-cloth makes a good substitute).

Measure the juice and weigh out 200g sugar for each 250ml of juice (this recipe should get you about 500ml juice). Place the juice and the sugar in a saucepan. Over a medium heat, gently bring the liquid to the boil and skim off any scum. Let it simmer for 5 minutes then remove from the heat and allow to cool for 5 minutes before pouring into a sterilised glass bottle. Either use a rubber-sealed bottle with a spring top or cork an ordinary bottle by soaking a cork in warm water for a few minutes and tapping it in. Seal the cork with hot wax (melt candle wax and dip the whole top of the bottle in).

Roasted rhubarb chutney
Makes about 6 x medium/350ml jam jars

1 tbsp pickling spices (see Basics, page 275)
1kg rhubarb
3 star anise
1 tbsp freshly grated ginger
300g onion, finely chopped
300ml distilled vinegar (clear not dark brown for a better colour)
100g raisins or sultanas
350g soft light brown sugar
½ tsp sea salt

Heat the oven to 180°C/gas mark 4. Put the pickling spices into a little bag (*see page 275*). Chop the rhubarb into 2cm chunks and place it in a roasting dish (preferably one that can also go on the oven top) with the star anise and the ginger. Roast for about 30 minutes with a lid or foil on top for the first 20 minutes or so, taking the foil off for the last 10 minutes, when the rhubarb should be soft but retaining its shape and surrounded by clear pink juices. Remove from the oven and set aside until it is time to add to the onion mixture.

Whilst the rhubarb is cooking simmer the onion gently in half the vinegar for 10 minutes. After 10 minutes add the raisins, sugar, the rest of the vinegar, the bag of spices and the salt. Stir until the sugar has dissolved and then simmer very gently until the mixture thickens and starts to look jammy. When this has happened, very gently add the rhubarb, mix it in gingerly and then simmer for about 10 minutes until nicely amalgamated. Some of your rhubarb chunks will disintegrate but hopefully a few will retain their shape to form abstract chunks of pink when bottled (my chutney looks like retro linoleum).

Spoon into hot, sterilised jam jars (*see Basics, page 266*). Leave the chutney in a cupboard for at least a month before eating.

SUMMER

SUMMER ON THE ALLOTMENT begins in May with a mass of self-seeded blooms. After the wet and mud of spring, I welcome the sight of the blue, star-shaped borage flowers and the clouds of red, pink, and white poppies which return in greater numbers each year. By early June both are engulfing any bed I haven't yet dug over. I have to force myself to pull up any poppies still flowering at the end of June. By then they have become great sprawling thugs and I need the space for the tender plants I have been raising on my bedroom windowsill. Before I bundle the poppy plants into the compost I hang up a few seed heads in the shed. A month or so later when they are dry (but before they have opened up and shed their seeds) I shake the seeds out onto paper and into a large A4 envelope. At Christmas I fill up small brown cash envelopes with poppy seeds and stick them on to parcels as an extra present.

Almost everything I grow from seed has to make the journey from packet to windowsill tray to seedlings in pots. To get the plants from windowsill to allotment in good condition requires vigilance. It's one of the times in the year when I really do have to pay attention. The second to last stage is the most difficult. I have to get the plants used to being outside but the only outside space I have at home is a tiny north-facing walled garden over which snails rampage. I have had entire trays of seedlings eaten down to a stalk in a single night. Rainstorms are the most dangerous times. One night the sound of heavy rain woke me. It was 4 a.m. and I remembered with a lurch of alarm that I had left my plants on the ground. (They spend their days in the one sunny corner of my back garden but should get moved onto a table at night.) I had forgotten to lift them to snail-free safety. Running outside in the pitch black, in the pouring rain, may sound a bit eccentric but I couldn't face the sad sight of little stubs of stalk glistening with snail trail. When the danger of late frost has passed in May, the plants are packed into the car in greengrocers' crates, driven to the allotment and then trundled down in a wheelbarrow.

For a brief moment in early summer the allotment is an orderly place. The potato plants are growing well, thick green leaves showing up against the dark earth pulled up around them. Tall garlic stems make neat rows of green, spikes curling over to reach the ground, with quick growing crops of salad and herbs sown between each row, and the broad beans are vigorous enough to need staking with hazel twigs. There is plenty of rhubarb to gather as well as tender young sorrel leaves. Healthy looking plants of squash, pumpkin and tomato dot the beds that very recently held poppies. Alongside the new arrivals, rows of rocket, spinach and salad are showing fingernail sized leaves and any tiny

weed seedling can easily be hoed away. The ground has not yet baked hard, the cockleshell paths have not sprouted weeds and the grass surrounding the beds is not too tall. This is the time for gazing with satisfaction.

Midsummer is a time of great fruitfulness at the allotment but it's not just the plants that grow fast, weeds do too. In June and July my attitude to my garden can become a bit embattled. If there is too much rain, weeds spring up everywhere threatening to choke my carefully reared plants. Too little rain and the job of watering the allotment must somehow be added on to the end of the day. Allotments don't allow sprinkler systems or hosepipes so each can of water must be filled and carried by hand from the mains-supplied water butt to the plot. When the entire plot is planted up it takes about an hour to water everything without allowing any time for harvesting or weeding. Happily, we have a damp climate with fairly consistent and plentiful rainfall, a good natural drenching once a week is usually enough to keep things going. I try to weed for an hour or two at least once a week but I don't always manage it. To counteract my erratic watering and give any crops that have failed a decent chance, I do repeat sowings staggered throughout the summer. In this way I can take advantage of changing weather patterns. This year, a wet May meant slugs got my first lot of cucumber seedlings but the next lot, sown a month later, were luckier. Rain in August meant green tomatoes but my neglected beds of chicory and cavolo nero survived without being watered whilst we were on holiday. This may not be the optimum way of gardening but it's one that fits in with the demands of work and family life. It means that the allotment can continue to be part of my life without taking too much time. My garden is far from perfect but it is fruitful despite its sometimes scruffy appearance.

Summer is not all about work; the heat, the flowers and the vigorous growth provide moments of great tranquillity. The ground may be dry and dusty but at the edge of my plot, under the shade of my neighbour's arbour, the light is subaqueous, filtered through a straggle of vines and tall green beans dotted with scarlet flowers. This summer I sat with my month-old daughter on my lap and watched the cabbage whites dance through my herb garden. I saw a gold and green scarab beetle nestled in the white cup of a cosmos flower. I picked striped collarette dahlias, their deep red, pink and purple petals ringed with a double row of petals streaked with contrasting stripes. I gathered a basket of soft felty broad beans, tightly furled artichokes and slim pale green finger-length courgettes. At summer's end, trying hard not to look at the weeds, I gathered a basket of pale lemon crookneck squash, knobbly pink fir apple potatoes, beetroot, tomatoes, sunflowers, baby spinach and rhubarb. My now two-month-old baby slept in her buggy, allowing me time to thin my cavolo nero and hoe my chicory seedlings, ensuring that this winter there will be something to harvest. That September lunchtime I had cherry tomatoes and knobbly skinned squash, steamed and eaten with chives and butter, a salad of bright yellow wild rocket flowers and mixed leaves, and a bowl of dark red raspberries crushed and swirled through thick yoghurt.

SALADS

I must give France its due. The French, I am told, have many failings, but they can make wine, coffee and salad. It is a great deal.
X. Marcel Boulestin – *Collected Recipes*

It would be hard for anyone who truly enjoys the pleasures of the table to choose between wine, coffee and salad, but as an indulgence salad does have one great advantage – no one has ever suffered from a surfeit of lettuce (apart from Rapunzel's mother who gave up her rights as a mother for a second taste of the lettuce growing in the witch's garden). Outside fairy tales, salad has been enjoyed, without hazard, for centuries. The French gastronome Brillat Savarin made great claims for salad in his witty treatise on food and life, *Physiologie du Goût*, first published in 1825.

This was followed by the salad – a finishing item which I recommend to the use of all who have faith in my teaching, for salad refreshes without fatiguing, and strengthens without irritating. I usually say it renews one's youth.

As great pleasure and a renewal of youth are large claims for a humble leaf, perhaps I should begin by defining what I really mean by salad, all salads being by no means equal. A good salad can be as simple as the heart of a sweet butterhead lettuce but it can also mean bowls of cooked, chopped vegetables smothered in mayonnaise or hot salads of cooked meats and vegetables mixed with leaves. Each of these has its place but the salad I am talking about is one that should be placed at the end of a meal. This salad is astringent and cleansing, it chases away any rich and cloying tastes leaving your guests feeling light and refreshed. It is a simple dish but one with great impact. However galling it may be for the cook who has slaved over a tart of the flakiest pastry, it is probably the freshly picked peppery leaves that your guests will comment on and remember not the delicate wobble of your savoury custard.

The first salads were just raw food sprinkled with salt (the word salad has its root in the Latin for salt – *sal*), the salt bringing out the essence of what was best and most flavoursome in the vegetable. In this case language gives us the key to a successful salad: simplicity and quality. For an essence to be savoured it must be really good quality, a quality that can only come with the freshest and tastiest of ingredients. This is where the just-picked home-grown leaf will always win the day.

For me the perfect salad is a simple green one, its leaves picked that day in the cool of the morning with a degree of thought as to its components and dressed with a basic vinaigrette. If you can be bothered to grow your own salad (and what in the end could be less bother when you weigh it up against the pleasure it will bring) then you will find that even the smallest plot can produce a surprisingly large amount of leaves. Added to which, the cost of a single packet of mixed leaves must surely be one of the best bargains around. Take a little care in choosing what to grow and when to grow it and you will enjoy a long summer of meals put together with little effort but resulting in maximum effect.

How to pick the perfect salad

> *The sallet-gatherer likewise should be provided with a light, and neatly made withy-Dutch-basket, divided into several partitions.*

This was John Evelyn's advice for the seventeenth-century salad gatherer but the chances are most of us will be armed with nothing more romantic than a plastic bag. When I pick salad leaves I walk around the vegetable garden taking a few leaves at a time and gathering them tightly in one hand to form a bouquet. Herbs and leaves gathered together in this way always look beautiful and quickly make a pleasure out of necessity, but it also allows me to compose the salad in my head. I usually pack my vegetables into an old wicker shopping basket, tucking the salad in around the edge at the last minute to hold the bunches together. If salad is the last thing picked it will have less time to wilt in the heat of the sun.

However you gather it in, the day you harvest your first salad will always be a happy one. Planning what to eat becomes easy when you are looking at living plants, the dishes decided by the quantities available. You might have a simple salad of Little Gem, chives and parsley, or of oakleaf lettuces spiced with hyssop flowers and the peppery blossoms of nasturtium. You may decide to take the handful of broad beans that are ready and add them to a bowl of green leaves, mint and fried lardons. Earlier in the season, over-wintered spicy mustard leaves, both the fronded spikes of golden mustard and the dark red thumbs of giant red make a bed for steak fried in butter, the meat's juices the only dressing the leaves need. If you are growing baby leaves in containers (greengrocer's wooden fruit trays are excellent for this) then shearing them off with a pair of scissors is the simplest way to harvest them. This method, called 'cut-and-come-again' by gardeners, ensures a second and sometimes third crop from a single seed. The other way is to grow individual lettuces and harvest only the outer leaves, leaving the heart and creating a little lettuce 'tree' which will stay productive for a remarkably long time. If you have a small space then concentrating your energies on a few really well cultivated lettuces is probably the best plan.

How to prepare your salad

If you don't have time to wash your leaves then put them straight in a plastic bag in the fridge and deal with them later. I try to wash mine as soon as I get back from the allotment, giving myself the illusion of effortless salad making later on when I come to prepare a meal. If you are careful when picking, taking the leaf and not the stalk, then the actual washing and sorting part will take much less time. If you leave your salad out on the side you will end up with a wilted mess of limp, unattractive leaves so it's always better to deal with salad first before lovingly washing your perfect courgettes and spiny cucumbers.

Fill the kitchen sink with water and tip all the salad leaves in. Scoop out the best looking leaves and throw them into a colander, discarding any weeds or bits of grass as you go along. When you have reached the end of the leaves (or your patience) empty the sink and refill it with clean water, wash the selected leaves a second time and then shake the salad dry. To do this you can use a salad spinner or, if you are lucky enough to find one in a junk shop or yard sale, an old wire salad basket. I have the latter as it takes up very little space hanging from my saucepan rack and I am always pleased to have an excuse to step outside. The action of swinging salad dry makes a whirling arc of water droplets over the garden. The garden is refreshed and waving my arms around my head always improves my mood (it's hard to be cross when you are looking vaguely foolish). You can then either wrap your salad in a clean tea towel or napkin, or put it in a plastic bag – it will keep for several days in the latter. If you are distracted and forget all about your salad, coming across it later in the day, wilted and woebegone, don't have a breakdown. You can refresh salad by washing it and drying it and putting it in a bag in the fridge. It will crisp up again and all your efforts will not have been in vain.

What salad to grow and when to grow it

Salad can be sown from April until late August and different varieties do better at different times.

For beginners, a packet of mixed leaves is a good place to start. Thompson and Morgan's mixture 'Saladisi' will provide you with five or six different varieties and get you started out painlessly without having to make any decisions about what to grow. It's a cheap way of discovering which kind of leaves you like best.

Little Gem has always been a fixture in my garden; it is easy to grow, makes attractive small leaves and is sweet and flavoursome. It makes a good base for many salads as well as a container for dips or pâtés of smoked fish, and it can also be cooked with peas.

Rocket is another staple. If you've ever picked a rocket leaf, popped it straight into your mouth and let the peppery explosion hit your taste buds you'll know it's one leaf no gardener should ever omit. The creamy filigreed flower of this plant is a beautiful way of decorating salads and pizzas. Rocket can be sown from February to April and again in July – any rocket sown in between those times will taste fine but may well end up peppered with holes from flea beetles. As you can have your pick of many other kinds of salad leaf at this time it seems sensible to keep rocket production for the cooler ends of the summer.

As with vegetables, it is good to grow a few old friends alongside some new things. This year I am trying *Umbriacona frastagliata*, or Drunken Woman, an Italian heirloom variety; giant red mustard; a purple crisphead lettuce called Pablo; as well as Catalogna, an oakleaf lettuce. This last leaf, also known as dandelion chicory, has a great taste and a lovely undulating shape. This year I am using both my own saved seed and some new seed.

There are so many types of salad leaves that it's very tempting to try a large number and why shouldn't you? For once you can safely throw caution to the wind. Apart from a very little money and some time, there isn't much at stake. As overwhelming compulsions go, splurging on salad seed is probably one of the cheapest and healthiest around. If you find you have grown too much you can always bag it up and give it away to friends.

Sowing lettuce

For a head start, sow each individual lettuce in its own module on the windowsill in April and transfer them to the garden when they've reached a decent size. Later on when the ground has warmed up you can sow your salad seeds directly into the earth. Growing a few individual lettuces in pots throughout the season allows you to slot plants in as bed space becomes available, which is useful if your gardening space is small, but sowing direct is a lot less effort if you have a decent-sized sunny plot.

Salad sowing

Spring – As soon as the ground has warmed up a little, sow rocket, spinach, chard and mustards, sorrel, beetroot for leaves, peas for their shoots.

Early summer – sow more lettuces, carrots, radishes, herbs such as hyssop, borage and nasturtiums for their flowers.

Mid to late summer – sow chicories, both outdoor hearting types and witloof for forcing (*see chicory section, page 55*), rockets and mustards.

End of summer – sow winter purslane, mustards, rocket and hardy lettuces for over-wintering.

If you're serious about edible leaves it is worth buying a comprehensive book such as Joy Larkcom's *The Organic Salad Garden* or Charles Dowding's *Salad Leaves for All Seasons*.

Dressings

It is hard to improve the freshest leaf with anything more than three parts oil to one part vinegar, with added salt and pepper. A good extra virgin olive oil and a decent white or red wine vinegar will do, as will lemon juice if you have no wine vinegar. Walnut oil makes a really superlative dressing for a green salad, as does the addition of a finely chopped shallot to a basic vinaigrette (leave them to macerate for half an hour before dressing your salad). I often add Dijon mustard for a creamier emulsion. Salad dressing should not be made too far in advance, definitely not in grimy bottles topped up day after day, and to be really correct, the seasoning should be mixed with the lemon or vinegar before whisking in the oil. I sometimes rub the inside of my salad bowl with a clove of garlic (in a method reminiscent of *salade au chapon*) which gives a taste of that pungent bulb without overpowering the other more refined flavours. Using wooden bowls may look nice and rustic but a ceramic or glass salad bowl ensures the flavours you are savouring are today's and not left over from salads of yesteryear.

Everyday allotment salad

Mixed lettuce leaves with baby sorrel, herbs and nasturtium flowers make up my standard bowl of salad throughout the summer. I take a few of whichever lettuces are growing well and mix them with chives, parsley, mint or very juvenile sorrel. At the last moment, after the salad is dressed I scatter over nasturtium or borage flowers if I have them.

Watercress salad

Remove the woody stalks from some watercress and dress the leaves with salt, pepper and lemon juice. Cook a roast chicken with lemon, thyme and plenty of salt and butter and surround it with the dressed watercress so that the dressing and the chicken's juices mingle. With fresh bread, this makes a wonderful early summer lunch.

Little Gem with *fines herbes* and spring onions

Take a bowlful of Little Gem leaves, 2 tablespoons of *fines herbes* (parsley, chervil and tarragon) and add 3 finely chopped spring onions. Dress with a simple vinaigrette.

Beetroot, chervil and Little Gem with a cream dressing

Peel and grate 1 large or 2 small beetroots. Place in the salad bowl with 2 or 3 Little Gem lettuces and the leaves from a small bunch of chervil but don't mix until you are at the table. Dress with 1 part lemon juice or vinegar to 3 parts single cream. Season with sea salt and pepper.

Pea salad with a creamy vinaigrette and cubes of Gruyère

Fresh peas, blanched and refreshed make a delightful side salad when mixed with little cubes of cheese and dressed with a simple cream dressing (*see above*). A slippery but flavourful morsel served in a teacup is a good side-dish for a ham and mustard sandwich and if eaten in front of an old film makes a very superior tv dinner.

Raw root vegetable salads

When grated, raw root vegetables make fine salads. Extremely vibrant in colour, they take minutes to prepare and when dressed with a lemon vinaigrette are a very punchy affair. Just don't grate them too fine or you'll end up with a soggy mess.

Grated carrot with lemon juice, oil and cumin

Serves 4 alongside two or three other dishes

4 youngish carrots, peeled and grated
juice of ½ lemon (more if you like things lemony)
1 tbsp extra virgin olive oil
1 tsp freshly toasted cumin seeds
sea salt and pepper

Elisabeth von Arnim's *Elisabeth and her German Garden* is a very funny book. In it she complains amusingly of the many things and people that threaten her rural solitude and in particular a houseguest, whose faults include a fondness for salads of carrot and cumin. Actually it's a rather good combination.

Peel and grate the carrot and dress with the lemon juice and the olive oil. Toast the cumin seeds in a dry frying pan until they start to smell nutty but don't let them burn. Toss the salad with the cumin seeds. Taste and season with sea salt and pepper.

Beetroot, crisp green apple and pumpkin seeds

Serves 4 alongside two or three other dishes

1 large or 2 small beetroot, coarsely grated
1 crisp apple, grated
lemon juice
extra virgin olive oil
1 heaped tbsp pumpkin seeds
sea salt and pepper

Peel and grate the beetroot and grate the apple (don't bother peeling it). Dress with a squeeze of lemon juice and a very little olive oil. Toss the salad with the pumpkin seeds. Taste and season with sea salt and pepper.

Variations

Use grated parsnip instead of beetroot, or you can substitute carrot for the apple.

For a creamier beetroot salad, whisk together 1 part horseradish sauce (the good quality creamed kind), 2 parts white wine vinegar and 4 parts sour or single cream. Season and mix well with grated beetroot.

Parsley salad

Serves 4

50g couscous
a knob of butter or 1 tbsp olive oil
a large bunch of parsley, leaves finely chopped
a bunch of mint leaves
2 spring onions, finely chopped
1 small cucumber, finely chopped
3 tbsps olive oil
juice of 1 lemon
sea salt and pepper

Put the couscous in a bowl with the butter or olive oil and a good pinch of sea salt. Boil the kettle and pour over enough boiling water to just about cover the couscous. Quickly cover the bowl with cling film. Leave to swell up for about 10 minutes whilst you chop up the herbs and vegetables.

Use a fork to break up the couscous. Put the fluffed-up couscous in a large bowl, add the herbs and mix well with the spring onions and cucumber. The ratio of green to grain should be about 10 : 1. Dress with oil and lemon juice and season. Test a teaspoonful of the salad and add more lemon or oil, to taste. If it's tomato time, add a chopped fresh tomato to the top of the salad.

Hot chick pea salad with spring onions and parsley
Serves 2

1 clove garlic
3–4 tbsps of extra virgin olive oil
1 x 240g tin chick peas, drained and rinsed
juice of ½ lemon (if you have very good new-season olive oil that really tastes of something, you can omit the lemon juice)
2 tbsps finely chopped parsley
3 or 4 spring onions, finely chopped
sea salt and pepper

New season olive oil is a taste to be savoured. In his autobiography, Richard Olney describes the owner of his local olive oil mill, Mme Gerfoit, preparing simple dishes for the truck drivers who came to transport her oil. On a table in front of an open fire she set out slices of thick peasant bread, bowls of chopped salted anchovies and a jug of new oil. The truck drivers would come in and warm their hands at the fire before taking the bread, spreading it with the anchovies, dribbling over the oil, spearing the slices with long-handled forks and toasting them in front of the fire. Other lunches included opaque newly-pressed oil served with individual dishes of hot chick peas, finely chopped garlic, onions and parsley, which were assembled by each diner into a salad at the table. No doubt Mme Gerfoit soaked and boiled her own chick peas but in this case tinned will do fine if you want a quick lunch.

Peel the garlic clove and crush it with the handle of a heavy knife. Heat the garlic in a small pan with 2 tablespoons of the olive oil. Allow the garlic to soften and flavour the oil for a couple of minutes but don't let it brown. Pour in the drained chick peas, season and heat through. Add the lemon juice and cook for another minute.

Remove from the heat and transfer to a bowl. Add the parsley and spring onions. Season with sea salt and pepper and add a little more olive oil.

Rice paper rolls with fresh herbs and salad

a plate of herbs, lettuce and julienned vegetables perhaps:

a small bunch of coriander (approx. 50g)

a small bunch of mint (approx. 50g)

a bunch of chives (approx. 25g), cut into roughly 10cm lengths

leaves of 1 Little Gem lettuce

a small bunch of Asian basil (approx. 50g)

6 spring onions, sliced lengthways into thin strips

1 small cucumber, sliced lengthways into thin strips

1 large carrot, peeled and cut into strips

Perilla sometimes called Shiso and Beefsteak plant – the leaf looks a bit like a nettle but it is a member of the mint family (optional).

50g rice vermicelli (prepared as per packet instructions)

12–15 pre-prepared rice papers

Now that Makbala has returned to Turkey, the plot next door to me is shared by a consortium of her female relatives, headed up by the two Hatifas. One sunny day at the allotment whilst working with my friend Claire, we were invited to lunch by two of these neighbours, a mother and her teenage daughter. We watched them carefully wash and arrange seasonal greens of sorrel, radish and onion tops on a plate before stuffing them into flatbreads with cucumber, boiled egg, tomato and feta. Our contribution was a courgette tart, freshly made by Claire (who arrived with it in her bicycle basket). Their presentation brought to mind Vietnamese herb plates. These are usually a combination of soft lettuce, cucumber, mints, bean sprouts, Asian sweet basils and perilla, all served alongside rice papers. The soft rice paper rolls are made up of *banh trang* (prepared rice papers), beef, pork or prawns, herbs, rice vermicelli (noodles) and vegetables. Each diner takes a rice paper, fills it with prawn or meat, some cucumber and some herbs, rolls it up into a cigar and eats it with dipping sauce. It's a novel way of using up the remains of your roast or can be cooked from scratch with beef or prawns.

You will need to visit a Thai or Vietnamese supermarket to buy the crackling discs of rice paper (embossed with the pattern of the bamboo they were dried on) and at the same time you can buy the more unusual herbs as well as using some from your garden. It's a wonderful way of presenting the bounty you have grown, beautifully arranged on a plate, but actually requires very little effort on your part (your guests do all the fiddly rolling up). *(cont.)*

Preparing the rice papers

Take a large flattish bowl or deep-sided frying pan and fill it with hand-hot water from the kettle. Take one rice paper disc and immerse it in the water. Use your hand to rub the water in gently until the rice paper is soft and malleable. Spread it out on a clean tea towel and soak up any excess water before placing on a large dinner plate. Stack up slightly more than you think you might eat as they are very moreish. You can make them at the last moment or cover them with cling film until you are ready to eat. They will stick together but pull apart again quite easily.

Serve with:

Dipping sauce (*nuoc cham*)

2 cloves garlic, peeled
2 bird's eye chillies or 1 large
red chilli, deseeded and finely
chopped
1–2 tsp caster sugar
2½ tbsps water
1 tsp rice vinegar
3 tsps lime juice
approx. 2½ tbsps fish sauce

Using a pestle and mortar smash the garlic and grind with the chillies to a fine paste, or use a knife to chop them up as finely as you can. Heat the sugar and water until the sugar has dissolved, pour the syrup into the pestle along with the chilli and garlic paste. Mix well and then add the vinegar, lime juice and the fish sauce (add this last ingredient a little at a time tasting as you go). The sauce should be hot and salty. Pour into a small shallow bowl to serve.

Fillings

500g cooked beef (*see page 85 for recipe*) or 500g cold shredded left-over roast pork, or chicken, or large prawns (freshly cooked).

Prepare the beef (*see page 85*) or shred the pork or chicken but leave the prawns whole. Set on the table with the herb plate, the julienned vegetables, the noodles, the sauce and the rice papers. Each person should take a rice paper and spread it out over their plate. Next arrange a little of each ingredient in the centre of the disc. All the matchsticked vegetables should be pointing in the same direction. Fold the top and bottom of the paper over and bring the sides in, rolling it up to make a fat sausage to dip in the sauce.

Beef and herb rice paper rolls
Serves 4

500g beef fillet,
trimmed of fat
1 tsp olive oil
sea salt and pepper
1 tbsp sesame seeds (toasted
in a dry pan) or 1 fresh chilli,
deseeded and finely sliced, to
garnish
a plate of herbs, lettuce and
vegetables (see page 83)

In Vietnamese restaurants they serve a dish from Northern Vietnam called Bò Nu `Ong. The meat is marinated with lemongrass, chillies and garlic then grilled and presented with a herb plate and a dipping sauce made with shrimp paste. The strong, fishy taste of shrimp paste may be an integral part of the dish but it's too much for me. So when I make the rice paper rolls with beef I serve the dipping sauce alongside with soy sauce.

My beef rice paper roll combines Vietnamese flavours with speedy Italian technique; there's no marinading and a whole beef fillet is seared so that the inside remains raw. The combination of very rare beef and fresh herbs is a good one. Children can eat the well-done bits on the side of the fillet – mine love both the taste of this dish and the thrill of making up their own rolls.

Lightly oil the fillet and rub it with sea salt and pepper. Heat a skillet very hot and very quickly blacken the outside of the fillet using tongs to turn it continuously. You are aiming for a crusty blackened exterior and a raw interior (3–5 minutes cooking time). Remove the fillet from the pan and allow it to cool. When the fillet is cooled, use a very sharp knife to cut it into very thin slices. You will find that if you pop it in the freezer for 5 minutes it will slice better. Spread the slices out on a platter. If it all starts to fall apart, just cut it into slivers.

In a heavy frying pan toast the sesame seeds until nutty and brown but not burnt, then set aside. Scatter the sesame seeds or the chilli over the beef and serve with the herb, lettuce and vegetable plate, noodles, dipping sauce and rice papers, as on page 84.

Carrot salad with chilli, mint and coriander

Serves 3–4, alongside the rice paper rolls

100ml rice vinegar
2 tbsps caster sugar
3 medium carrots, peeled,
cut into thin matchsticks and
salted
approx. 2 heaped tbsps
coriander leaves, finely
chopped
approx. 2 heaped tbsps mint
leaves, finely chopped
1 bird's eye chilli, deseeded
and finely chopped
3 spring onions, peeled
and shredded
sea salt and pepper
sprig of mint or coriander, to
garnish

for the dressing
1½ tbsp soy sauce
2 tbsp rice vinegar
½ tsp sesame oil
a pinch of caster sugar

Heat the vinegar and the sugar until the sugar has dissolved. Allow to cool. Pour the sugar vinegar over the carrots and leave to soak for an hour or so. Lift the carrots out of the mixture and mix with the coriander, mint, chilli and spring onion. Season.

Whisk together the ingredients for the dressing. Pour the dressing over the carrots and toss well. Garnish with a sprig of mint or coriander.

Green garlic dolmades

Serves 4 as part of a picnic lunch

40–45 fresh young vine leaves (this includes extra leaves as a decorative bed for your dolmades and some larger, tougher ones to put underneath the parcels as they cook)

8 green garlic plants (use 1 shallot, a bunch of 8 spring onions and a clove of garlic if you can't find green garlic)

Later on one fat bulb will do with some greens

4 tbsps olive oil

4 tbsps chopped dill (you could also use mint)

4 tbsps finely chopped flat-leaf parsley

150g shortgrain rice (risotto will do)

juice of 2 lemons

sea salt and pepper

Late spring and early summer are the best times to make dolmades. Vine leaves are young and tender then and, by a happy coincidence, this is about the time when you can start to harvest a few of your young garlic plants, which should be looking like baby leeks. The delicate flavour of the young garlic really shines in these clean-tasting dolmades, which are stuffed very simply with rice and herbs. Pick an extra bag of tender vine leaves and freeze them to use in winter – they are very resilient and freeze well. If you can't find fresh vine leaves use the pickled ones sold in delis. Vines are a fairly commonly grown plant in urban gardens so keep your eyes out for any growing against warm city walls in your neighbourhood. This year we found an old vine growing in the elder tree beside our shed. We freed the vine of hogweed and nettles and after we had tacked a simple wooden arbour onto the side of the shed we trained the vine over it. The dead-looking vine burst into life, I had somewhere shady to sit with my new baby and we ate vine leaves all summer. In the autumn we harvested our first crop of allotment grapes, small, round globes with a green taste – not sweet but not sour either.

In a large pan of salted boiling water, blanch the vine leaves for about a minute (you can probably do about 5 at a time) then refresh them in a bowl of cold water. If you are using preserved vine leaves soften them in boiling water for about 10 minutes, then drain and refresh them in cold water. Spread the vine leaves out on a clean tea towel ready for use.

Trim the roots and outer leaves of the garlic plants

keeping as much of the green as possible. Wash them well and finely chop the white and the tender parts of the green.

Heat 2 tablespoons of olive oil in a large, heavy bottomed pan and cook the garlic very gently (or the shallot, spring onion and garlic which should all be very finely chopped) until soft and transparent. Add the herbs, the rice and the juice of 1 lemon and, stirring continuously, cook for about a minute. Remove from the heat. Season and stir well.

Take a vine leaf and place it veiny-side up. Be gentle, they tear easily. Snip off the tough stalk and place a heaped teaspoon of mixture on the stalk end of the leaf. Fold the bottom up over it and then bring in the sides of the leaf. Keep rolling all the way up to the top and you should end up with a nice fat cigar shape. As you make the dolmades, put them seam-side down in a circular pattern on a plate. This will give you the best idea of what size of saucepan you need.

Line a heavy bottomed pan with the older tougher vine leaves or any that you have broken. Place the dolmades seam-side down starting from the edge and making circles into the middle. Pack them nice and tight as this stops them from unravelling. Cover the vine leaves with about 2cm water, squeeze over the other lemon and pour over 2 more tablespoons of olive oil. Place a plate that is slightly smaller than the pan on top of the vine leaves. Weight it down with a couple of tins or large pebbles. Bring the liquid up to the boil then turn it down to a very low simmer, cover and cook for 30 minutes. Do keep an eye on the liquid to make sure it doesn't boil dry. After 30 minutes the rice will be cooked and the liquid almost all gone. Very carefully, use tongs to remove the dolmades and transfer them to a plate. Reserve any liquid that is left, let it cool and then mix with a little Greek yoghurt and some olive oil as an accompaniment to the vine leaves. If you don't have any liquid, make some tzatziki to go with the vine leaves (*see page 117*).

Spring onions

Next to my plot is my neighbours' shed, a large rectangular structure the size of some London bedrooms, with a covered space for a table and chairs and a long bench built into one wall. The shed is made of old doors and large sheets of plywood and is connected to their vegetable beds by a rickety framework of salvaged wood. A mass of dead looking brown twigs covers it in winter. In spring these buds miraculously unfurl, forming a roof of shiny green vine leaves. Seated on the ground in front of large enamel bowls my neighbours harvest the tops of their onions. These they stuff into large flatbreads along with sorrel, radish tops and feta for lunch. The onion greens give a spicy heat to the pepper and lemon of the other leaves.

Spring onions offer a subtler, sweeter take on the same sandwich and washed and sliced along with some of their greens together with a strong-tasting cheddar they make a traditional sandwich filling that is hard to improve on.

For a French treatment of spring onions, chop them finely and add them to a salad of green leaves and *fine herbes* dressed with a lemon and oil vinaigrette. If boiled briefly, then grilled, spring onions make a good tart-filling with eggs and goat's cheese.

Sweet pickled spring onions
Makes 2 x medium/350ml jam jars

300g spring onions (roots trimmed, outer skin and green parts removed)
6 tbsps caster sugar
200ml water
200ml distilled white malt vinegar
4 fresh red chillies
1 tsp mustard seeds
1 tsp coriander seeds

Use spring onions with a decent sized bulb to make this sweet pickle, bathed in a brine spiked with chillies.

Place the spring onions in sterilised jam jars (fresh out of the dishwasher is fine). In a small pan, heat the sugar, water, vinegar, chilli and spices. When the sugar has dissolved, bring the spiced vinegar to the boil and remove from the heat. Allow to cool slightly, then pour over the onions. Put on lids. Place in a cupboard and eat after one month.

Globe Artichokes

No kitchen garden should be without artichokes; quite apart from their taste, they are beautiful in their own right, the outline of their jagged, pewter leaves stands out like wrought iron against the earth, a welcome silhouette in the months when the rest of the garden has sunk back down into the ground. You can buy plants or sow seed but the simplest way to grow artichokes, which are very easy to propagate, is to look out for friendly neighbours who have them and take cuttings. This is done by sliding a knife down the side of the outside leaves to the root, to remove a new shoot (they should look like a little V of about five or six leaves with a bit of root attached). Plant them with a good metre of space between each, keep them well watered and they should take. Even if you have your own established plants you can still make new plants and provide yourself with a longer run of artichokes as the plants will bear fruit at different times. They can be eaten very simply, boiled until the outer leaves come away easily and served with melted lemon and butter, or as part of a picnic, eaten cold with a vinaigrette. They can be griddled, roasted, stuffed or pared down to the heart and sautéed with white wine and thyme.

Stuffed globe artichokes
Serves 4 as a starter

4 medium-sized artichokes
lemon juice
2 medium-sized very ripe
tomatoes, skinned
2 cloves garlic
10 wrinkled black olives,
pitted and coarsely chopped
4 anchovy fillets
1 tbsp capers
1 tbsp stale bread that has
been soaked in water,
squeezed and coarsely
chopped
a small glass white wine or
the juice of 1 lemon
4 tbsps olive oil
sea salt and pepper

Though they are tastiest with early summer specimens, stuffed artichokes can be made with any size – you'll just need to increase the cooking time from 20–25 minutes for small to medium artichokes to 45 minutes for large ones.

Remove the tough outer leaves of the artichokes and trim the stalks so that the artichokes sit flat. Working from the outside, tease open the artichoke, by rubbing your fingers back and forth across the centre. Use a small spoon to scrape out the choke (the thistly hairs in the centre of the artichoke) and rinse with water to dislodge any small hairs you might have missed. Rub the centre with lemon juice and drop into a bowl of acidulated water (water with the juice of half a lemon squeezed in).

De-core the tomatoes and chop to a fine pulp on a large board. Crush the garlic into the tomatoes and with a heavy knife chop the olives, anchovy fillets, capers and bread into the mixture, using the flat side of the knife to draw it together and chopping repeatedly until you have a glossy mess. Season, taste and then stuff each artichoke. Pack them tightly into a small saucepan and pour in enough water, with the wine or lemon juice, so that there is liquid halfway up the side of the artichokes. Add 1 tablespoon olive oil into the top of each artichoke. Simmer, covered, for 20–25 minutes or until tender.

Serve each artichoke in a bowl with a little of the cooking liquid spooned over it. This is a messy dish best eaten with the hands and plenty of bread. Encourage your guests to tear off an outside leaf and use it to scoop out each mouthful of stuffing.

Artichokes baked in foil with garlic and thyme

6–8 globe artichokes (not too big)
a few sprigs thyme
2 cloves garlic, sliced
olive oil
sea salt and pepper

Preheat the oven to 220°C/gas mark 7.

Trim the artichokes as on page 92 and lay them down in one layer on a large piece of foil. Scatter over the thyme, garlic and seasoning and a little olive oil. Seal up and place in a roasting dish. Bake for 1 hour.

This method also works well with small beetroot and wedges of pumpkin.

Beans

Pesto with green beans and new potatoes
Serves 4

6–8 very small new potatoes per person
200g spaghetti
about 10 thin green beans per person
3–4 tbsps homemade pesto (see Autumn page 197)
2 tbsps extra virgin olive oil
Parmesan
sea salt and pepper

If you are the impatient type and can't wait for your potatoes to be properly ready before you dig them up, then this dish, common in Liguria, in Italy, provides the perfect excuse, as it needs very tiny new potatoes. If you have only a few potato plants then this rather decadent approach might not suit; it's best kept for those with a surplus. If you have planted French beans then with any luck you might have some ready at about the same time. You can make this recipe with your own basil at the other end of the season when you will inevitably end up with lots of small potatoes in the bottom of your sack.

Place the potatoes in a large pan of salted water and bring to the boil. Boil for 2 minutes and add the spaghetti and cook for approximately 10 minutes, or according to the packet instructions. Add the green beans 4 minutes before the end (feel free to cook the green beans separately if all the timings are giving you a headache).

Put the pesto in the bottom of a large bowl and thin with the olive oil. When the pasta is ready, drain and add to the bowl. Mix well, season with sea salt and pepper and serve with plenty of freshly grated Parmesan.

Autumn variation
Before your basil comes into season you can try making pesto with rocket and walnuts instead of basil and pine nuts.

Broad beans with feta

A very simple salad can be made with broad beans, podded, briefly boiled in salted water and then slipped from their skins. The inner bean has a marvellous green sheen to it and is very good dressed with olive oil, lemon juice, ribbons of freshly chopped mint and a few shavings of feta or pecorino. I sometimes eat them with pesto, new potatoes and spaghetti in place of the french green beans used on page 94.

Dorothy Wordsworth's journals have a transporting effect on me: they place me right in the heart of nature. She has an artist's eye for detail and a poet's facility for precise, unadorned prose and to read her is to step directly into her world. She took on many roles in the life she shared with her brother but one of the happiest seems to have been as a gardener. The garden Dorothy worked at Dove Cottage was an erratically cared for tangle of plants, both domestic and wild. In her diary Dorothy records bringing lemon thyme down from the hillside and planting it by moonlight, gathering lilies and periwinkles from a neighbour's garden and nailing up the trailing honeysuckle. On other days she records the scarlet beans scrambling up poles and Coleridge uncovering a seat covered over with brambles. Some days, and this is when I feel closest to her, she just 'saunters'. Dorothy's garden is created with love and one can easily imagine its half-wild ramshackle beauty. It was obviously a source of comfort to her. Like any gardener, Dorothy faces moments of despair but, unlike most, even in despair she has a graceful eloquence few of us could match:

> *July 5th*
> *It came on a heavy rain . . . The Roses in the garden are fretted and*
> *battered and quite spoiled, the honeysuckle, though in its glory is*
> *sadly teazed. The peas are beaten down. The Scarlet Beans want*
> *sticking. The garden is overrun with weeds.*

In the first year she spends at Dove Cottage, Dorothy writes frequently about peas. Her entries provide a pretty comprehensive lesson in pea husbandry. I have to admit I have found peas difficult in the past but this year with Dorothy's help (and two separate sowings), I grew just enough peas for tarts, frittatas and risottos or to be eaten straight out of the pod, their sweetness a constant revelation.

> *May 15th*
> *Thursday A coldish dull morning – hoed the first row of peas, weeded etc.*

> *Monday May 19th*
> *Sauntered a good deal in the garden, bound carpets, mended old*

clothes. Read Timon of Athens. Dried linen. Molly weeded the turnips, John stuck the peas.

June 10ᵗʰ Tuesday
I made tarts, pies etc. Wm stuck peas. After dinner he lay down. John not at home. I stuck peas alone. Molly washing. Cold showers with hail and rain, but at half past five, after a heavy rain, the lake became calm and very beautiful. Those parts of the water which were perfectly unruffled lay like green islands of various shapes.

July 31ˢᵗ
Gathered peas, and in the afternoon, Coleridge came, very hot; he bought the second volume of the Anthology. The men went to bathe and we afterwards sailed down to Loughrigg.

August 3ʳᵈ, Sunday morning
I made pies and stuffed the pike – baked a loaf. Headache after dinner – I lay down. A letter from Wm roused me, desiring us to go to Keswick. After writing to Wm. We walked as far as Mrs Simpsons and ate blackcherries. A Heavenly warm evening, with scattered clouds upon the hills. There was a vernal greenness upon the grass, from the rains of the morning and afternoon. Peas for dinner.

August 4ᵗʰ
Rain in the night. I tied up Scarlet beans, nailed the honeysuckles, etc. etc . . . I pulled a large basket of peas and sent to Keswick by a returned chaise.

August 6ᵗʰ Wednesday. A rainy morning. I ironed till dinner time – sewed til near dark – then pulled a basket of peas, and afterwards boiled and picked gooseberries.

August 22ⁿᵈ Very cold. Baking in the morning, gathered pea seeds.

Dorothy planted her peas in April, which is fine, but this year I had more success with my later sowing in late May when the ground had warmed up. I had tried to give my first sowing of peas a head start by burying vegetable peelings in a trench and covering the ground with hessian (to feed and warm it respectively) but it didn't seem to help that much. Dorothy harvested her peas two months later in June, leaving a few plants to grow on and provide seed for next year. As the first pea tendrils appeared, one of the Wordsworth household would have carefully placed a pea stick alongside to support the plant; I use the brushy top growth from a hazel or hornbeam hedge. You can grow your peas up netting, but the sight of a spiky forest of hazel twigs, their lower parts feathered with bushy green pea plants, is a delightful one. I get my pea sticks from a wild bit of my parents' garden in Wiltshire, where later in the year I also cut taller, thicker hazel sticks to support cucumbers, tomatoes and sunflowers. (Using bamboo from the other side of the world is really absurd when you think how much native wood there is available in Britain. If you can't forage for your own then suppliers of native woods can be found at www.allotmentforestry.com.)

I sow 'Wrinkled' or marrowfat peas with varying degrees of success. Homegrown peas are very tasty but they are also tricky. The ground needs to be warm before you put them in and then they need to be well watered. You can always cheat and start a few in pots on the windowsill. As peas don't like their roots being disturbed, some people sow them outside in lengths of guttering which they then slide, soil and all, into the ground once the peas have sprouted.

Pea tendrils can be used in salads and risottos before the peas are ready or you can serve your peas in the pod for your guests to snack on raw. When the pods are split open, children and adults seem equally as entranced by the sight of the fat shiny peas tightly squeezed inside as they are by the sweet taste of freshly pulled peas. Peas, like freshly dug potatoes, give you something money can't buy, a taste only available to those who grow their own. Peas start converting their sugar into starch the moment they are picked and are always better on the day of harvest; your own freshly picked and podded pea has a quality that no shop-bought pea can ever hope to emulate.

Petits pois à la Française

(Peas braised with salad, spring onions and mint)

Serves 4 as a side-dish

150g Little Gem or other sweet lettuce leaves (not too leathery, please)
8 spring onions, cut into quarters and then halved
2 tbsps chopped mint leaves
2 tbsps chopped parsley leaves
200g peas (as the season for lettuce is much longer than that of peas you can get away with using frozen here)
2 rounded tbsp (40g) butter)
pinch of caster sugar, if needed
2 tbsps water
sea salt and pepper

This recipe is a good way of using up the outer leaves of Little Gem or any lettuces not quite tender enough for salad but too good to compost. The slow braise results in wilted lettuce with a little bite to it and very tender peas bathed in a herby butter. It goes well with slices of cold ham and some good mustard.

Take a small to medium-sized saucepan and lay the lettuce leaves in the bottom to form a lettuce flower of two or three layers. Strew the spring onions and chopped herbs along the inside of lettuce leaves and then add the peas. Dot the butter over the peas and season adding a pinch of sugar if you think the lettuce needs it. Add the water and draw the outside leaves of lettuce into the centre to cover the tops of the peas. Put the saucepan lid on and simmer gently for 15–20 minutes. Have a look after 10 minutes to make sure there is still water in the bottom of the pan and add another tablespoon if it looks dry.

Pea and globe artichoke heart frittata
Serves 4 as part of a picnic lunch

1 tbsp butter (approx. 20g)
6 medium-sized artichokes,
trimmed down to their
hearts (see page 92)
juice of ½ a lemon
1 rounded tsp finely chopped
fresh thyme leaves
250g fresh peas (unpodded
weight)
3 eggs (4 if they are small)
2 tbsps milk
a good knob of butter
(approx. 20g), for frying
a few chopped mint leaves,
to garnish
sea salt and pepper

If you grow your own artichokes you may find yourself suddenly overwhelmed by abundance in early June. This recipe only requires the hearts and so uses up lots of artichokes in one go. Artichokes and peas are ready at the same time and combine to make a rather luxurious frittata.

In a small heavy-bottomed saucepan heat the butter and add the prepared artichoke hearts. Shake the pan to coat the hearts with butter and then squeeze over the lemon juice and add the thyme. Add 1 tablespoon water and season with salt. Cover and turn down to steam for about 10 minutes (or until the hearts are soft). Remove from the heat and add the peas. Mix well and season with pepper and more salt if necessary.

Beat the eggs and add the milk and then the vegetables. Mix well. Wipe out the frying pan, return it to the heat and add a good knob of butter. When the pan is hot and the butter is melted but not brown, swirl it round the pan a bit and then add the egg and artichoke mixture. Allow to cook over a medium heat until the sides have solidified and the top is not too runny. Take a plate that just fits the inside of the frying pan and place it upside-down on top of the mixture. Using a tea towel to protect your hand, flip the frittata onto the plate and then slide it back into the pan to cook the new underside. When the underside is cooked (after a couple of minutes) slide the frittata out onto a plate and sprinkle with a little sea salt and a few fresh mint leaves. Serve hot or at room temperature.

Pea and mint risotto
Serves 4

1 tbsp butter (20g)
1 tbsp olive oil
2 shallots (or 1 onion)
300g risotto rice
50g ham (optional)
1 litre chicken stock (kept hot on the stove)
500g fresh peas, podded weight
approx. 4 tbsps freshly grated Parmesan
2 tbsps chopped mint leaves (plus a little more chopped mint to finish)
1 tbsp crème fraîche
1 tbsp butter (20g)
Parmesan, to serve
sea salt and pepper

Melt the butter and olive oil in a heavy-bottomed saucepan and gently sweat the shallots. When the shallots are soft add the rice and ham and stir for a minute until every grain of rice is coated. Add a little of the hot stock (a ladleful at a time) stirring well each time and adding a little more as it is absorbed. After about 15 minutes add the peas. After about 20 minutes the rice should be tender but have a slight nuttiness when bitten into. If your stock runs out just use a little bit of hot water from the kettle.

Take the risotto off the heat and add the Parmesan, mint and crème fraîche, mix well and season. Add another tablespoon of butter, to finish. Allow to sit for a minute or two. Taste again and adjust the seasoning if necessary. Serve with a little more chopped mint scattered over the top and a hunk of Parmesan for people to grate on more if they want.

Variation
Skip the crème fraîche and add 6 artichoke hearts (prepared as on page 92) with the peas for a risotto that captures the essence of early summer.

Black (or red) radish tzatziki
Serves 2 as a side-dish

1 small bunch of red radishes thinly sliced or 1 medium-sized black radish, grated
3 tbsps Greek yoghurt
a squeeze of lemon juice
1 tbsp olive oil
1 tbsp chopped mint leaves
sea salt and pepper

Black radishes have a charming sooty appearance that brings to mind a small mole (the underground kind). I have only ever seen them at the TFC (the Turkish Food Centre in Dalston) and in my allotment neighbour's plot. They are not instantly appealing but a very positive reference to 'Spanish radish' in *Cooking with Pomiane* by the French scientist and cookery writer Edouard de Pomiane, encouraged me to make this dish. De Pomiane notes that in Germany and Austria they used to serve long spirals of black radish as an appetizer with beer. He suggests making them into a salad with cream but yoghurt makes a lighter dish perhaps more suited to modern palates. You can substitute white radish (called mooli or daikon) or the more readily available scarlet radish.

If you are using a black radish then peel and grate it, and salt with a light touch. Leave for a couple of hours, then drain off any juices.

Mix the radish with the yoghurt, lemon juice, oil and mint, then season with salt and pepper.

Courgettes and squash

Some people object to courgettes, sensing a reproach in the speed at which they grow. I don't think of them as bullies; their miraculous fruitfulness is a safeguard against the failure of trickier crops. That a single seed can produce such a quantity of vegetables never fails to amaze me. I pick mine constantly, the smaller the better, and they hardly ever get a chance to grow longer than a hand span. But just occasionally, a plant will revenge itself on me for continually thwarting its growth and hide a monstrous marrow beneath its grey-green leaves; if this happens I make piccalilli (*see page 201*).

Courgettes and squash provide that great luxury of the home vegetable grower – blossoms. Dipped in batter, fried, salted and eaten with cold glasses of beer, they are as much a part of my summer as strawberries and cream. I start my courgette plants off in trays on my bedroom windowsill, sowing in two batches, one month apart to ensure a longer growing season. In the past I have had success with the green Italian varieties, Bambino and Nero di Milano, as well as the bright yellow Soleil and custard or patty pan squashes. This year I am growing the knobbly yellow Crookneck squash, which has a similar taste to courgette, and the pale green Verde di Italia, an early variety with a delicate flavour and ridged skin. The crookneck squash are slow to get going but continue well into September when the rest of my courgettes are over.

Courgettes can be eaten raw, in ribbons dressed with mint and vinegar; steamed and dressed with lemon, butter and chives; sliced and fried and bound with egg to make frittata or quiches; stewed with tomato; shredded, squeezed and mixed with ricotta to make a stuffing for roast chicken; or turned into the following fritters which can be eaten hot or made ahead of time as part of a picnic.

Courgette fritters

Serves 4 as a starter

4 small or 2 medium courgettes (about 350g)
1 tbsp plain flour
2 eggs, beaten
1 tbsp finely chopped herbs (mint and chives or thyme)
zest of 1 lemon
1 clove garlic, finely chopped
2 spring onions, peeled and shredded
olive oil, for frying
75g feta, cubed (optional)
mixed lettuce and herbs and lemon segments, to serve
sea salt and pepper

The Pelion peninsular in mainland Greece is the mythical home of the Centaurs. Their hooves once thundered through the beech forests that cling to the area's surprisingly dramatic cliffs and craggy hills. We ate these fritters on the terrace of a restaurant up in the hills and they came with a bowl of tzatziki, which was a perfect accompaniment. If you find yourself eating a lot of them you may like to try shaping the courgette mixture round small cubes of feta for the sake of variety.

Grate the courgettes coarsely. If you have time, salt and leave them to drain in a colander. Don't worry about this bit too much if it's nearly lunch- or dinner-time and your courgettes are nice and tiny.

Take a clean tea towel and place the courgette pulp in the middle. Wring the tea towel out over the sink. The pulp should collect in a fat bulb and a surprising amount of water will come out.

Place the flour in a bowl and add the beaten eggs, herbs, lemon zest, garlic, spring onions and courgettes. Heat a large frying pan with a couple of tablespoons of olive oil. When the oil is hot, take a heaped tablespoon of mixture and drop it into the pan, flattening it out slightly with the back of the spoon. Don't muck about with it until the bottom is golden brown (a couple of minutes) or the whole thing will disintegrate. Flip it over with a spatula and give each fritter a couple of minutes before draining them on a plate lined with paper towel.

To serve, arrange some mixed leaves of mint, sorrel, Little Gem and mustards on a large plate, and place the fritters around the edge of with some radish tzatziki (*see page 102*) in the middle and a few lemon segments.

The fritters can also be served rolled-up in a soft flatbread with salad and tzatziki and eaten like falafel, for a more portable picnic dish.

Fried courgette flowers

(stuffed and unstuffed)

Serves 4 as a starter

20 courgette flowers
vegetable oil, for frying

for the batter
50g flour
a pinch salt
1 egg (separated, white reserved)
1 tbsp olive oil
150ml lager (you can substitute milk and water mixed half and half)
Vegetable oil for frying

for the stuffing (optional)
200g ricotta
2 tablespoons freshly grated Parmesan
1 tbsp finely chopped sage or 1 tsp chopped thyme leaves
1 tsp lemon zest
sea salt and pepper

Early morning is the right time to pick courgette flowers, before the blossoms start to wilt in the sun; filling a bag with a mass of egg-yolk orange flowers is also a great way to start the day. Back home again, I shake off any dirt and arrange them carefully in a shallow bowl to form one enormous bloom. As a salty appetiser the combination of crisp batter and the tender, slightly vegetable bite of the petals is almost miraculous, and that's before you reach the slightly molten cheese within. Serve with a very cold beer or a glass of Prosecco.

Courgette flowers are male and female. If you pick the male flowers (which won't turn into courgettes) you are not denying yourself any fruits. The two are easy to tell apart as the male flowers have no fruit swelling at the base of the petals where they meet the stalk. When I have lots of courgettes I pick some with the blossom still attached and fry the whole thing. The general rule is the thinner the batter, the crispier the coating – with the caveat that thinner batter won't cling on so well. Feel free to adjust the amount of liquid to your own tastes.

To prepare the courgette flowers, wipe with a kitchen towel and check inside for insects, then pull off the sepals – the spiky bit on the outside – and the green stamens within. The quickest way is to snip off the bottom of the flowers with scissors but this spoils the look of them a little so you may prefer the fiddlier option of going in from the top.

To make the batter, whisk the flour and salt together with the egg yolk, oil and lager. Leave this mixture to rest for at least 10 minutes, then whisk the egg white until stiff and gently fold it into the batter just before you are ready to start frying. The batter will keep for a day in the fridge.

If you are making stuffed flowers, mix the ricotta and Parmesan together in a bowl with the herbs, lemon zest and seasoning, taste and adjust the seasoning but remember you'll be adding salt at the end. Stuff a rounded teaspoon into each flower and pull the petals back together to seal in the cheese.

Heat a wide frying pan with about 1 cm vegetable oil. When it's hot simply dip the flowers (stuffed or unstuffed) into the batter. Shake off a little of the batter and pop the flower into the hot fat. Fry each flower for about 2 minutes (or until golden and crunchy) before draining on kitchen paper and seasoning with sea salt. Sometimes I squeeze a bit of lemon over too. When cooking, don't crowd the pan with dipped flowers as this will lower the temperature of the oil. Aim to do 3 or 4 at a time, or 5 in a big frying pan.

Courgette ceviche
Serves any number

1 small courgette per person, topped and tailed and sliced into thin ribbons (a potato peeler gets the thinnest strips)

approx. 150ml dressing, made with 3 parts extra virgin olive oil to 1 part balsamic or sherry vinegar

small bunch fresh mint leaves, finely chopped (summer savory or marjoram would also be nice)

sea salt and pepper

Ceviche is a South American way of eating raw fish 'cooked' in citrus dressings. You can apply this process to the very tenderest of courgettes, sliced into ribbons and dressed instead with balsamic or sherry vinegar and fresh herbs. Eaten raw like this, alongside charcuterie, they make a very elegant start to a meal. This recipe really needs to marinade for at least an hour (30 minutes at a pinch) to let the flavours develop. For a very colourful effect use a mixture of yellow and green courgettes or summer squash.

Make the dressing, reserving a few leaves to garnish with. Place the courgettes in bowl and pour over the dressing. Mix well, cover and leave to marinade at room temperature.

Courgette and marjoram frittata

Serves 4 as part of a picnic or 2 with a green salad as a main course

1 tbsp olive oil
1 clove garlic, peeled and crushed with the flat side of a knife
4 baby courgettes, trimmed and sliced into thin coins
3 eggs (4 if they are small)
2 tbsps water or milk
a good knob of butter (approx. 20g)
1 rounded tsp fresh marjoram, finely chopped
sea salt and pepper

A frittata is a thicker, flatter Italian version of an omelette. It makes a fat cake, which can be cooked ahead of time and cut into wedges as part of a picnic or summery meze-style lunch.

In a heavy frying pan, heat the olive oil together with the garlic. When the oil is hot add the courgettes and fry on both sides until slightly coloured. Remove from the heat and drain the courgettes on kitchen paper, discard the garlic. Season.

Beat the eggs and add the water or milk. Add the courgettes. Mix well. Wipe out the frying pan and return it to the heat, adding a good knob of butter. When the pan is hot and the butter is melted but not brown, swirl it round the pan and then add the egg and courgette mixture. Allow this to cook for a couple of minutes. Take a plate that just fits the inside of the frying pan and place it upside-down on top of the mixture. Using a tea towel to protect your hand flip the frittata onto the plate and then slide it back into the pan to cook the new underside. After a couple of minutes slide the frittata out onto a serving plate and sprinkle with a little sea salt and a few fresh marjoram flowers (or leaves).

Frittata can be eaten hot or at room temperature.

Variation

Beetroot greens or artichoke hearts (prepared as on page 92) that have been lightly sautéed in butter can be added earlier in the season instead of courgettes.

Slow-cooked courgettes with lemon and mint

Serves 4 as a side-dish

8–10 small courgettes (10cm maximum)
3 cloves garlic, peeled and crushed roughly with the flat side of your knife
6 tbsps olive oil
juice of 1 lemon
2 tbsps finely chopped mint or parsley leaves
sea salt and pepper

On the Greek island of Sifnos we came across a family-run seaside restaurant where we ended up eating almost every night. The children played on the beach in the moonlight whilst we drank endless tin jugs of very cold white wine. This salad of braised courgettes was one of several vegetable first courses that they offered, along with the *horta* and *salata horiatiki*. For this salad you really do need the smallest courgettes and as such it is ideal for the home grower who can pick them whatever size they want (picking them small also avoids a glut). When you get bored with mint try dressing it with parsley.

Preheat the oven to 180°C/gas mark 4.

Top and tail the courgettes. Take a large heavy-bottomed casserole and arrange the courgettes in a single layer. Throw in the garlic. Season and then pour in a cup of water (200ml) and 3 tablespoons of the olive oil. Put the lid on the casserole and bake in the oven for one hour (turn over the courgettes halfway through).

Take the casserole out of the oven, remove the lid and allow the courgettes to come to room temperature. When you are ready to eat, dress them with the remaining oil and the lemon juice (add the latter gradually and adjust according to your own taste).

Sprinkle over the mint and serve. Eaten with fresh bread and feta, this dish makes a light and simple lunch.

Courgettes with Indian spices

*Serves 4 alongside 2 or 3 other curries
and rice or chapattis*

*6–8 small courgettes, topped
and tailed and cut
lengthways into four*

for the spice paste
3 cloves garlic, peeled
*1 fresh red chilli, deseeded
and roughly chopped*
1 tsp ground cumin
½ tsp ground coriander
½ tsp turmeric

2 tbsps vegetable oil
½ tsp whole cumin seeds
¼ tsp whole mustard seeds
½ tsp salt
juice of ½ lemon
chat masala, to serve

In a pestle and mortar grind the garlic and chilli to a paste (or chop them finely together with a knife) and add the ground cumin, ground coriander and turmeric.

In a large heavy frying pan heat the vegetable oil. When it is hot, add the whole cumin seeds and the whole mustard seeds. When they start to pop add the curry paste mixture and stir for 1 minute before adding the courgettes, the salt, 100ml water and the lemon juice. Cover and cook very slowly for 10 minutes.

Serve in a bowl with a pinch of chat masala on top and some lemon wedges.

Courgette stuffing for roast chicken
Serves 4

1 medium free-range roast
chicken (approx. 1.5kg)
sea salt and pepper
2 tbsps olive oil
1 tsp fresh thyme leaves

4 small courgettes, grated,
salted and left to drain for 30
minutes
1 tsp of fresh marjoram
1 tsp of lemon zest
3 tbsps freshly grated
Parmesan
2 tbsps softened butter
1 egg, beaten
1 tbsp fresh white
breadcrumbs
sea salt and pepper

Most people think of stuffing the cavity of the bird but stuffing placed between the skin and breast is another way of adding flavour to the meat. This recipe takes its inspiration from Richard Olney's split, stuffed and baked chicken recipe in *Simple French Food*.

Take a large pair of kitchen scissors and cut the chicken along one side of its backbone (the underneath). Lay it on a chopping board, breast up, and hit it with your fist to flatten it, breaking the leg and thigh joints where necessary. Very carefully slide your hand between the skin and the flesh of the bird. You will feel lots of tiny membranes, which will break easily. Try not to rip the outer skin. If you keep pushing your hand gently further in you can loosen the skin of the thigh and leg joints just as easily as the breast. Season the chicken and anoint on both sides with the oil, scatter over the thyme leaves and leave to rest for 30 minutes.

Preheat the oven to 230°C/gas mark 8.

Squeeze the grated courgettes in a tea towel over a sink to get rid of as much water as possible. Mix the remaining ingredients with the courgettes to make a stuffing, forcing a handful at a time between the chicken skin and the meat. When you have finished stuffing the chicken, sit it in a roasting tray, patting it back into shape.

Season the bird and roast in the preheated oven for 15 minutes. Turn the oven down to 180°C/gas mark 4 and cook for another 45 minutes to 1 hour, basting occasionally.

Courgette and lemon risotto
Serves 4

3 tbsps butter (75g)
1 clove garlic, peeled and roughly crushed
600g courgettes and/or summer squash (topped, tailed and diced)
10–15 courgette flowers (wiped clean, green sepals and stamens removed)
1 tbsp olive oil
1 litre chicken stock
1 onion
300g risotto rice
juice and grated zest of ½ a lemon (keep them separate)
4 tbsps crème fraîche
125g freshly grated Parmesan
approx. 2 tbsps finely chopped basil
sea salt and pepper

In a heavy frying pan heat 2 tablespoons of the butter along with the clove of garlic. When the butter has melted, fry the courgettes and/or squash over a medium heat. When they have browned a little and are tender but with bite, remove and set aside. Slice the courgette flowers into ribbons (reserve 2 tablespoons for garnish).

In a heavy-based saucepan gently heat the remaining tablespoon of butter and the olive oil. In another pan heat the stock so that it is barely simmering. Sweat the onion very gently in the butter and oil until soft (about 15 minutes). Add the rice and stir for 1 minute so that every grain is coated. Add a couple of ladlefuls of stock and stir well. After a couple of minutes the rice will have absorbed the stock, then add more gradually. After 10 minutes add the lemon zest, the courgette and the sliced flowers. Continue cooking for another 10 minutes until you have used up the stock and the rice is cooked but retains some bite.

While the rice is cooking, beat the lemon juice with the crème fraîche and the Parmesan. When the risotto is cooked, take it off the heat and add this mixture. Stir well, letting the flavours mingle before seasoning with lots of black pepper and a little salt (the Parmesan is quite salty). Stir in the basil, keeping the odd leaf to sprinkle on top with the courgette flowers you have saved. Serve with a dish of grated Parmesan.

Variations
Earlier in the season you can use mint, parsley, chives or marjoram if you have no basil.

Cucumbers

We eat an awful lot of pickles, the crunchier the better. Whether they are slender warty cornichons or bulbous cucumbers crowned with dill, an opened jar of gherkins usually lasts about a day in our house. To satisfy demand (and to use up the mountain of empty pickle jars), I grow a small gherkin cucumber that is perfect for pickling. It's a centuries old variety, bred specifically for growing outdoors in cooler climates, so even if you don't have a greenhouse you can still enjoy the subtle charms of a really fresh cucumber, which if you are only used to the bitter, watery greengrocer variety will be a revelation.

I grow an heirloom variety, the Parisian pickling cucumber, first developed by nineteenth-century French market gardeners who were eager to supply the craze for cornichons. This one crops well in our cooler, shorter northern summers with lots of early fruits produced without too much nurturing. Plant them on your windowsill in May and outdoors in June, taking care to handle the fragile sappy stems delicately when you transplant. This year, I made a triangular frame out of hazel poles and grew them up a string (gravity helps them to grow straight), but you can let them scramble along the ground. If you have a compost heap, try growing cucumbers on that. If not, mulch well with compost when you put them in, to give them a bit of warmth and protection – slugs are horribly prone to eating up juicy cucumber and gourd seedlings and I have sometimes lost all mine in the past. If you want to get things off to a really good start place a cloche over the seedling. You can make a disposable cloche (cloches are usually bell shaped and made of clear glass) by cutting the bottom off a 2 litre plastic water bottle and putting the rest of the bottle over the plant. The cloche forms a mini greenhouse providing warmth but keeping out pests.

When it comes to being harvested, cucumbers have a chameleon quality that allows them to hide behind leaves, so, just like courgettes, they require regular, vigilant picking. Cornichons are supposed to be small but I let my cucumbers grow big. We eat them in salads right through till September and I also make them into dill pickles, the largest ones sliced into four lengthways.

Saving cucumber seed

At the end of the summer you will probably end up with a couple of over-ripe yellowish monsters. Don't throw them away as, if you have grown real varieties and

not hybrids, it is easy to save seed for successful crops the following year. Scoop out the seeds and put them in a jam jar full of water for 2 days. The bad seeds will float, being full of air, but the good ones will sink. Pour off the water, getting rid of all the bad seeds. Pour the remaining good, heavy seeds into a sieve and then spread them out on a sheet of newspaper. When they are dry put them in an envelope and store in a cool, dry place.

Pickled cucumbers

enough small cucumbers to fill a large 2 litre pickle jar or Kilner jar (approx 500g)
2–3 tbsps sea salt
6 sprigs dill including stalk, roughly chopped (use dill crowns if in season)
2 bay leaves
3 garlic cloves, peeled
400ml clear distilled malt vinegar
400ml water
2 tbsp pickling spices (see Basics, page 275).
3 tbsps granulated sugar

Use either gherkin cucumbers or the small stubby cucumbers sold in Turkish and Middle Eastern shops.

Sterilise the jar in the oven (*see Basics, page 266*).

Wipe the cucumbers with a damp cloth and lay them in a large shallow dish. Cover generously with sea salt. Leave for 24 hours, moving them around occasionally. When you are ready to make the pickles, brush off the salt and pour a kettleful of boiling water over the cucumbers. Allow them to sit for 5 minutes before draining.

Pack the cucumbers down into the jar (small ones will be in layers, larger ones will have to stand upright). Sprinkle in the dill, and push the bay leaves and garlic amongst them.

Make a pickling vinegar by bringing the vinegar and the water to the boil along with the pickling spices and the sugar in a non-reactive (stainless steel) pan. Simmer for about 10 minutes, then taste. You don't want to make it too strong as some of the spices are to remain in the jar, gradually increasing in flavour over the months of storage. Strain and set the spices aside, removing any really strong ones like cloves or star anise. Sprinkle a tablespoon of the remaining spices in the jar and pour over the vinegar. Seal and put away for a month before trying.

If you're growing your own onions you can always include some of the very small ones too; just peel them first and add at the salting stage.

Cucumber salad
Serves 4

1 small cucumber (approx. 150g)
sea salt
1 tbsp wine or rice vinegar
½ tsp nigella or black onion seeds

Peel and slice the cucumber into slender batons. Sprinkle with a little sea salt and dress with either white wine vinegar or Japanese rice vinegar. Leave for an hour or so. Before serving, sprinkle over some nigella or black onion seeds.

Tzatziki
Serves 2

2 small or 1 large cucumber (peeled but only seeded if they are big)
sea salt
6 tbsps yoghurt
1 tbsp chopped mint leaves
1 clove garlic, finely chopped
pepper

Slice the cucumber into small cubes, salt and leave to drain for an hour or two. Mix the yoghurt with the mint and garlic, add the cucumber and season to taste. Tzatziki goes very well with *borek* (*see page 118*).

Spinach

Borek (spinach and feta triangles)
Makes about 18–20 borek

1 tbsp olive oil
1 clove garlic, peeled and crushed lightly with the side of a knife
2 spring onions, white parts roughly chopped
1 large bunch of spinach, leaves only, weight when stalks removed about 250g
200g feta cheese, crumbled
1 egg
leaves from a small bunch of parsley, chopped
leaves from a small bunch of dill, chopped
black pepper
nutmeg
1 x 200g packet of borek *pastry (like filo only thicker; 2 doubled up sheets of filo will do if you can't source the* borek *pastry, which is found in Turkish shops)*
olive oil for brushing
1 tbsp sesame seeds (optional)

Whenever I feel that my children haven't been eating enough vegetables I make these – the crunchy pastry and delicious herby cheese conceal the fact that they are inadvertently eating large quantities of leafy greens. *Borek* are feta cheese and herb pastries popular in the near East; I always make them with spinach to counteract the saltiness of the feta. They are very good for picnics, packed lunches or for when you know you are going to be busy but need something to grab and eat quickly.

If you are unsure about the folding-up part of the recipe, practise with a piece of A4 paper first. Cut the paper in half lengthways and use one tall rectangle. Fold the bottom right-hand corner away from you to make a diagonal, then fold over and over making triangles all the way up.

In a large, heavy-bottomed saucepan heat the oil and the garlic. When the pan is hot, add the spring onions and fry for a few minutes before adding the spinach. Move the spinach around the pan for a couple of minutes until it is completely wilted. Remove from the heat and drain in a sieve, pushing the spinach hard with the back of a wooden spoon to get rid of as much liquid as possible. Leave to cool.

Crumble the feta into a mixing bowl, crack in the egg and add the herbs. Mix well and season with black pepper and some freshly grated nutmeg (4 or 5 passes along the grater should do it). When the spinach has cooled, add that and mix well.

Preheat the oven to 180°C/gas mark 4. Line a baking sheet with non-stick baking parchment.

Take a sheet of the pastry (returning the rest to the packet so it doesn't dry out as you work) and brush with olive oil. If you are using filo, lay another sheet on top. Cut the pastry, either with scissors or by scoring it with a heavy knife, into pieces roughly 25cm long by 10cm wide.

Place about a good rounded tablespoon of mixture into the bottom right-hand corner of the rectangle. Take the bottom right-hand corner and fold up to the opposite edge, making a right-angled triangle, diagonal-side nearest to you. Fold over and over making triangles all the way up, brushing every other triangle shape with oil as you go. Keep going until you have reached the last fold. Give the inside of the final flap a very good brushing with oil (this is the glue for your parcel). Place the pastry on the baking sheet and give it a brush all over with oil. Keep making parcels until you have used up all your mixture. If you have some pastry left over just seal it up well and put in the fridge (it keeps quite well for a week or so).

If you like, you can scatter the sesame seeds on top before putting the triangles in the oven.

Bake for about 20 minutes or until crisp and golden brown. Remove from the oven and place the pastries on a cooling rack. You can eat them warm but be careful as the inside stays molten-hot for a good 10 minutes (greedy, impatient mouths will get burnt).

Variations

When I am short of time I make a quick version of these by putting the spinach into the parcels raw. Take a bunch of spinach leaves and roll it up into a cigar then slice it into very thin ribbons and combine with the egg, herbs and cheese as above. They are slightly trickier to roll up but if you compress the spinach as you fold the pastry over you should be able to get a decent amount of mixture into each one.

Chana dhal with spinach
Serves 4-6

450g chana dhal (split yellow lentils)
½ tsp turmeric
3 thick slices unpeeled ginger, smashed with the handle of a knife
½–1 tsp salt
a pinch of garam masala (see page 245 for homemade mix)
a small knob of butter (15g)
2 cloves garlic, unpeeled, smashed with the flat side of a knife
2 green chillies, deseeded and finely sliced
a small bunch of spinach leaves (approx. 125g)
a handful of chopped fresh coriander or mint leaves (or both)
juice of 1 lime

There a many different kinds of dhal. This is a very basic one made with split yellow lentils. They don't require soaking and the last-minute addition of some wilted spinach makes it almost a meal in itself.

Put the chana dhal in a saucepan and cover with 1 litre of water. Bring to the boil and remove any scum. Add the turmeric and ginger and cook for at least 1½ hours. Keep your eye on it during the last 30 minutes and add a little more water if it is too dry, stirring occasionally. You are aiming for a thick purée, with the lentils very soft to the touch. Add the salt and garam masala.

Just before you are about to serve the dhal, heat the butter in a heavy frying pan. Add the garlic and the chillies, quickly followed by the spinach. Keep the spinach moving round the pan so that it wilts but does not burn, then tip the whole lot into the dhal with the herbs. Squeeze over the lime and stir well. Let it sit so that the flavours combine for about 10 minutes before serving.

This recipe makes quite a bit of dhal but it freezes very well.

Wilted spinach with chillies and garlic
Serves 2

a bunch of spinach (leaves only, approx. 250g)
1 tbsp olive oil
1 clove garlic, smashed with the flat of the knife
½ tsp chilli flakes
½ tsp salt

Happily one of the best ways of cooking spinach also happens to be one of the easiest. When you wilt spinach by cooking it fast over a high heat you preserve all the flavour and freshness of the uncooked leaf before adding the pungency of chilli and garlic. You can combine wilted spinach with pasta and make a meal of it.

Wash the spinach and trim off the stalks. Don't be too rigorous about drying it. In a large heavy frying pan heat the oil over a high heat with the garlic. When the garlic starts to sizzle, throw in the spinach. Sprinkle over the chilli and salt. Keep the spinach moving around the pan for 2 or 3 minutes, until the spinach wilts and turns glossy. Remove from the pan with tongs and serve.

Variation
You can add some lemon juice or a teaspoon of grated lemon zest alongside or instead of the chilli flakes.

Potatoes

There are recipes that use potatoes scattered throughout this book, but the following are the tried-and-tested everyday ways we eat potatoes at home – and we eat a lot of potatoes.

Potato Dauphinoise
Serves 4

600g waxy yellow potatoes (Charlotte are good), peeled
200ml single cream
100ml milk
1 clove garlic, peeled and lightly crushed
a little butter, for greasing
nutmeg
1 small tbsp butter (approx. 15g)
3 tbsps Parmesan (Gruyère is more correct but as Parmesan is what you probably have in the fridge that will do fine)
sea salt and pepper

Preheat the oven to 180°C /gas mark 4.

Slice the potatoes into very thin coins (using a mandolin is quickest). Put the potatoes in a colander and rinse under the cold tap, stirring them around with your hand. Toss the slices in a clean tea towel until dry.

Whisk together the cream and the milk in a bowl.

Rub the garlic over the inside of a gratin dish (a deep ovenproof ceramic dish) making sure you don't leave any lumps of garlic behind (just the juice). Butter the dish. Put a single layer of potato slices over the bottom of the gratin dish. Season lightly and add a few scrapes of nutmeg but don't overdo it - a little goes a long way. Repeat until you have used up all your potato slices. Dot the top of gratin with small pieces of butter and pour over the creamy mixture.

Cover the top with grated Parmesan. Cover with foil and bake for 45 minutes, then take the foil off for 15 minutes, to bring it up to 1 hour in total. Test the middle with the point of a knife to make sure all the potato is cooked through and give it another 10 minutes if you need to (an underdone gratin is very unsatisfying).

Richard Olney-style mashed potato
Serves 4

My first meal in Paris was in a glum little dining room for boarders, in the Hôtel de l'Académie, at the corner of the rue de l'Université and the rue des Saints-Pères. The plat du jour was 'gibelotte, pommes mousseline' – rabbit and white wine fricassee with mashed potatoes. The gibelotte was all right, the mashed potatoes the best I had ever eaten, pushed through a sieve, buttered and moistened with enough of their hot cooking water to bring them to a supple, not quite pourable consistency. No milk, no cream, no beating. I had never dreamt of mashing potatoes without milk and, in Iowa, everyone believed that, the more you beat them, the better they were.

Richard Olney – *Reflexions*

6 largish potatoes, about 500g (any non-waxy maincrop variety will do)
75g butter
sea salt and pepper

Peel the potatoes and cut into quarters. Place in a pan of cold salted water and bring to the boil. By gradually bringing them to the boil you are ensuring they cook more evenly but if you are in a hurry you can use boiling water from the kettle.

When the potatoes are well cooked but not falling to pieces, drain them, after placing a measuring jug in the sink to collect the cooking water as you do so.

Either sieve the potatoes or use a potato ricer to get a smooth purée. Stir in the butter and gradually mix in the water, a tablespoon at a time (up to approximately 4 tablespoons), using your eye to judge when you have achieved a good consistency: silky-smooth but not too runny. Season with sea salt and pepper.

Oven chips for children
Serves any number

1 medium-to-large potato
per child
2 tbsps olive oil
sea salt

This recipe is so simple I hesitate to write it down, but as a regular accompaniment to hot dogs, steaks, fried eggs and ham it is part of our family life, so here it is. Adults are welcome to try it.

Preheat the oven to 180°C/ gas mark 4.

Wash the potatoes and cut them into thick wedges lengthways (roughly eighths). Pour the oil onto a heavy metal baking sheet and pop into the oven 3 minutes before you are ready to start cooking. When the fat is hot, take out the baking sheet and very carefully slide the potatoes onto it. With a pair of tongs, turn the potoatoes in the oil. Season with sea salt.

Cook for about 15 minutes then turn the potato wedges (you may have to use a metal spatula to prise them off the baking sheet). When the potatoes are crispy and golden on both sides (25–30 minutes) slide them onto a plate lined with paper towel and shake them around a bit. Serve immediately.

Shoestring potatoes for two

2 large potatoes (large
maincrop, such as Maris
Piper, Desiree or
King Edward)
approx. 250ml vegetable oil
sea salt

A small bowl of crispy, well-salted shoestring potatoes makes a great appetiser but goes equally well with meat dishes, especially steaks or burgers.

Peel the potatoes and slice into very thin matchsticks. This is much easier if you have a mandolin with a julienne attachment or else a food processor. Rinse the sticks in cold water and shake dry in a clean tea towel.   *(cont.)*

Heat the oil (it should be about 4cm deep) in a small saucepan. Have ready a plate with a couple of sheets of paper towel on it. When the oil is hot, add the potatoes. (To test it is hot enough, put a 2cm cube of bread in the oil. If it browns in 30 seconds, it is ready.) Don't overcrowd the pan; you will probably have to do two or three batches. Let them cook, stirring them around from time to time. When the shoestrings are golden and crunchy-looking lift them out with a slotted spoon or tongs and drain on the paper towel. Season with sea salt. Either eat them whilst cooking the rest of the potatoes or pop them in a warm oven until you have done them all.

Pommes Anna
Serves any number

about 2 medium potatoes or 4 smaller ones per person (very roughly 100g per person)
25g butter per person
sea salt and pepper

I first read about *Pommes Anna* in Elizabeth David's *French Provincial Cooking*, and her rather more brusque instructions lie behind the ones below. Any waxy yellow potatoes suit this dish but home-grown Charlottes would make it something really special.

Preheat the oven to 180°C/gas mark 4.

Peel the potatoes, wash them and using a mandolin or a sharp knife slice them into thin rounds. Put the sliced potatoes in a colander and rinse under the cold tap, stirring them around with your hand. You must do this to remove the starch. Toss the slices in a clean tea towel until dry.

Butter a small ovenproof dish or skillet. Build up layers of potato, seasoning and dotting with butter as you go. Cover with buttered baking parchment and cook in the oven for 30 minutes.

Take the dish out and remove the parchment. Press down the potatoes with a spatula and return uncovered to the oven for another 15 minutes, or until the tip of a knife pierces the centre of the potatoes easily.

Baked potatoes

Everyone has their own way of baking potatoes. I like mine crusty with sea salt. Rub the potatoes with olive oil and scatter over some sea salt. Stick a table knife (with an ovenproof handle) or skewer through the potato and roast at 180°C/gas mark 4 for 45 minutes to 1 hour (depending on the size of the potato).

New potatoes in parchment
Serves any number

about 6 small or 4 medium
new potatoes per person
15g butter per person
sea salt
a few sprigs of thyme or
leaves of mint

It goes without saying that new potatoes are at their best simply scraped clean with a knife, boiled and served with butter, salt, black pepper and a few chopped chives. But if you really love new potatoes and find yourself eating a lot of them then this recipe is a good one for the evening when you are finally sated by perfection and fancy something a little bit different.

Preheat the oven to 220°C/gas mark 9.

Clean the potatoes under the tap with a knife (the skin should peel off very easily if they are fresh). Small ones can be left whole, anything slightly larger should be cut in half.

Take a large sheet of baking parchment and place the potatoes in the middle and dot over the butter. Scatter with salt and herbs and seal up by folding over the parchment and rolling up the edges securely.

Cook in the preheated oven for about 45 minutes to 1 hour.

Sorrel and new potato salad
Serves 4

400g new potatoes (pink fir apple or Charlotte are very good)
2 shallots, finely chopped
8 tender leaves of sorrel, cut into fine ribbons
sea salt and pepper

for the vinaigrette
3 tbsps extra virgin olive oil
1 tbsp good red wine vinegar
sea salt and pepper

Place the potatoes in a large pan of salted water and boil until cooked but not overcooked. Drain the potatoes and run a cold tap over them to take the heat out a little so you can peel them. Cut into quarters and place in a large bowl. Make the dressing by whisking together the oil and vinegar with the seasoning. Toss the potatoes in the dressing. Sprinkle over the shallots and just before you serve the salad add the sorrel. Mix well and serve. This makes a good accompaniment for steak with a salad of peppery mixed leaves on the side.

Potato omelette
Serves 2

4 or 5 medium-sized waxy new potatoes
a small knob of butter (approx. 15g)
1 tbsp olive oil
3 eggs, beaten
chives or sorrel, to garnish
sea salt and pepper

Egg and potato tortillas are good but if they are to be cooked correctly they take time. This dish has the advantage of being far swifter to rustle up.

Thinly slice the new potatoes into coins. Wash them well and toss dry in a clean tea towel. In a heavy frying pan heat the butter and the olive oil. Carefully place the potato discs in the bottom of the pan so they form a single layer with each disc slightly overlapping the next. Season well and cover the frying pan (a bit of baking paper weighted down with a saucepan lid does fine). Let the potatoes cook for about 10 minutes, on a low heat, keeping an eye on them to make sure they are not burning. *(cont.)*

Take away the paper, turn up the heat to a medium flame and pour over the beaten egg. Tilt the pan so that the egg mixture runs around the frying pan and give it a helping hand by lifting up the edges of the potato cake with a knife. After a minute or two, when the egg on top is runny but not too liquid, place a plate over the top of the pan and using a tea towel to protect your hand quickly flip the saucepan over. The top side of the potatoes should be golden and crispy. Slide the omelette runny-side down back into the pan and give it another minute. Don't worry if you lose a bit of egg on the way – it will still be delicious.

Serve garnished with a few chives or ribbons of sorrel on top. This is good with a green salad and some ham for a simple lunch.

Tomatoes

In a day in June, at the hour when London moves abroad in quest of lunch, a young man stood at the entrance of the Bandolero Restaurant looking earnestly up Shaftesbury Avenue—a large young man in excellent condition, with a pleasant, good-humoured, brown, clean-cut face. He paid no attention to the stream of humanity that flowed past him. His mouth was set and his eyes wore a serious, almost a wistful expression. He was frowning slightly. One would have said that here was a man with a secret sorrow.

William FitzWilliam Delamere Chalmers, Lord Dawlish, had no secret sorrow. All that he was thinking of at that moment was the best method of laying a golf ball dead in front of the Palace Theatre. It was his habit to pass the time in mental golf when Claire Fenwick was late in keeping her appointments with him.

P G Wodehouse – *Uneasy Money*

I don't have a secret sorrow and I don't play mental golf but I do have my own way of passing the time. I try to work out what I would grow if I was suddenly expelled from my down-at-heel Eden and reduced to a single sunny windowsill. It is not something that can be decided in a hurry but one thing is certain, it wouldn't be a flower. My solitary plant would have to deliver a lot more than just beauty. Quite often I end up deciding on a tomato. After which, I go on to imagine just what kind of tomato would provide the greatest satisfaction to a gardener in such reduced circumstances, for few vegetables offer such variety. Tomatoes can be perfectly round and red like ping pong balls but they can also be curved like bananas, monstrous ribbed beefsteak tomatoes or delicate tapered plums; they can be egg- or heart-shaped, small as a cherry or as big as a baby's head; and they come in every colour – red, yellow, purple, shocking pink, striped green and red, black and even white.

The earliest memory I have of eating a really good tomato is when I was ten, sitting at a little beach bar in the seaside town of Rapallo in Italy. My sister and I had spent the morning swimming and playing on an improbably thin strip of pebbles, parasols and sun beds. The beach bar waiter served up the tomatoes, which were sliced and sandwiched between two thin squares of salty, oily focaccia. They were sweet, melting and full of sun – I felt sure no tomato would ever taste as good again, that is until I grew my own. Now I cannot imagine late summer without home-grown tomatoes. Biting into a tomato still warm from the sun is at the top of my list of allotment luxuries. It is a pleasure worth any number of digging visits, on cold wet days when the mud sticks to my boots and the roots of weeds go down and down for ever.

How to grow tomatoes

Really good tomatoes are a luxury we can all afford; all you need are a packet of seeds, a flowerpot and some compost. They are very robust and easy to grow and will do well in tall flowerpots outside your front door

You can grow vine tomatoes (tie them to a stick) or bush tomatoes but, as the latter sprawl, those with a limited amount of space are better off sticking to the tall kind.

Start the seeds off any time from March onwards. I usually aim for March and end up doing it in April. I grow mine in plastic seed trays split into small squares (modules). I cut the trays down so that they will fit onto my very narrow windowsills. Before I put the trays there I line the sills with strips of tin foil and folded newspapers to avoid damaging the paintwork when I water. Each tray is filled with compost and watered well. I then place a seed on the surface of the soil (one per module) and lightly cover with more soil. Finally I stretch some cling film over the top and place the tray on my sunny bedroom windowsill. After a few days when the seed starts to germinate I remove the cling film. I keep the soil moist and when each plant has got its second pair of leaves and is looking strong (after a week or so) I pot it on to a slightly bigger pot. At this stage

I put the plants outside for a few hours every day but bring them in at night until they've toughened up – gardeners call this process 'hardening off'. In another couple of weeks they will be ready to go down to the allotment.

When the plants look robust, you can plant them in their final pots. Most big garden centres sell tall terracotta flowerpots about 30cm high, which are perfect for tomatoes. Cover the top of the soil with pea gravel, pebbles or shells and you won't have to water them so often. But even if you do forget to water them, tomatoes like a bit of abuse – starving and under-watering means better-flavoured crops.

Take care to pinch out the side shoots so you are left with tall plants with not too many fruits; although you can always thin them out at the green stage. I grow my tomatoes mixed in with marigolds, cucumbers, acorn squash and pumpkin in one big bed. I stake them with lengths of hazel, winding string around the plants as they grow.

Eating tomatoes

When tomatoes are at their very best it is almost possible to subsist on them, simply oiled, salted and eaten with bread. Aside from this most basic rendering there are an almost infinite number of ways to use them in salads (and see p.142–146 for preserving and making sauces).

Tomatoes with tapenade

tomatoes, sliced

sea salt

olive oil

basil

On a large plate lay out the flat circles of sliced tomatoes, salt them and pour a thin stream of olive oil back and forth across the plate, and decorate with a few torn up leaves of basil.

for the tapenade
(makes enough for a small pot that serves 4 as a starter)

2 tbsps capers, drained

6 anchovy fillets

1 tbsp black olives, stoned

1 clove garlic, crushed

roughly 3–4 tbsps extra virgin olive oil

juice of 1 lemon

pepper

Pound the capers in a pestle and mortar with the anchovies and olives and still pounding add the garlic. If you don't have a pestle and mortar, chop all the ingredients to a pulp with a heavy knife, or in a food processor. When it is well amalgamated start adding the olive oil, slowly, until you have a thick, glossy sauce, add the lemon juice, taste and add a little more if you wish, season with freshly ground black pepper.

Place a small pot of the tapenade on the table along with some fresh bread and your lunch is ready. If you don't have any tapenade just scatter over a few shiny, wrinkled black olives.

Greek salad
Serves 4

2 large tomatoes

1 small cucumber, peeled and cut into chunks

1 shallot or ½ red onion, cut into thin rings

100g feta

½ tsp dried oregano

extra virgin olive oil

It may be a cliché of tavernas up and down the Adriatic but anything that can transport me instantly to the Greek islands earns itself a permanent place on my summer menu. One bite calls up the memory of hot sun, clear seas, tree-shaded terraces with square tables and paper tablecloths flapping in the wind.

Take the tomatoes, cut into quarters and mix with the cucumber and onion. Lay a slab of feta cheese on top and crumble over the dried oregano before anointing the whole lot with olive oil.

Tomatoes with chorizo
Serves 4

2 large tomatoes
1 tbsp sherry vinegar
black pepper
2 cooking chorizo (approx.
250g in total)
a handful chopped flat-leaf
parsley leaves (approx. 2
tbsps)

Tomatoes with sherry vinegar and parsley is a great combination with or without the chorizo.

Cut the tomatoes into rough cubes. Pour over a tablespoon of sherry vinegar and add a few grindings of black pepper.

Cut the chorizo into 5cm chunks. Heat a frying pan, rubbed with a very little oil, and fry the chorizo rapidly until crispy. Add to the tomatoes, along with a little of the oily red juices the chorizo has released into the pan. Scatter over the flat-leaf parsley.

Old-fashioned skinless tomato salad with chives and winter savory
Serves 4

2 large ripe tomatoes
1 tsp chopped leaves of
winter or summer savory
a few chives, finely chopped
1 clove garlic, finely chopped
½ shallot, finely chopped
1 tbsp white wine vinegar
3 tbsps extra virgin olive oil
sea salt and pepper

This was a great favourite of my grandmother who ate it every day in the summer.

Cut a cross in the bottom of two large ripe tomatoes, place in a bowl and pour over some just-boiled water to cover. Leave for 10–20 seconds. Drain the tomatoes, skin, core and remove the seeds and chop finely.

Put the herbs in the bottom of a glass bowl along with the garlic and the shallot. Pour over the vinegar and the olive oil. Mix well and then add the tomatoes. Season at the last moment – salting tomatoes ahead of time draws out the water and makes them soggy.

Catalan *pa amb tomàquet* (bread with tomatoes)

Serves 1

1 slice robust country bread,
fresh or lightly toasted
1 clove garlic, peeled
and cut in half
1 very ripe and sweet tomato
(preferably your own)
extra virgin olive oil
a little chopped parsley or
basil to garnish, if you wish
sea salt and pepper

When tomatoes are at their peak this simple snack is probably the easiest and tastiest way to enjoy them. It is eaten by working men all over the Mediterranean but most famously in Catalonia. With the right ingredients, this is convenience food at its most sublime.

Rub the bread or toast with the cut side of the garlic. Cut the tomato in half and rub the flesh and juices out onto the bread. Repeat. Pour a thin stream of olive oil over the tomato bread in a zigzag motion. Season, sprinkle over the herbs, if you are using them, and eat.

Tomato granita

Serves 4

8 large (or 12 medium) ripe,
sweet tomatoes
extra virgin olive oil
a few fresh basil leaves
1 tsp of sherry vinegar
a little caster sugar, if
necessary
sea salt and pepper

Granita is normally made out of strong-tasting syrups such as coffee or lemon, but by roasting the tomatoes in this recipe you can take their flavour to the same level of intensity. The effect is similar to gazpacho but on a really hot day the sparkling red crystals of this tomato water-ice win the day. This is only worth making with really flavoursome tomatoes otherwise it will be too acidic.

Preheat the oven to 140°C/gas mark 1.

Cut all but one tomato in half and place them cut-side up in a large casserole or gratin dish. Sprinkle a little sea salt and a few drops of oil onto each tomato. Roast very slowly for about 1½ hours.

(cont.)

Remove the tomatoes from the dish and rub them through a sieve. Taste and season again, this time adding a few chopped leaves of basil and ½ teaspoon of the sherry vinegar. Taste again. If you think they need it, you could add a scrap of sugar at this point.

Spread the mixture into a shallow tray and place in the freezer for 30 minutes.

Take the tray out of the freezer and break up the ice crystals with a fork. Return to the freezer. Do this 3 more times at 30 minute intervals. Don't worry if you forget and leave it too long – you'll just have to be a bit more vigorous with your fork.

Serve 4 small glasses topped with a few leaves of basil and the final tomato (skinned, deseeded and chopped into very fine dice) and a few drops of olive oil and the remaining sherry vinegar.

Variations

You can make a slightly spicier granita by substituting the following for the basil:

1 red chilli (deseeded and finely chopped); add half then taste before adding the other half as chillies vary in strength.
juice ½ lime
a few drops of Tabasco
a handful of fresh coriander leaves, finely chopped

Toasted cheese and tomato sandwich
(to be truthful I should say fried but don't let that put you off)
Serves 1

2 slices of bread (sourdough or robust country bread)
butter
Cheddar or other hard cheese
1 ripe but not soft tomato
sea salt and pepper

This may seem like an odd thing to put in a recipe book but sometimes the simplest things are the hardest ones to get right and a really fine toasted cheese sandwich can make a humble lunch for one into an interlude of pure pleasure. To succeed you need no kitchen gadgetry, just some good bread that won't fall to bits, soft butter and a heavy cast-iron frying pan. You'll end up with a buttery, crunchy sandwich that oozes melted cheese and fills the kitchen with the wonderful smell of toasting cheese and fresh hot tomato juices. This year I am growing a densely fleshed plum tomato purely to make the ideal toasted sandwich.

Heat a heavy frying pan whilst you slice and butter 2 pieces of bread.

Cover 1 slice of bread with thin slices of Cheddar cheese and top with 2 slices of tomato from which the pips and core have been removed. Season and top with the other slice of bread. Now butter the bottom of the sandwich only. Slide the sandwich, butter-side down into the pan and squash it with a plate with a weight on top. Pay very close attention and after about 2 minutes your nose will tell you that the cheese has melted and the bottom is browning nicely. Remove the plate and pick the sandwich up with a spatula. Add a dot of butter to the pan and let it melt. Flip the sandwich over and return to the pan. This time press the top down with a fish slice or metal spatula (putting the plate back on top gets it all a bit too sweaty).

When the bottom is as brown and crunchy as the top remove from the heat and cut in half. Feel free to add a little ham, mustard or mayonnaise as the fancy takes you.

Breakfast of champions

Tomatoes seem to have a special affinity with breakfast. You could do a lot worse than simply halving one and sprinkling it with salt before taking alternate nibbles of tomato and buttered toast. You'll find that it's a strangely pleasing way to start the day. If you feel like going to a bit more trouble and have a good supply of ripe tomatoes at hand, try making fresh tomato juice in a juicer, which is also very good if a bit paler than what you might be used to.

Fresh tomato sauces

Fresh tomato chutney for Indian dinners

*3 tomatoes, peeled, deseeded
and finely chopped
1 small bunch of coriander,
finely chopped
2 spring onions, thinly sliced
2 red chillies, deseeded and
finely chopped
a pinch of cayenne
½ tsp freshly roasted and
ground cumin seeds
2 tbsps lemon juice
sea salt, to taste*

This goes well with root vegetable pasties or as a side-dish with curries.

Combine all the ingredients. Store in the fridge until ready to use (but it is best eaten on the day you make it).

To make harissa use the same ingredients but simply replace the lemon juice with 1 tsp of smoked paprika, add one clove of finely chopped garlic, double the chillies and omit the fresh coriander. Then blend and season. This fiery North African relish goes well with cous cous and roasted vegetables or with merguez sausages.

Salsa fresca
Serves 2

*3 tomatoes, peeled, deseeded
and finely chopped
1 small bunch of coriander,
finely chopped
2 spring onions, thinly sliced
1 avocado, diced
2 red chillies, deseeded and
finely chopped
juice of 2 limes
a dash of Tabasco
1 tbsp extra virgin olive oil*

Combine all the ingredients and season. This recipe should be made an hour or two ahead of time to allow the flavours to mingle. You can eat it with black beans, rice and chicken or with a big bag of corn tortilla chips and some cold beers.

Gazpacho

Serves 4 as a starter or part of a picnic

1kg tomatoes
1 medium cucumber (peeled and deseeded – but don't bother if it's small and home-grown)
1 shallot or 4 spring onions or ½ sweet white onion
2 cloves garlic, finely chopped
4 tbsps extra virgin olive oil
1 tbsp sherry vinegar
sea salt and pepper

You can serve gazpacho with garnishes (chopped peppers or hard-boiled egg, croûtons or cucumber) but I prefer to serve it in a glass before meals. If I'm going on a picnic I will often make up a batch of gazpacho and put it in a large pickle jar with a few cubes of ice. It is hard to better when served outdoors on a hot summer's evening.

Slice the tomatoes in half and de-core. Top and tail the cucumbers and cut into chunks. Peel and roughly slice the onions. Blend the garlic, tomatoes, cucumber and onion in a food processor. Push the purée through a sieve or vegetable mouli into a mixing bowl. If you like your gazpacho really smooth you may like to do this twice but I can never be bothered.

Measure the oil out into a jug and then pour into the soup very slowly in a thin stream, whisking as you go. Alternatively you could rinse out the food processor and add the oil with the blender running but this just seems like too much washing up for me. Whisk in the sherry vinegar and season. Cover and place in the fridge for at least 2 hours.

Roasted feta and tomato
Serves 1

½ tbsp olive oil
1 tomato
pepper
a pinch or two of dried
oregano
1 small shallot, thinly sliced
into rings
25g feta, in a 1 cm-thick slice

On chilly, overcast days I need something piquant to pierce the gloom and recall the memory of hot Mediterranean holidays. This dish of roasted feta is quick to make and soon fills the kitchen with the irresistible aroma of roasting cheese. When I make it, the smell instantly transports me to the Greek island of Sifnos. My lunchtime view may not be the same (no limpid sea, no whitewashed monastery against an azure sky) but the taste is almost as good. It's best eaten with warm Turkish flat bread, or your own sourdough, and a green salad.

Preheat the oven to 220°C / gas mark 4.

Swirl a little olive oil into the bottom of a small ovenproof dish (I bought some flat terracotta dishes with long handles back with me from Greece). Lay 2 medium-thick slices of tomato over this, season with pepper and sprinkle with oregano. Add a few rings of shallot and then lay the slice of feta over the tomato. Give it another turn of the olive oil bottle and with a bit more pepper (no need for salt as feta is so salty). Roast in the oven for about 10 minutes, or until the cheese is melting a little and giving off a good savoury smell.

Eat immediately. This works well as part of a meze lunch.

RICHARD OLNEY'S LAST MEAL

Very few of those who have spent their lives thinking and writing about food get to cook themselves their last supper. Richard Olney is one exception. On a summer afternoon on his peaceful Provençal hillside, Olney went to lie down after a light lunch and never woke up. When his brothers arrived from America to arrange the funeral, they found evidence of Olney's last meal. A plate stacked next to the sink held traces of tomato pilaff and there was an empty wine glass beside it.

Tomato pilaff may seem like a modest meal for such a skilled cook to bow out with; but it was fitting. Prepared carefully with the freshest, seasonal ingredients, it is very good and could be said to stand for much of what Olney believed cooking was about. His pilaff was made with tomatoes he had grown himself in the garden he had wrested back from wilderness over forty years before. Olney's brothers found the rest of the pilaff in the fridge; they heated it up and toasted him with a good wine from his cellar.

Tomato pilaff
Serves 4

2 tbsps olive oil
1 shallot, finely chopped (or 1 small onion)
200g long-grain rice
1 tsp sea salt
1 clove garlic, peeled and crushed
450g tomatoes, peeled, deseeded and finely chopped (roughly 4 medium tomatoes)
1 tbsp butter
a small bunch of fresh basil
pepper, to taste

You can serve the pilaff with fresh basil as a meal in itself or eat it alongside roast chicken or lamb.

In a heavy-bottomed pan warm a tablespoon of the oil and fry the shallot very gently. The onion should be soft but not coloured. When the onion is soft, stir in the rice, cook for about a minute until all the rice is coated with oil and transparent.

Pour over 500ml of just-boiled water from the kettle and add the salt, cover and leave to simmer very gently for about 10 minutes. About 5 minutes before the rice is ready, heat a tablespoon of oil in a frying pan and fry the garlic and the tomatoes over a high heat. Add to the rice with the butter and basil leaves torn up into smallish pieces. Season with the pepper.

SUMMER SYRUPS AND PRESERVES

Tomatoes

I cannot think of any greater argument for the selfish pleasures of seasonal eating than the tomato. The spherical, bullet-hard examples on sale throughout the winter are sour and utterly lacking in any kind of juiciness. Compare them with a freshly picked tomato, perfumed with its distinctive musky smell, and you will never eat another out-of-season tomato again. This has nothing to do with environmental concerns – it's purely a matter of taste. There is just no point. Out of season I only use tinned tomatoes, which at least have the advantage of being canned when ripe. The best of all possible worlds is to preserve them yourself.

Tomato gluts

Whether or not you end up with a bumper tomato crop may have very little to do with your skill as a gardener and everything to do with the weather, especially if you are growing tomatoes outdoors. In the past I have grown an old variety called Pink Brandy Wine whose soft, fondant, almost pipless flesh tasted of all the best, never forgotten Mediterranean holiday tomatoes. This year I am growing a fat, red, ribbed Italian tomato, Costoluto Fiorentino, which makes similar claims to superlative flavour, and a giant plum tomato, Amish Paste, which is ideal for cooking down to a most flavoursome sauce.

All these tomatoes are chosen for their taste rather than any hope of reliable cropping in an English summer. So I usually grow something fail-safe too, such as Gardener's Delight or Alicante. But, even so, if the end of the summer is cold, instead of a cupboard lined with jars of homemade sauce I will be left with a lot of green tomatoes, some of which I bring home to ripen on my kitchen windowsill. Some people make green tomato chutney but I like chutney made with over-ripe fruits. If an Indian summer arrives and you find yourself overwhelmed by your tomato harvest, count your blessings and preserve them in one of three or four ways. It's a great way of prolonging the pleasure.

Preserving tomatoes

To help you decide on the best method of preserving your precious crop, consider how you will use it, how much storage space you have and how much time you have to set aside for this purpose. Each method has something to recommend it; some will save time later on, others are less of a fiddle now but require more cooking later on when you come to use the tomatoes up. First of all, consider what it is you use tomatoes for most. If it's pasta sauces then ready-made sauce will be the key to a winter of quick suppers. For those who cook a lot of Indian, Thai, Chinese or South American food, sauce that is already flavoured with Mediterranean herbs may not be the most suitable. A pure tomato passata may be better. Having limited time in August could mean that making vats of sauce may not be an option. In this case passata is again your best choice. If the winter is busy but you have August off, then make as much sauce as you can now to save time later. Finally, sauce is probably the best use of space for those short on storage because the tomatoes have cooked down and are more concentrated. These are all important considerations but, if this is your first year, then why not make a little of each kind and see which proves to be most useful.

There can be no comparison between a ripe, freshly picked, home-grown tomato and one you buy in a shop. It follows that any sauce or purée made from decent home-grown fruits will elevate even the very simplest of meals to something wonderful. The thought of a store cupboard full of homemade passata (puréed tomatoes), ready-made sauce or simple bottled tomatoes will keep me buying tomato seeds even after disastrous summers when too much rain spoils the flavour and spreads blight through my entire crop. Don't despair if your harvest fails you, or you don't have space to grow them in the first place. You can still buy a crate of good tomatoes from a farmers' market or reliable greengrocer at the peak of the season and preserve them yourself. My local Turkish Food Centre in Dalston, London, sells whole trays of tomatoes (about 5kg) at a discount so even if you don't grow your own you can still seek out a bulk supplier and make your own sauce.

Tomato Sauce

One of the most useful things to do with excess tomatoes is to make and bottle your own sauce. An afternoon set aside to make sauce will mean months of easy meals later in the year. The preparation time of everything – soups, sauces, lasagnes and gratins – will be halved and you will have provided yourself with convenience food of the most superior kind, transforming winter evenings of snatched, hurried suppers into brief but happy reminders of summer.

Every year my aunt spends a whole day sitting outside in her garden, pipping and skinning tomatoes ready to make sauce. In the past she has made huge amounts of sauce in oil drums on an open fire but these days she makes do with a large saucepan. (It helps that she lives in Italy but it is not essential.) She uses a special depipper and skinning gadget (I'm getting one for Christmas) but a sharp knife and a blending wand will do the job just as well.

Simple sauce for preserving tomatoes
Makes 4 x 1 litre Kilner jars

4kg tomatoes
4 tbsps olive oil
4 onions
4 cloves garlic (optional)
fresh herbs – a bundle of
fresh sprigs of oregano
or winter savory
juice of 2 lemons (extra
acidity increases your
chances of successful
preservation)
2 tsps sea salt
a little caster sugar, if
necessary
a small bunch of basil
(optional)

It is only worth making this sauce if you can get your hands on ripe, tasty tomatoes. Use your nose to sniff out the most aromatic varieties, set aside some time and get skinning.

Cut a cross in the bottom of each tomato. Blanch the tomatoes by pouring boiling water over them. After between 10 and 30 seconds drain and then use a small knife to peel back the skin from the cross to the stem end. Remove the hard green cores and quarter each tomato.

Add the oil to a pan and heat gently. When the pan is medium hot, add the onions and the garlic if you are using it and cook very gently until the onions are pale and soft, then add the tomatoes, the herbs, the lemon juice and the salt. Cook gently for an hour or so, stirring frequently to stop it sticking.

When the sauce has cooked down to a thick purée, remove it from the heat and discard any tough herb stalks. Taste the sauce and adjust the seasoning. You may want to add a little sugar, unless your tomatoes are nice and ripe. If you wish to add basil, tear the leaves roughly and add to the sauce. Blend using a hand-held wand in the pan or in a food processor.

Put the sauce in 4x1-litre Kilner jars and sterilise (*see Basics, page 266*) or else it freezes well.

Simple passata

The Italians call it passata, the Greeks *perasti* – either way it's one of the simplest ways of preserving tomatoes. Wash the tomatoes (they should be whole, undamaged fruits), skin and remove the green core as on page 144, then quarter them. In a large pan, heat the tomatoes gently with a very little water and some salt (optional). When the tomatoes have cooked down to a soft purée, let it settle, then pour off any watery juices. Bottle and sterilise *(see Basics, page 266)*. (Or you can add the tomatoes to the pan unskinned, passing them through a mouli after they have cooked down and then proceeding as above.)

Bottling whole tomatoes

The most basic way of preserving tomatoes is to bottle them whole, in the same way that you would bottle peaches. It is quick but the fruit is not cooked down so takes up more space (it does look lovely though) so perhaps do 1 or 2 jars only. You will be surprised by how fresh the tomatoes taste. Take whole, firm but well-ripened tomatoes and skin them as on page 144. With a small, sharp knife cut out the core in a cone shape then squeeze them gently to release a few seeds and a little juice. Pack them down into sterilised jars, leaving a couple of centimetres at the top. Sprinkle over a little salt, seal and sterilise *(see Basics, page 266)*.

You can add sliced onion, peeled garlic, sprigs of basil, thyme, savory or bay and whole fresh chilli peppers to your jar if you wish.

Oven-drying tomatoes

The methods I've suggested could seem far too much like hard work, in which case try slow-drying your tomatoes using your oven and then freezing them. This is a very easy but still flavoursome way to preserve tomatoes. In the south of Italy this is done out of doors on a hot roof or a rack, with old ladies on duty all day to shoo away the flies.

Cut the tomatoes in half and scoop out the seeds with your finger or a teaspoon (don't be overly zealous), then place them cut-side up in a large casserole or gratin dish. Dot with herbs (chopped fresh oregano or torn basil), add a few drops of olive oil to each tomato and then season them with sea salt and pepper. Roast them very slowly (about 1½–2 hours at 120°–140°C/ gas mark ½–1. When they are cool, place them on a rack to dry off, before bagging them up and freezing. Use them in sandwiches, sauces and on top of pizzas. If you want to eat the dried tomatoes straight away, keep them in the fridge with a thin covering of olive oil (they should last a week or two).

Chutneys, jellies and syrups

Tomato chutney with home-grown chillies
Makes about 5 x medium jars (350ml)

1.5kg tomatoes (about 10 medium tomatoes)
1 tbsp pickling spices (see Basics, page 275)
400g onion (2 good sized onions), finely chopped
450ml distilled vinegar (clear not dark brown for better colour)
6 red chilli peppers, deseeded and finely chopped
3 cloves garlic, peeled and lightly crushed
250g sultanas
1 tbsp freshly grated ginger
500g soft light brown sugar
1 tsp mustard seeds
1 tsp sea salt

Chutney is the traditional British response to a vegetable glut and this recipe is a good one for those who grow their own chillies. There are so many to choose from but this year I am growing the traffic-light-coloured pepper called Ring O Fire. Using fresh chillies results in a sweet, spicy and very moreish chutney. Just don't eat too much of it in one go.

Blanch the tomatoes *(see sauce recipe on page 144)*. Skin, chop roughly and set aside. Put the pickling spices into a little bag. Put the onions and half the vinegar in a large stainless steel pan. Simmer for 10 minutes then add the chillies, garlic, tomatoes, sultanas and ginger. Simmer until the tomatoes have broken down and the chillies have started to soften. Add the sugar, the rest of the vinegar, the mustard seeds, the bag of spices and the salt. Stir until the sugar has dissolved and then simmer very gently until the mixture thickens and starts to look jammy.

Spoon into hot, sterilised jam jars *(see Basics, page 266)* Leave the chutney in the cupboard for at least a month before eating.

Gooseberry and elderflower 'muscat' syrup
Makes 1 x 75cl bottle

8 elderflower crowns
250ml water
750g granulated sugar
1kg gooseberries (under-
rather than over-ripe) topped
and tailed using scissors

Hard green gooseberries and the sweet-scented creamy white blossoms of the elder are ready at the same time (around the beginning of June). Together they combine to make a syrup that magically tastes of the Muscatel grape used to make sweet pudding wines. This is not news; muscat syrup has been around a long time and I owe my discovery of it to Constance Spry. You can use this syrup as a cordial, to make a very superior slushie or it's delicious over ice with fizzy water, as well as in the fool on page 148.

In Hackney is the AK Convenience Store or, as the sign over the door says, 'Di Likle Pati Shop'. As well as newspapers and milk, the owner sells meat patties, squares of molasses toffee in waxed paper and, on hot summer weekends, snow cones. He uses a small plane to scrape ice off a big block and then squeezes over the shavings some very sweet, very lurid syrup, coloured purple, orange or red. To get the same effect at home, freeze a plastic container full of water to make a small block. When it has set, pop it out and wrap it in a tea towel. Use a rolling pin to crush the ice, drizzle over the gooseberry syrup and serve with a straw.

If you want to make a lot of this syrup, the best way of preserving it is to freeze it in plastic juice cartons, but as this recipe only makes a bottle just keep it in the fridge – you'll find it will go pretty quickly. You can also use it as the basis for a very delicate-flavoured dessert jelly.

Sterilise a glass screwcap wine or juice bottle *(see Basics, page 266).* *(cont.)*

Pick over the elderflowers and remove any insects. Do not wash them, as you will lose much of the flavour. Remove the bitter stalks and tie the flowers up in a muslin bag.

In a heavy-bottomed pan heat the water and the sugar very gently, stirring all the time until the sugar has dissolved. When you have a thickish syrup add the gooseberries and cook on a low heat for about 10 minutes or until the fruit starts to break apart. Turn off the heat and add the elderflowers in their bag. Allow the flowers to infuse the syrup. Taste after 5 minutes and if they have given a good flavour to the syrup take them out. You may like to leave them in for a little longer; this is a matter of taste but remember that the flavour will be less intense when it is cool. Drain the syrup through a jelly bag or muslin (a sieve lined with a clean J-cloth will do). When it has definitely stopped dripping (after an hour or two) pour into the clean, sterilised bottle. Store in the fridge.

Gooseberry and elderflower fool
Serves 4

400g gooseberries, topped and tailed
100g granulated sugar
2–3 tbsps elderflower cordial
150ml thick cream

You can use your elderflower cordial in this recipe, though you could also use a good shop-bought one.

Top and tail the gooseberries (I use a pair of kitchen scissors) and place them in a pan with a little water (so it goes about halfway up the fruits) and the sugar. Simmer gently until the fruits burst apart and are soft. Remove and leave to cool. Mash up the fruits with the cordial, taste and add a little more sugar if it is too tart. Whip the cream if it is not really thick and swirl into the gooseberry mash. Chill the fool until it is very cold.

Gooseberry fool goes well with homemade madeleines *(see page 263)* or cat's tongue biscuits.

Green gooseberry 'muscat' jelly

Makes about 2 litres of jelly (roughly 6 x medium/350ml jars)

1kg green gooseberries (big but not overly ripe)
1 litre water
approx.1kg granulated sugar
10 elderflower crowns – picked over and tied up in a muslin bag (if you miss the elderflower season use 100ml elderflower cordial)

If you like the idea of the muscat flavouring try this conserve instead. For a more thorough description of jelly making see page 203.

Sterilise the jam jars *(see Basics, page 266)*.

Place the gooseberries in a large preserving pan and add the water, simmer until the gooseberries have burst. Drain through a jelly bag (don't squeeze!) and measure out 500g of sugar for every 500ml of juice. Put the juice and sugar back into the (cleaned) pan over a medium heat. Stir until the sugar has dissolved and then add the elderflowers in their bag (or the cordial). Taste the jelly mixture now and again (start after 5 minutes) to make sure the Muscat taste is not becoming too intense. Remove the flowers when you are happy with the taste, and boil until the setting point is reached *(see Basics, page 270, for the flake test)*. Pour into hot, sterilised jars.

Roasted-blackcurrant jelly

Makes approx. 6 x medium/350ml jars

1kg blackcurrants (ripe but unblemished fruits)
approx. 1kg granulated sugar (500g for each 500ml of juice you collect)
water
sterilised jam jars (see Basics, page 266)

See the wild apple jelly recipe on page 203 for a more thorough explanation of jelly making.

Preheat your oven to 150°C/gas mark 2. Wash the fruit and place in a large casserole dish and bake, covered, for about an hour until it is soft. Remove the dish from the oven and using a wooden spoon or potato masher crush the fruit.

(cont.)

Having placed a large bowl underneath your scalded jelly bag, pour in the pulp and the juice. The jelly will run through very quickly at first and then slow to a dribble. Don't be tempted to squeeze the bag as this will make your jelly cloudy. When it has all dripped through, measure the juice and set aside.

If you have more blackcurrants than you know what to do with, skip this next part as this second cooking of the pulp is really good for making the most of a smaller crop rather than dealing with a glut.

If you have a small crop, take the pulp and put it in a pan. Just cover with cold water, bring to the boil and let it simmer for about 20 minutes. Return the fruit and juice to the jelly bag and repeat the straining process above. Combine the two juices and measure.

You will need to add 500g sugar for every 500ml of juice.

In a cleaned saucepan combine the sugar and juice. Stir until the sugar has dissolved and then turn up the heat and boil rapidly, skimming off any scum that forms (if you keep the jelly half off the heat it will collect on one side of the pan, making it easier to skim off). The setting point should be reached within 10 minutes. To know when it is ready, you can use a sugar thermometer or do the flake test *(see Basics, page 270)*. Remove the jelly from the heat and skim off any last remaining traces of scum. Pour into the hot, sterilised jars *(see Basics, page 266)*.

Cut out little circles of greaseproof paper and put one on top of each jar before sealing down by screwing on the lids tightly. Store in a coolish dark place. It keeps for ages but store in the fridge after opening.

Blackcurrant tea

One of the best things about preserving is that it provides a link between seasons. Blackcurrants picked the previous summer, when the leaves of the bush give off a warm musky scent and the fat dark berries are full of juice, make a very dark purple jelly with a firm set that is packed with high-summer vitamin C *(see previous recipe)*. The first few jars will probably get eaten up immediately on toast but slide one to the back of the cupboard where it will wait quietly, until mid winter. Use it as a hot cordial, when throats are rasping and all the senses are crying out for sunshine.

Blackcurrant's use as a medicinal plant goes back centuries. Geoffrey Grigson records in his *Englishman's Flora* that wild blackcurrants, in the form of wine, jelly and syrup were used as a folk remedy for sore throats (the quinsy or squinancy) long before they took a place in the domestic garden. Blackcurrant tea crops up in Dorothy Wordsworth's journals too. She and Coleridge drink it after a blustery day out in the Lake District.

To soothe a throat or clear a head-cold, pour just-boiled water over one tablespoon of the jelly in a mug, and stir vigorously (don't worry if you're left with a few solid bits at the bottom). Drink as many mugs as you need throughout the day.

Cassis

1kg blackcurrants
500g granulated sugar
approx.1 litre vodka
2 x 1 litre Kilner jars,
sterilised in the oven (see
Basics, page 266)

A kilogram of blackcurrants will fill two large (75cl) screwcap bottles with this syrupy liqueur. It keeps well (unopened indefinitely, or if opened use within 3 months). Use it to make Kir *royal* (champagne, or sparkling wine, and cassis) or to increase the appeal of cheap white wine as an ordinary Kir. It is also very refreshing when drunk over ice with fizzy mineral water.

As you would expect of a traditional liqueur, there are lots of ways of making cassis. Jane Grigson has an excellent old Burgundian recipe in her *Fruit Book* in which the berries are steeped in wine and cooked very slowly. The resulting syrup is then thinned with vodka. The result is a densely-flavoured almost jelly-like syrup. The following recipe has the advantage of not involving any cooking, which in high summer is a good thing. This recipe is very easily scaled down but if you decide to make a lot, small bottles of cassis make very welcome presents – just get into the habit of saving up interesting little glass bottles.

Wash the fruit and remove any obviously over-ripe or damaged berries. In a bowl squash the berries with the back of a wooden spoon before packing them into the jars, stop about 4 fingers width from the top and cover with vodka. Put them in the cupboard for at least 2 months (4 will give you an even greater depth of flavour if you can wait that long). Give them a shake now and again when you remember.

When autumn is definitely with you, get the jars out of the cupboard and strain the contents through a scalded jelly bag (you may have to make your own larger bag – *see wild apple jelly recipe, page 203*). You are allowed to give it a squeeze to help it along. A few hours later, when all the juice has dripped through, start adding the sugar to the juice, stirring well. Keep tasting, and stop when you think it is sweet enough (you might not use all the sugar).

Put back in the cupboard for another month or two, shaking every other day for at least a fortnight. You'll know when it's ready because the liquid will be clear and the sugar will have completely dissolved. You can use it straight away but keep a bottle back so you can see how the flavour improves.

Apricot and cardamom chutney

Makes approx. 5 x medium/350ml jars

pickling spices
½ tsp cumin seeds
½ tsp mustard seeds
½ tsp coriander seeds
1 stick of cinnamon
4 cloves
a few flakes of dried chilli
6 cardamom pods

for the chutney
450g onions, finely chopped
(weight after chopping)
400ml distilled clear vinegar
1kg apricots, halved and
stoned
1 walnut-sized piece of
ginger, peeled and
finely grated
150g raisins
2 fresh red chillies, deseeded
and sliced thinly
350g soft light brown sugar
sea salt and pepper

A perfectly juicy apricot, its skin smudged with red freckles, is sadly harder to find than you might think. Any apricots not quite worthy of being eaten fresh should be made into chutney; they cook down to make a sticky chutney that's close to mango in texture and is a good relish for Indian and Middle Eastern meals. Apricots and cardamom complement each other well. To get the best result possible I threw out my jar of last year's cardamom and bought a fresh packet of tight green pods from The Saver Plus supermarket on Bethnal Green Road. Outside the shop, boxes of Alphonse mangoes were stacked up; the kidney-shaped yellow fruit nestling in shredded paper, sent out a powerfully perfumed scent. Inside there was cardamom tea (a delicately spiced version of chai), coconut oil, ugly limes, giant frozen fish and racks of unknown vegetables. It's a good idea to buy small packets of whole spices and be ruthless about any that have been lingering too long in the cupboard. Using fresh spices that you grind yourself will make a big difference to your cooking.

Place the spices in a pickling bag (*see Basics, page 275*).

Peel and slice the onions. Put them in the bottom of a large stainless steel saucepan with half the vinegar. Simmer gently for 10 minutes. Keeping the heat low, add the apricots to the pan along with the rest of the vinegar, the pickling bag of spices, the ginger, raisins, chilli, sugar and a little salt and pepper. Keep stirring the mixture until the sugar is fully dissolved. Cook the mixture at a gentle simmer for between 30 and 45 minutes, stirring from time to time. You are aiming for a thick jam-like texture. Taste the chutney and adjust the seasoning if you feel it necessary. Remove from the heat and spoon the chutney into hot sterilised jars *(see Basics, page 266)*. Use a chopstick to slide two or three cardamom pods down into each jam jar next to the glass for appearance and to add a little flavour whilst storing.

Seal and store in a dark cupboard for at least a month. This gives the flavours a chance to develop and the vinegar time to mellow before eating.

OUTDOOR FEASTS AND CAMPING

In praise of picnics

'Hold hard a minute, then!' said the Rat. He looped the painter
through a ring in his landing stage, climbed up into his hole above,
and after a short interval reappeared staggering under a fat, wicker
luncheon basket.

'Shove that under your feet,' he observed to the Mole, as he passed it
down into his boat. Then he untied the painter and took the sculls again.
'What's inside it?' asked the Mole, wriggling with curiosity.
'There's cold chicken inside it,' replied the Rat briefly;
'coldtonguecoldhamcoldbeefpickledgherkinssaladfrenchrolls-
cressandwidgespottedmeatgingerbeerlemonadesodawater –'

'O stop, stop,' cried the Mole in ecstasies: 'This is too much!'

'Do you really think so?' inquired the Rat, seriously. 'It's only what
I usually take on these little excursions, and the other animals are
always telling me that I'm a mean beast and cut it very fine!'

Kenneth Grahame – *The Wind in the Willows*

In the summer months I live to picnic. For me there is as much pleasure in the planning and preparation as there is in the consumption. Kenneth Grahame must have been an expert picnicker and his imagined picnic is one well worth emulating. One hundred years on, it still reads like an ideal. The joy that this picnic brings both Rat and Mole encapsulates all that a picnic should be. Rat has gone to a degree of trouble for his new friend Mole yet in the best tradition of true friendship, he wears this lightly. The picnic's success is a combination of Rat's solicitude and the delight Mole feels in seeing his pal nonchalantly triumph over the elements, combined with the excitement of surprises and the pleasure that dining in new and unexpectedly beautiful surroundings, in this case the mossy riverbank, brings. There is an air of Christmas morning as Grahame goes on to describe Mole's delight as he unwraps the 'mysterious packets one by one' gasping 'Oh my! Oh my!' at each fresh revelation. It would be a very hard-hearted friend who could turn up their nose at such a feast.

A picnic should only be undertaken joyfully – there is nothing worse than a martyred host – and it should always have a festive air. While not offering breathtaking scenery (a must for those most dedicated of picnickers, the nature-worshipping Romantics) the city holds many advantages for the modern picnicker, above all the diversity of ingredients available – the world really is on your doorstep, and on top of this, in a city, you are never that far from a green space or park. I try not to get too hung up on finding the perfect place. Fixing your sights on an ideal can be very defeating, as Patience Gray notes in her book *Work, Adventure, Childhood, Dreams*:

> *To find the ideal place in which to finish a novel is like looking for the ideal picnic place: one ends up either writing or picnicking anywhere or gives up the idea of writing or eating altogether.*

I love the wilder parts of Hampstead Heath in London. One of my favourite midsummer picnic spots is on the north-east side of the Heath close to the Ladies' pond. Before we eat, my friends and I leave our picnic and whet our appetites with a swim in the pond's rushy green waters. Afterwards, hungry and a little chilly, we sit on a blanket to devour a herby, salty roast chicken still warm from the oven, torn up and eaten with Kentish flutes (sourdough baguettes), glasses of pale pink wine, and courgette fritters seasoned with lemon zest and served with a dollop of tzatziki. As a flock of escaped green parakeets flies overhead we watch the golden harvest moon rise and listen to the distant sounds of music coming from Kenwood House. We pack our things and bundle up tired children into picnic blankets and, with them draped over our shoulders, we wade through the long grass as the fireworks pop up above the trees to mark the concert's end.

Menus

I didn't do it consciously or realise it until afterwards, but I got my inspiration for one of my best ever Heath picnics from Sybille Bedford's account of her own preparations for a journey to Mexico:

> *And there is always food. I had packed a hamper and a cardboard box. Whenever I can I bring my own provisions; it keeps one independent and agreeably employed, it is cheaper and usually much better. I had got us some tins of tunny fish, a jar of smoked roe, a*

hunk of salami and a hunk of provolone; some rye bread, and some
black bread in Cellophane that keeps. That first night we had fresh
food. A chicken, roasted that afternoon at a friend's house, still gently
warm; a few slices of that American wonder, Virginia ham; marble-
sized, dark red tomatoes from the market stands on Second Avenue;
watercress, a flute of bread, a square of cream cheese, a bag of
cherries and a bottle of pink wine. It was called Lancer's Sparkling
Rosé, and one ought not to be put off by the name. The wine is
Portuguese and delicious. A shining, limpid wine, full almost, not
growing thin and mean on one in the way of many rosés. It has the
further charm of being bottled in an earthenware jug, so that once
cooled it stays nicely chilled for hours. I drew the cork with my
French Zigzag. The neatest sound on earth.

Sybille Bedford – *A Visit to Don Otavio*

An easy picnic can consist of good (if expensive) deli produce, of bought olives, salami and fresh bread, but a picnic can take wing if you have the time to prepare it carefully yourself. For the sake of your guests' digestion it's a good idea to stay specific (roughly) to a single country. I have listed a few different menus all loosely inspired by a different region's cuisine, in this case Greece, Sweden, France, Britain and Spain.

Eastern Mediterranean picnic
  Crusty flat breads
  Olives
  Tzatziki
  Taramasalata
  Courgette fritters
  Spinach and feta triangles
  Tomatoes on the vine
  Cold lamb and cumin cutlets
  Peaches, cherries or plums
  Baklava

Swedish
  Home made gravadlax
  Rye sourdough
  Potted shrimp with paprika
  Herb cream cheese
  Pickled cucumber
  Madeleines
  Gooseberry yoghurts
  Icy lager or a good pink wine

Chicken roasted with thyme
and lemon

Homemade tapenade

Cherry tomatoes on the vine

Parsley salad

Small lemon custard tarts

Raspberries

White wine

British

Potted crab

Pork pies or any good cold pie
(these can be bought)

Sourdough bread

Crudités with vinaigrette

Quails egg with celery salt or

salted paprika

Cheddar cheese, spring onion and
chutney sandwiches

Strawberries (cream in a jam jar)

Rosé or cider

Spanish

Gazpacho

Tortilla

Olives

Crusty baguette

Whole chorizo

Bought Iberian custard tarts
(the kind with the blackened tops)

Bag of apricots or peaches

Bottle of icy fino

Autumn picnic for walkers or workers in the garden or on the allotment

This picnic was made for a digging party I had at the allotment. Inviting friends to help you dig and making them lunch in return is a good way of getting the plot ready for winter without breaking your back. I was fortunate in that one of my friends is Claire Ptak, a master cake maker who brought with her an enormous box of the cupcakes she sells in Broadway Market with which we ended our picnic.

Steak and ginger pasties

Cold bottles of beer (ale not lager)

Chutney or mustard

A bag of good British apples, I like
Egremont Russets and Spartans

Plums

Hard cheese (Caerphilly or Cheddar)

Sticky gingerbread or cupcakes

Coffee in a flask

Dark chocolate

Steak and ginger pasties

Serves 4–6

2 tbsps vegetable oil
450g beef steak, chopped
into very small dice
a knob of butter (20g)
150g onion, chopped
1 thumb of ginger, peeled
and chopped very fine
1 tbsp soy sauce
1 tbsp plain flour
500ml stock (beef if you
have it but chicken will do)
1 x quantity shortcrust
pastry (see Basics, page 273)
300g swede, peeled and cut
into 5cm-ish cubes
400g potato, peeled and cut
into 5cm-ish cubes
egg wash (one egg whisked
with 1 tbsp of milk)

Pastry lids and wrappings around meat and vegetables made some of the earliest examples of portable food. The pasty has long been a standby of working men and picnickers. This recipe might not please Cornish traditionalists (they like their meat to go in uncooked) but it is great food for windswept walks. Serve with a grated celeriac and horseradish salad if you are eating at home. These also freeze well if you have any left over.

In a heavy saucepan or casserole heat the oil and fry the meat over a medium to high heat until well browned. Remove the meat to a bowl with a slotted spoon, turn down the heat and add the butter and then the onions. Fry gently until softened and then add the ginger, cook for another minute, stirring constantly, and then deglaze the pan with the soy sauce. Return the meat to the pan and sprinkle over the flour. Cook for 1–2 minutes, stirring all the time, then add the stock and bring up to the boil. Simmer gently on top of the stove for 1–1½ hours with the lid ajar.

If you need to go out, you could put the casserole into a slow oven (150°C/gas mark 2) for 3 or 4 hours. If you do this you will need to reduce the gravy. Strain the meat and onion mixture and return the liquid to the pan. Bring slowly to the boil, skim, then boil hard to reduce down until you have about 2 tablespoons of concentrated silky, dark gravy.

While the meat is simmering, make the shortcrust pastry (*see Basics, page 273*). Leave it to rest in the fridge for at least 30 minutes.

(cont.)

Bring two pans of salted water to the boil and cook the swede and potatoes separately until just tender – about 8–10 minutes (the swede will take slightly longer).

Drain the vegetables and combine in a large mixing bowl. Add the meat mixture and set aside to cool.

Preheat the oven to 180°C/gas mark 4.

Flour a board and roll out the pastry to about 4mm thick. Using a saucer or a small bowl to draw round, cut out as many circles as you can. Paint a line of egg wash around the edge of the circles and place a heaped tablespoon of filling into the middle of each. Pick each pasty up gently and cradle it in one hand whilst using the other hand to pinch the edges of the pastry together. (You can leave it on the counter if you prefer.) If it is all getting a bit sticky dip you fingers in flour. Place each pasty on a baking tray lined with baking parchment (or a non-stick tray) and brush all over with egg wash. Make a little slit in the top of each pasty to let out steam.

Use up any pastry scraps to roll out again until you have used up all the pastry. Bake for 35 minutes or until golden brown. Remove and place on a cooling rack.

Potted crab
Serves 4

2 dressed crabs or one large boiled crab from your fishmonger (approx. 600g crab meat)
¼ tsp ground mace or 1 blade
¼ tsp ground nutmeg
½ tsp cayenne pepper
juice of 1 lemon, if small or ½ if big (you want 3 tbsps)
zest from ½ lemon
250g butter
sea salt and pepper

Travellers have always needed easily portable food that won't perish too quickly. Potted meats were one of the first convenience foods, becoming popular in the mid-seventeenth century as a more durable alternative to the pastry piecrust. Potting food has the advantage of also helping to preserve it. The idea is a simple one: meat is pounded, seasoned, packed down into a ceramic pot and then sealed with clarified butter. When it comes to the provenance of your butter, in this case local isn't necessarily better. Jane Grigson notes in *English Food* that Danish butter was traditionally used in the Lancashire potting industry, as it is creamier and less salty than British butter and therefore better for clarifying.

When you've got the time and the inclination, buying a whole crab from your fishmonger and picking the meat out yourself will always be better than buying a dressed crab – it will be fresher and you will get more crab meat for your money. Always buy fresh dressed crab and avoid the horrid, watery frozen ones.

To dress a whole crab, crack it open and remove the dead man's fingers (the feathery pointy bits that ring the edge of the shell just below the crab's mouth), then pick out the meat – how much you get will depend on how patient you are. I usually lose the will to live halfway through the central part of the body where all the white meat is. It's worth keeping the crab shell, claws and legs for making shellfish bisque.

In a bowl mix the crab meat with the spices, taste, and add the lemon juice and zest. Don't be too heavy-handed with your seasoning; crab has a delicate flavour, which the spices are there to enhance, not overwhelm. Melt 125g of the butter and pour over the crab meat, mix well. Pack the crab meat down into an ovenproof earthenware dish or, if you are feeling dainty, individual ramekins.

If you are not going to eat your crab immediately you must poach and re-sterilise it so that you can keep the crab in the fridge for 3 or 4 days or take it on a picnic safely. Skip this next part if you are potting and eating on the same day.

Place the dish or ramekins in a roasting tin or deep-sided gratin dish. Fill the tin with just-boiled water from the kettle so that it comes halfway up the side of the dishes. This is known as a *bain marie*.

Place in the oven at 150°C/Gas mark 2 for 25–30 minutes. Remove the dish or ramekins from the *bain marie* and allow them to cool.

Melt the rest of the butter and pour over the crab pots, but leave the white residue behind at the bottom of the pan. Cool and then chill in the fridge.

Serve your potted crab with sourdough toast, lemon quarters and a sharply dressed green salad. A real treat that any guest will thank you for.

Potted shrimps
Serves 4 as a snack or starter

100g butter
¼ tsp ground mace
¼ tsp smoked paprika
a grating or two of nutmeg
a pinch of cayenne pepper
200g brown shrimps
50g butter for clarifying
(optional)

On a summer holiday in Southern Sweden my then three-year-old daughter and I spent a very languid long afternoon endlessly dipping a flimsy bamboo shrimping net into a mill-pond smooth Baltic. After about 4 hours we had a bucket full of translucent finger-nailed sized shrimp. Once boiled up and laboriously shelled there was about a teacupful, enough for one bright-pink and brown sandwich. I didn't think of it then but they would have been perfect for potting. In landlocked Hackney we don't get much opportunity for shrimping, but luckily my nearest fishmonger, Steve Hatt, sells packets of ready-shelled brown shrimp which pot up beautifully. Potted shrimp usually have the same spices as potted crab (mace, nutmeg, cayenne) but I like adding a little smoked paprika too. Potted shrimp, watercress, brown toast and a pot of tea make a fine end to a chilly afternoon but they are equally good as part of a picnic.

Put the butter and spices in a small pan and heat gently. When the butter has just melted add the shrimps and heat through very gently for a minute or two. Pour into a ceramic pot. Press the shrimps down a little. I usually find there is enough butter on top but if your shrimps are poking out you might want to clarify a little butter (melt butter and tip into a bowl leaving the white residue behind) and pour that over.

Cooking in the ashes

*We sit there, imbibing incense smells and eating food whose
excellence is due to neolithic skill. When the flames, that play around
the twigs like leaves of fire, subside we grill our supper. And
crouching there one can't help realising that the best cooks in the
other world are trying to emulate this prehistoric art without the
means, which here, are the only ones to hand – the quick fierce
resinwood, the olive oil, marjoram newly sprouting from terrace
walls, the twigs of thyme flung on the fire, which give an acrid savour
to little lumps of mountain sheep or fish that an hour ago were in the
sea, succulent titbits sprinkled with juice from lemons picked in
nearby groves.*

Patience Gray – *Ring Doves and Snakes*

Enjoying my life in the city means getting out of it sometimes. I like camping with my children, partly because they love it so much but mainly because I love cooking outdoors. We have spent afternoons on Exmoor gathering wortleberries to sprinkle onto our morning porridge. We've fried whitebait caught on the North Devon coast and spent a long weekend in a Kentish field cooking every meal on a giant fire and learning how to make dampers (dough cooked on a stick and eaten with jam).

Campfire cookery always involves an element of improvisation and in this sense it is more creative than any other kind. Cooking on an open fire is cooking with your wits. It is a primal act and one in which all your instincts as a practical cook must be brought to bear as you observe the wind, the rate at which the fuel burns, the fluctuating heat of the fire and the speed at which the food is cooking. It is a good way to hone your skills and become a cook who really understands the process of cooking. The spirit in which you approach it is key: it requires attention and a high degree of adaptability if things don't go according to plan. It may be primitive but at its best this way of cooking achieves results that far eclipse food cooked indoors in the conventional manner. There is an excitement and a triumphant sense of occasion attached to outdoor cooking that is entirely unique. Any meal, however humble, has the air of a feast and you will find that – provided it's not raining – it is very hard not to enjoy a meal cooked in the open air.

Fuel

The ways of cooking were very primitive (and in many parts of the South West of France they still are); that is to say they were perfect, and gave results which I did not appreciate enough then, and which we try now, often in vain, to imitate. The roasting was done on a spit, and the rest of the cooking on charcoal.

X. Marcel Boulestin – *My Two Countries*

You don't have to rely on bought barbecue fuel. It is easy to collect enough wood for a single meal even if you live in the city. The wilder parts of city parks are a good source of windfall wood or you can look out for scraps that builders are throwing out in skips. (Although if you are getting wood from skips make sure you don't use anything that has been treated or painted as this may taint the taste of your food.) If you are near woodland you can forage for windfall wood from aromatic trees such as pine, hazel or beech. When cutting back your garden in springtime, keep any vine clippings and dry them as these burn well with an intense heat. Thyme or rosemary thrown onto the fire just before cooking adds a lovely flavour to meat cooked over it.

You don't even need a garden in which to cook; fires can be built in barbecues raised off the ground. Last spring I ate a very fine razor clam and asparagus paella cooked by this book's photographer, Jason Lowe, in the car park of an old school house in Homerton, East London. The firewood was foraged from Victoria Park and burnt in a giant paella dish the size of a tractor wheel with a slightly smaller dish sitting on top. We were well away from any cars and only received one complaint from another tenant alarmed by the cloud of smoke travelling up past her window. When the rice was cooked through and a crisp, crackly bottom had formed, the pan was carried three floors up to my friend Claire's flat. She had laid the table with a linen cloth and decorated it with hand-drawn name cards and Sicilian lemons still on the branch; the latter looked lovely and were also perfect for squeezing over the paella.

Lemongrass and coriander chicken with sticky rice
Serves 8

for the marinade
1 tsp black peppercorns
9 coriander roots
3 stalks of lemongrass
(outside leaves removed)
6 cloves garlic
2 tbsps light soy sauce
2 tbsps Thai fish sauce
½ tsp caster sugar

2 medium free-range
chickens (1.5kg each),
jointed into 8 pieces each

1 big bag of Thai jasmine
rice from which you will
measure out ¼ cup per adult
and ⅛ cup per child (50g
and 25g if you want
to weigh it out before you
set off)

1 large bottle hot sweet
chilli sauce

Street food from south-east Asia makes excellent camping food. There's something about the combined heat of the fire and the flavours that works really well in the open air. The marinade for this recipe can be made in advance and the chicken bought on the day to avoid food poisoning brought on by lack of refrigeration. Cooking on an open fire is hot and demanding work but the end result is fantastic. On one very memorable camping trip this meal was cooked for four families and eaten under starlight in a sloping Kentish field edged on one side by an ancient hazel wood and on the other by a meadow.

That night we cooked our chicken, rice and squash (*see next recipe*) on a big open fire of foraged firewood using a purpose built metal grill, but if you're camping in more formal conditions, where fires are not allowed, a barbecue and camping stove will do just as well.

Before you leave home, pound the peppercorns, coriander roots, lemongrass and garlic to a paste in a pestle and mortar or pulse in a food processor. When you've worked it to a smoothish paste add the soy sauce, fish sauce and sugar to make a marinade. Pour it into a jam jar and pack into your camping condiments box.

On the day, find a good local butcher and purchase your chicken. Get him to joint it into decent barbecue sized portions for you. When you get back to camp put the chicken in your largest saucepan, pour over the marinade and mix well. Use your hands to really work the marinade in. Put the lid on the pan and move it to a cool place (in the shallows of an icy river would be best but under a very shady tree will do). Weight it down with a rock if you're worried about animals.

Leave to marinade for at least 3 hours. About an hour before you're going to start cooking, light your fire (30 minutes or so for your barbecue).

About half an hour before you put the chicken on the grill make the sticky rice.

Measure out the rice and wash it in a sieve. Try and get the water to run clear. Pour into the bottom of a large heavy-bottomed saucepan and cover with fresh cold water to the level of one finger joint above the rice. Put on the hottest part of the fire without a lid and bring to the boil. Put the lid on loosely and move to a cooler part of the fire (or turn down the heat). Simmer for about 10 minutes until all the water is absorbed (you should be able to see little steam holes in the rice). Put the lid on very tightly and move to the edge of the fire (or a very, very low heat). Let it steam for another 10 minutes. Then wrap the whole pan in a big towel and leave for about 20 minutes or whenever the chicken is cooked.

When the rice is on, get the chicken onto the grill. If you're cooking a lot of chicken you'll need a big fire, a big grill and a helper.

Use tongs to get the chicken over coals that are glowing red rather than actually flaming. You'll need to keep turning the chicken and occasionally damping down the fire if it looks as if it's getting out of control. When the chicken looks well browned, attack a thick bit with a knife to check it's cooked through and the juices run clear – the last thing you want is pink, under-done chicken.

Eat the chicken and rice with custard squash (*see next recipe*) and plenty of sweet chilli sauce.

Custard squash with marjoram and vinegar

4 large custard squash
6 cloves garlic, thinly sliced
3 tbsps olive oil
1 small bunch of marjoram
(2 heaped tbsps of roughly
torn or chopped leaves)
2 tbsps red wine vinegar or
sherry vinegar
sea salt and pepper

1 large bottle hot sweet
chilli sauce

Just before we left to go camping I found I had a glut of these custard yellow squash on the allotment. Their treatment here is more Italian than Thai but it seemed to work well on the day and after all Kent is a long way from Bangkok. Both red wine and sherry vinegar are effective in this recipe.

Slice the squash into thick (1cm) slices and toss with the sliced garlic and 1 tablespoon olive oil. Heat 2 more tablespoons olive oil in shallow frying pan. Season the squash well and fry them rapidly. When the squash have taken on a good colour, but before they get too soft, remove from the heat and place in a large dish. Tear up some marjoram and scatter over the squash. Sprinkle over the vinegar before you serve.

Serve this with the slightly caramelised chicken above and a good spoonful of the rice. Make sure there is a big bottle of sweet chilli sauce to hand.

Pit chicken
Serves 4

Camping and cooking with small children can be an alarming experience. No matter how vigilant you are, there will undoubtedly be a moment when the smallest and least rational person takes a determined run straight at the fire, seemingly hell bent on self-immolation. The prehistoric method of pit cookery is one way of getting around this problem as all the heat is hidden away, buried underground. Pit cookery isn't quick; a chicken takes about five hours. If you're the kind of cook who likes to keep peeping to check how things are going then this is not for you.

I have to admit that my first attempt at pit cookery was a dismal failure. I dug my hole, built my fire, and after rubbing oil, thyme, lemon and salt into a beautiful free-range chicken, I wrapped it lovingly in baking parchment and tin foil. When I dug it up five hours later it was still pretty much raw. I don't think my rocks were hot enough and on top of that the water table was very high after a week of torrential April showers, so with that in mind it's probably best to keep this recipe for dry spells and high summer. Approach the whole thing in the spirit of experimentation (and caution) and make sure you have a back-up plan, in my case a big fire and plenty of steaks.

Preparing the chicken

Season the chicken well inside and out with sea salt and pepper. Rub the chicken's skin with butter or olive oil and squeeze over the juice of a lemon. Stuff lemon halves inside the chicken along with a small bunch of thyme.

Wrap the chicken in two thicknesses of baking parchment, tie it up with string and then surround the whole thing with tin foil. To make the chicken easier to get out of the ground you can also wrap it in chicken wire. If you are camping you could do all this at home before setting out. Set the chicken aside whilst you prepare the fire.

If you have a banana tree growing in your garden and want to be more authentic then you can use the leaves to wrap up your meat instead of parchment and foil.

Dig a hole twice the depth of your chicken (roughly 70cm wide and 45cm deep). If you are cooking in your garden and think you might use the pit again you can make the sides secure by embedding stones in the soil as a lining but this is not strictly necessary. The sides should slope gently outwards from the bottom. Take care that there is no dry grass too near your pit. Make a fire in the pit, building it with small dry sticks with larger pieces of wood stacked around the edge. Place rocks on top of these pieces of wood so that as the fire burns the rocks heat and then fall into the middle of the pit. The only caveat with rocks is that shale explodes when heated so should be avoided.

Before you attempt to cook your chicken the stones should be glowing white-hot; this may take at least two hours, but not more than three. You may have to add more wood during this time. When the rocks look ready, use tongs to pile them on top of the glowing coals. Add a layer of branches, taking care not to choose plants that will affect the taste of your meat or are poisonous; native hazel will do nicely. Lay the chicken on top of the branches and cover with more branches. Soak some sacks (old coffee sacks are perfect) in water and lay these on top of the branches. You are trying to keep the steam in so make sure they overlap. Cover the sacking with a plastic sheet, or a board or some flattened cardboard boxes. Cover all of this with soil, leaving the perimeter of the sheet or board exposed so that you can easily lift it up at the end of cooking.

After five or six hours (you can't rush it) lift the board away and carefully remove the branches. If you have done it properly, steam should still be rising from the pit. If you find you like cooking meat this way try cooking a joint of pork for a more traditionally Polynesian experience. Add an hour on the cooking time to bring it up to at least six to seven hours depending on the size of your joint.

Dampers

1 camping mug per person (approx. 250ml) plain flour water jam or honey butter 1 long stick per damper

Cooking outdoors takes much longer than you imagine. Your fire may be lit but, as you must wait for it to die down to a decent bed of coals, supper could still be a way off. Dampers give children (and adults) something to do and take the edge off their hunger. This is bread-making at its most basic: the dough is mixed and formed into a sausage, which is then twisted in a spiral onto the end of a stick; the stick is held over the flames until the outside is brown and crusty. If your arms grow tired put a log next to the fire and lean your stick on it.

In a bowl pour out about half a cup of flour per person, pour in a little water slowly until you have a sticky dough. It's best to use a spoon at the beginning to get things going or you may discover how hard it is get dried dough off your hands when you are stuck in the middle of a field without a tap. Add a little more flour so that you can work the dough without it sticking to your hand. Once you have worked your dough to a fairly soft and flexible condition, twist off a lump about the size of an apple and roll it into a sausage before wrapping and stretching it around the end of the stick in a spiral shape. *(cont.)*

Hold the damper over the fire trying not to let it get too burnt or ashy. You are aiming for golden brown not charred. When the damper is cooked (it will always remain a little doughy in the middle) smear it with jam or honey and butter and gnaw.

Camping potatoes

6 new potatoes per person
olive oil
2 cloves garlic per person
thyme or rosemary
sea salt

Potatoes have always been cooked in campfires, but the traditional approach of simply tossing a whole potato into the embers in a single layer of foil usually results in a solid lump of charred black coal with a nugget of very tender potato in the middle. My camping potatoes are cooked in the glowing coals of an open fire but sealed in several layers of foil first, ensuring that each camper will get more than a teaspoon of potato. They are, however, almost as good cooked in a conventional oven.

Either preheat your oven to 200°C/gas mark 6 or wait until at least one part of your fire has burnt down enough to give you a solid bed of coals.

Clean the potatoes and toss with some olive oil and the garlic, herbs and salt. Sprinkle a little water over the potatoes and wrap up in three or four thicknesses of foil. Place the packet in a part of the fire where the coals have made a thick layer and are glowing red with a grey ashy coating. Pull some of the coals over the top of the packet. About every 20 minutes or so turn it over. Keep an eye on things – you may have to move the packet around a bit as the fire burns down. About 45 minutes to 1 hour after you started, your potatoes should be ready. You can always squeeze the packet with some tongs, if you are worried about them being under-cooked, to see if they are soft.

Egg in a spoon

Your fire may look cold and grey when you wake up in the morning, but if you poke about underneath the ashes you may find the odd coal still glowing. Blow on the coal and take a few minutes to build the fire up with dried grass and twigs. For me there is something satisfying about not having to resort to a match but you may not agree. When it's blazing, boil a kettle for your coffee and wait for the flames to die down a little. Get ready a long-handled metal serving spoon, an oven glove or tea towel, a little butter and an egg. Slice and butter a piece of bread.

Crack the egg into a cup or bowl. Put a little nugget of butter into the spoon and hold it over the coals. If you have some herbs with you or nearby, put a small sage leaf into the spoon with the butter. When the butter has melted, gently pour your egg into the spoon. Our photo shows me making this over a gas flame – not ideal but it works. If you have had the forethought to bring a ladle, you could use that instead of a spoon, as does Alice Waters (from whom I got this idea).

When the egg has cooked use a knife to gently loosen it and slide it on to your slice

of bread. If you have no sage you could add a little bit of parsley or some chives at this point. Season with sea salt and pepper and eat straight away.

A marinade for meat

Good quality meat doesn't need much more than a little oil, white wine or lemon juice, seasoning and some fresh herbs. An hour or two of marinating is usually enough to add some extra flavour to the meat.

Fish in vine-leaf wraps

I use vine leaves to make dolmades when they are young and tender but later on in the summer, as they toughen up, I wrap them around small fish (very fresh red mullet or sardines if I can get hold of them) and barbecue on site. Fish this small need not be scaled, just brush each with olive oil and season before wrapping it up in a vine leaf and grilling over a fire. When the fish is ready and you remove the vine leaf, it will take off the scales.

Cooking *à la plancha*

When I visit the Soho tapas bar Barrafina, I take the opportunity to get a great lesson in cooking *à la plancha* while I wait for my food. I ask for a seat at the window end of the long counter, order a glass of ice-cold Fino and pay close attention as the tapas chefs throw some of London's finest seafood onto the grill.

A *plancha* is a flat metal plate, a little like a griddle but without the ridges, that is used throughout Spain to flash-grill vegetables, lean meat, fish and shellfish (basically anything that doesn't render a lot of fat). At Barrafina they use the *plancha* to grill shellfish in their shells (razor clams or mussels) or to sear squid or fish. The flat surface is very lightly oiled and then heated until it is just smoking to give an even crisp surface to the food. Outside the tapas bar, this is a method of cookery that is ideally suited to seaside camping (or anywhere with lots of very fresh seafood where you can build a fire). You need to keep the fire burning nice and hot and remember to take a flat, heavy, iron skillet with you. You can buy a *plancha* but there's really no need to splash out as a heavy frying pan works just as well. You can of course cook like this at home too, dressing the seafood with chilli, lemon, garlic and parsley and serving it straight away.

AUTUMN

MAKING DO AND MENDING
– SOWING FOR THE WINTER

In an ideal world my vegetable garden would be right outside my house, the ingredients for the day's meals just a few steps beyond the back door. In reality I have to drive or cycle down a thundering arterial road to get there. I am often snatching a harried visit from the teeth of other obligations. I have barely enough time to weed or water before it's time to go and all I can do is hastily shove a few herbs or a bit of salad into a plastic bag.

But any time at the allotment is better than no time, and in the summer if I go any less than twice a week the plot soon starts to slide into neglect. The line between a relaxed approach and not doing enough is a fine but frequently very weedy one. Plants and weeds often look a bit out control but somehow it stays productive. I've realised that it is important not to be too hard on yourself; feeling guilty won't make your vegetables grow better, so approach your garden in the spirit of a love affair: a little intermittent neglect is fine as long as the passion remains.

For most gardeners, especially those with families, holidays are an inevitable part of every growing season. Long school holidays and reluctant children mean that in August I often can't give my garden enough attention. Last year, coming back from holiday in early September, I expected weeds but also bounty; in my mind I saw buckets heaped up with tomatoes, bunches of shiny green basil leaves and perhaps a few slender yellow courgettes. What I found was rampant, unwanted growth – thistles and dandelion clocks dotting every bed, hip-high weeds everywhere I looked, each one waving a triumphant plume of seeds. The tomatoes, inadequately staked, now mildewed, were lying sideways on the ground and a single giant courgette, shrivelled and monstrous, protruded from beneath withered leaves silvered with mildew. The ground was dry and dusty and my cockleshell paths were lost beneath clumps of grass and burdock. Everywhere there was devastation and decay.

The only thing to do when faced with such a horrible scene is pick and run: the happiness that comes from a carefully filled basket is usually enough to dispel my feelings of inadequacy as a gardener. So, trying not to feel too wretched, I began by gathering some tomatoes – the miniature plum had stood up well to the damp and there were a few tigerella (a striped red and orange variety), but of my charismatic Black Russian, an heirloom variety planted with great expectation, there was no sign. I added a big bunch of sunflowers, some lemon yellow some a dark rusty dried-blood red, some stained black with a ring of fire across their bright yellow leaves. I filled a bag with edible flowers of rocket, each creamy white flower traced with a delicate looping filigree; star-shaped blue and violet borage blooms; and peppery hot red and yellow nasturtiums. I picked chives and filled a courgette leaf with raspberries. I added a few last sticks of rhubarb and my harvest was not so paltry. I pulled up the largest and most seed-heavy weeds and, grabbing my basket (which by now had a pleasing weight to it), I vanished.

Digging

> To lift and penetrate and tear apart the soil is a labour – a pleasure – always accompanied by an exaltation that no unprofitable exercise can ever provide. The sight of upturned soil makes every living creature avid and watchful. The finches followed me, pouncing on the worms with a cry; the cats sniffed the traces of moisture darkening the crumbling clods; my bitch, intoxicated, was tunnelling a burrow for herself with all four paws. When you open the earth, even for a mere cabbage patch, you always feel like the first man, the master, the husband with no rivals.
>
> Colette – *The Break of Day*

Autumn is traditionally the time when gardeners dig over their patch, cover it with muck and let it sleep but it can also be a time when you plant crops to keep you going through the colder months. A week after my disastrous return from holiday I went back to the allotment and looked around. I saw that others, with more forethought (and perhaps more time) were growing great blowsy green cabbages, tight round heads of broccoli and sheaves of black cavolo nero. Instead of giving up and coming back in spring I decided to sow myself a winter salad garden. Dispiriting moments are part of having a garden and it is the ability to rise above them that distinguishes true gardeners from dilettantes. Gardens are wonderfully forgiving, no mater how lax you have been, they will, unlike friends, repay your renewed attentions without bearing a grudge.

I chose a bed that had last held potatoes and wasn't too weedy. I dug, I pulled, and soon there were weeds piled high on the paths. The bed that last week had presented me with a withered, weed-blown aspect was now a clean, dark black rectangle raked to a pleasing smoothness. Laying down the hazel rods I had cut earlier in the year as supports for tomatoes and sunflowers, I marked out eight squares to make up a quilt of winter salad. I raked the warm soil and watered it using a fine rose, before dribbling the seeds onto the ground and carefully pulling the earth back over them. I sowed a mixture of winter varieties of spinach, lettuce, chicory and oriental mustards, as well as claytonia (winter purslane) also known as Miner's Lettuce, and Texel greens, an Ethiopian mustard.

A few weeks later, in early October, I harvested my first leaves. Everything except the chicory had come up. The spinach was too small, the Little Gem had been nibbled by slugs but the mustard – dark thumb-shaped leaves and thin spiky golden mustard – looked vigorous. I gathered a bagful, enough to make a bed for some chilli-spiked crab cakes and, after adding a few sprigs of rosemary and some sage for warming dishes of beans and potato, headed home.

The most successful winter crops were the mustards and the purslane. These both kept me going when everything else was dormant. In the spring, the late-planted Little Gem and spinach suddenly burst into action and brought a welcome early crop of tender leaves, and in April the mustards shot up and into flower providing bright yellow blooms for salads and spicy omelettes.

Cockleshell paths

Mary Mary quite contrary
How does your garden grow?
With silver bells and cockleshells
And pretty maids all in a row.

Or in my case cockle, oyster and whelk shells. Paths are a bit of a problem on my allotment. I just can't stand the look of old carpet, despite its marvellous weed-suppressing qualities. So instead, when the demands of cultivation decrease, I pay attention to the framework of the plot; I buy big bags of cockle, whelk and oyster shells from Leigh-on-Sea (which still has a thriving cockle trade) and spread them out in long, pearly white rows. Most seafood suppliers are happy for you to take shells away for, if not nothing, then very little. As well as looking pretty, the shells gradually crush down into the earth, feeding the soil and adding structure. It is far from being a weed-free solution but when the odd poppy grows up through your shells it's hard to worry too

much about it. When I go to collect my bags of cockleshells I order a big plate of freshly-steamed cockles with lemon and black pepper. Bought fresh and eaten straight away with a bit of bread and butter, they are a far cry from the rubbery specimens sold in little polystyrene pots at East End seafood stalls. If you buy extra to take home they also make a great *spaghetti vongole*.

Garlic and a rose

The rack above my kitchen sink is hung with fat plaits of home-grown garlic; the different varieties striped pink, red and purple. My crop is never enormous but it's surprising how long four or five short plaits last. Garlic isn't difficult to grow – if you have a sunny bit of earth you can just push a clove into the ground. After that it doesn't need much attention (bar the odd bit of weeding and feeding).

As long as it's well into autumn it doesn't matter when you plant, just wait for a fine, clear day to offer itself. Last year it was October 30th. Beside the road leading to the allotments, against a brilliant blue sky, the yellow leaves of a young maple stood out, bright as flags. The ground was just right and a single red rose was blooming beside my shed. Above me a flock of starlings threw endlessly changing shapes against the sky. I chose the bed that had until a week before held withered plum tomato plants and a great towering mass of sunflowers gone to seed. I had picked six very miniature plum tomatoes, then pulled everything up, digging and raking until I had made it as smooth as I possibly could. I then made shallow drills 45cm apart in which I would plant the garlic 15cm apart. This would leave me space to interplant other crops in the spring.

I broke the garlic out of its newspaper wrappings, and a pungent smell rose up. The bulbs released from their papery white casing revealed the beauty of the thick white cloves artfully streaked with colour. With the help of a friend I popped the garlic into its earthy bed, pulling the warm soil over each clove so that they were just covered. I hoped that by Christmas perhaps the odd green spike would have appeared to reassure me that something was happening underground. Afterwards we sat in the sun on the edge of a flowerbed and drank coffee from a thermos whilst nibbling on some cake.

Garlic grows over the winter – it can be planted in the autumn or after Christmas for harvesting the following summer. I like growing garlic because I find it encouraging that something is growing away even when the weather is too grim for me to visit my garden. If you've dug over and prepared a bed for next year then you might as well grow something other than weeds, plus you'll have new green growth to look at in spring. The best thing about growing your own garlic is that you will have the opportunity to observe how garlic changes in taste (from mild yet pungent to increasingly bitter) throughout its life and which dishes are best suited to each stage.

Which garlic to sow

Buying your seed garlic from the supermarket may not yield the best results. You won't be able to choose your variety and those on offer in shops aren't always suitable for growing in British weather. Buying from a seed merchant also guarantees that your seed garlic is free from virus and fungus. I buy my seed garlic from a lady called Jennifer Birch in Stroud. The imported garlic is grown to standards set by the French government, a bit of officialdom I find oddly encouraging. You may only make contact by Royal Mail. Once Mrs Birch has received your cheque she posts the garlic from her home, Garfield Villa. I imagine her surrounded by reeking strings of garlic in a suburban bungalow, shunned by the neighbours. Whatever her personal circumstances, she has a gift for describing the varieties she sells that is worthy of a tulip merchant and makes choosing very difficult.

This year I grew Germidour ('rich purple head with ivory clove skins'), Cristo ('a white head with pale red clove skins'), Arno ('a white head with pink cloves') and Corail ('large white head and huge cloves'). Each description ends with the invocation 'string or plait', words that hold out the promise of a good crop. Germidour, a traditional, early variety, was by far the most successful and I'll definitely be growing it again. A good crop of large purple and white streaked bulbs was ready in June, freeing up the plot for other crops.

There are two kinds of garlic: those which have to be planted in the autumn and those that can either be planted in autumn or January and February. The first kind includes the broader-leaved short-dormancy types (these last from harvest until December when they start to sprout), which produce bigger bulbs. The latter kind lasts longer (into the following spring) but grows slower and produces a narrower leaved plant and a smaller bulb. If you grow both kinds you should have a year-round supply. I plant my garlic all at the same time (any time between end of October and mid-November). Garlic needs at least one month in the ground under 10°C and planting in the autumn is a good guarantee of getting this. A wet spring and lots of direct sunshine in the last few weeks before harvest are the ideal growing conditions.

Germidour is harvested as 'wet' new season garlic from late April and into May. At this youthful green stage the garlic looks a bit like a leek or a giant spring onion. It has a clean, distinct yet mild taste and should be stored in the fridge once lifted.

Keep the rows weed free (running a hoe down them now and again is all it takes) and make sure they get plenty of water during the main growing season, from April onwards. Don't worry if your garlic looks a little brown around the leaves in late spring, this is just wind-burn. I give my garlic a good feed with bone meal and wood-ash in March.

If your garlic flowers (some hard-neck varieties always do, the soft-neck variety only when a dry spring makes growing difficult), then cut off the flower stems when they reach 10cm tall. Don't treat garlic like onions and leave the bulbs in until the green leaves have fallen over – if you do this you may well find your garlic bulbs have split when you dig them up. Start digging away the earth at around the approximate harvest time (from June to end of July/August depending on the variety) to see if your plant has produced a nice-sized bulb. You could use the space between rows to intercrop fast-growing plants like lettuce, spring onions, spinach or rocket that you can sow in April and May and harvest six weeks later.

On a nice dry day, lift your bulbs and hang them up (a dry well-ventilated shed would be perfect) or spread them out over chicken wire. This creates an airy environment to enable your garlic to dry out prior to stringing. When it's good and dry, trim the stems down to about 6cm and cut off the roots. Rub away the dirty outer layers of skin with your thumb and plait the stems (using string to bind the whole together).

The best thing about growing garlic is that, as well as using the dried bulb, pulling the young plant when it is green throws up all kinds of culinary possibilities. The greens can be cut like chives to flavour soups, tarts and risottos. Whole heads of new season garlic can be wrapped in foil, seasoned, anointed with olive oil and baked in the oven – when the cloves are soft they can be squeezed out of their papery skin and made into a purée (*see page 182*) which can be added to mashed potatoes, used to season purées of root vegetables such as carrot and sweet potato, added to aubergine caviar (as an hors d'oeuvre), spread on toasts and topped with other grilled vegetables, stirred into bean soups to add depth of flavour, or used in homemade tomato sauces.

Roasting garlic for puréeing

Tin foil method

Preheat the oven to 180°C/gas mark 4.

Take several heads of garlic and lay them flat on a sheet of tin foil. Zigzag a thin stream of olive oil over the garlic, add some sprigs of fresh thyme, season and seal up the foil.

Roast for just over an hour or until the cloves are soft (test with the tip of a knife).

Push out the soft, sweet pulp and mix with olive oil to get a smooth purée. Either use it straight away or store it with a thin layer of olive oil on top in the fridge.

If you want to present your beautiful browned heads of garlic at the table for guests to squeeze out themselves, roast them in an earthenware dish and they will look more attractive. Pack the garlic in an earthenware dish that holds the heads snugly and push a few sprigs of thyme in between the cloves. Pour a tablespoon of water or chicken stock over each head of garlic, and a little olive oil. Scatter some sea salt over. Cover with foil and roast for 30–45 minutes, taking the foil off after 30 minutes.

Serve with a soft goat's cheese, bread and a tomato and parsley salad, or with a roast chicken and a watercress salad.

For green garlic recipes see pages 53–55 in the Spring section.

Onions

Growing onions

Onions are easy to grow especially if you start off with 'sets' (bulbs rather than seeds). All you have to do is push them into the ground, leaving the tip showing, about 15cm apart. Keep them well watered and weed free. Birds may pull the odd one out – just push it gently back in. Last year I planted tiny red and white seed onions in candy cane stripes amongst my garlic, in single rows, and got bunches and bunches of fat, shiny onions, which I strung up above my sink. Next year I will try to copy the market gardeners of Naxos whose onion planting Patience Gray describes in *Honey From A Weed*. The island gardeners planted their onions in steep fields, in raised-up rows, scored with a rough version of the intricate Greek key or wave pattern more usually found decorating pottery. This method kept the plants irrigated as rain water was forced to run this way and that. The 'meander' pattern is one often found on ancient Attic jars, showing, says Gray, that primitive decoration was also a way of communicating knowledge. Planting onions in this way may well not make any difference on my flattish Leyton plot but regardless of what it does to my onions, I will enjoy carving the pattern into the earth and it will give my Turkish neighbours something to laugh at.

SAVING SEEDS

*A certain crackling noise the dry seeds make in their paper packet is
enough to sow the very air around me with their flowers.*

Colette – *Flore et Pomones*

The whisper of seeds in a packet is the magic that pulls me back to my garden each spring no matter what disasters have struck in the previous seasons. Ordering seeds is exciting enough but saving seed at the end of the growing season is even better – endless renewal in its simplest and most rewarding form. By saving some of your own seeds you instantly become part of the earth's eternal cycle of growth and regeneration – no small achievement if you're living in the heart of one of the world's biggest cities. Obviously most seed merchants won't encourage you to save seed but it's definitely worth a try. Aside from the pleasure of getting something for nothing, there is a quiet industry to slowly disentangling seeds from pods that is very pleasing, and if your seeds fail to germinate you've lost nothing more than a little of your time. I started with the easy things, vital plants with easy-to-collect seeds such as dark-purple morning glory, rusty-coloured sunflowers, striped marigolds and poppies. From a single packet of each of these I have had five years' worth of flowers and given away dozens of packets of seeds.

Saving your own seed allows you to be really profligate with flowers. My patch of sunflowers is the size of some vegetable gardens. By late summer a great host of nodding yellow flower heads greets me every time I walk down the central path to my plot. I pick an enormous bouquet of them on each visit; arranged in a blue glass jug on my kitchen windowsill they blaze out, providing a deep well of colour from August to October. Every year a vast colony of poppies takes over an entire section of the allotment. Early morning visits reveal a sea of pink and red flowers, each fragile new bloom shaking itself free of the pod like a scrumpled silk handkerchief. These I cut and combine with the air-brushed sheen of bright orange California poppies and the velvet of dark red roses.

Saving seed isn't hard. The general rule is to wait until the flowers have bloomed and faded and the pods have set but not yet shed their seeds.

To save sunflower seed you have to wait until the petals have withered away. At the end of each summer I make sure I cut and take home two sunflower heads well before the birds have a chance to get at them. I always hang the sunflowers up above my sink but anywhere dry and safe from rodents will do. A month later, I rub the seeds free of

the remains of the dried flower head and store them in an envelope in my seed box, clearly marking the variety on the outside of the packet. I use a biscuit tin but anywhere cool, dark and dry is fine.

Poppy heads should be cut when the stalk and head are dry. Hang them upside down in a paper bag or large envelope. The minute seeds will drop out of their own accord into the bottom.

Marigolds should be picked and stored in a similar way but the seeds are more delicate. Pull the small filament-like little seeds away from the remains of the flower head. Pot marigolds can simply be rubbed apart to reveal the curly black seeds.

With morning glory (*Ipomeaea*), wait until the round pods have changed from green to hazel. Cut down the plant and spread it out over some newspaper – the hard black triangular seeds are easily rubbed clear of the papery seed-casing.

Rocket is a particularly easy plant from which to save seed. Last year I hung up a couple of plants that had run to flower and made big green pods. I don't have a greenhouse so I simply tied them up with string and hooked them over a nail on my garden wall. I was staring out of the window some time in early December, trying to think of a way to put off some more pressing task, when I saw them. Amazingly they hadn't shed their seeds or rotted. When I rubbed the pods apart the newspaper filled with very small round balls the size of fleas. With the seeds gone, each stalk still held up a spear of crinkly membrane, which had formed the separation between the two pods. They had a strange silver beauty with the light behind them and I put them in a vase on the kitchen windowsill. They stayed there for months.

Saving vegetable seed

As long as you don't try to save seeds from hybrid varieties (seed that is the product of two heavily inbred parents), you should have success. Hybrid seeds are often sterile or produce poor weedy specimens. Saving seeds from heirloom varieties makes you part of a tradition of seed-saving that stretches back over thousands of years. Some seed companies that specialise in heirloom varieties provide instructions on the back of the packet, allowing you to preserve the tastiest and most vigorous plants for next year.

AUTUMN FOOD FROM THE VEGETABLE GARDEN

Beetroot soup with courgette flowers
Serves 2

1 bunch of beetroots
(4 medium or 8 smallish)
1 tbsp olive oil
1 clove garlic, peeled and
lightly crushed
1 small onion or shallot,
finely chopped
1 thumb ginger, peeled and
finely grated
1 tsp cumin, freshly ground
1 medium potato, peeled and
cut into cubes
4 courgette flowers, sepals
and stamens removed, cut
into strips
cream or plain yoghurt to
finish (optional)
sea salt and pepper

Home-grown beetroots make a soup that is coloured a purple so deep you wonder why it doesn't stain your teeth. The colour contrasts spectacularly (for once that isn't an overstatement) with the bright yellow-orange of the courgette flowers – colour therapy in a bowl.

Scrub the beets and trim them, leaving a little of the stalks. You want to avoid cutting into the flesh as this makes them bleed. Put the beetroot in a medium-sized heavy-bottomed pan and cover with cold water. Add a pinch of sea salt and bring to the boil. Simmer, covered but with the lid slightly ajar, until the beetroots are tender (45 minutes to 1 hour depending on their size). You may need to add more water from the kettle. Drain the beetroots and, when they have cooled, trim the tops and bottoms and rub off the skin; it will slip off very easily. Use gloves or peel under a running tap if you are worried about staining your hands. Slice the beets (they will look beautifully shiny) and set aside. *(cont.)*

Heat the olive oil in a medium-sized pan and sweat the garlic and the onions very gently for about 10 minutes. When the onions are soft, but not coloured, add the ginger and the cumin. Cook for 1 minute then add the potatoes, stir well and cover with hot water from the kettle. Simmer for about 10 minutes and then add the beetroot. Cook together for another couple of minutes. Using a hand wand or a blender, blend until smooth. Taste and season. Garnish each bowl with courgette flowers. Add a swirl of cream or yoghurt if you like your soups creamy.

You can garnish with chives or mint if you have no courgette flowers.

Pumpkin curry with *panch phoron*
Serves 4 as a side dish with other curries

for the panch phoron
25g fennel seeds
25g fenugreek seeds,
25g nigella or kalonji
(black onion) seeds
25g cumin seeds
25g brown mustard seeds
Mix the spices together.
Store in a jam jar to be
used as needed.

for the curry
2 tbsps vegetable oil
1 heaped tsp panch phoron
1 thumb of ginger, peeled
and finely grated
450g pumpkin, peeled and
diced into small cubes (seeds
and fibres removed)
1 tsp amchoor (sour dried
mango) powder or 2 tbsp
lemon juice
a knob of butter (20g)
sea salt and pepper

This year I grew a gnarled beauty of a pumpkin called Burgess Vine Buttercup. It's perfect for small plots; the vines don't grow too big and each knobbly pumpkin, veined a dark greeny blue, is only about nine inches in diameter. I took a pumpkin weighing just under a kilo and made chick pea and pumpkin soup with one half and used the other half to make a pumpkin curry cooked with *panch phoron*, a classic Bengali mix of spices (*panch* is Bengali for five, *phoron* means spices). This superbly aromatic mixture is almost always used whole to flavour oil rather than ground to a powder. You can make your own very easily (*see below*). It goes well with bean, potato or cauliflower curries or in this recipe, where the pumpkin takes the flavour of the spices beautifully and is 'melted' by slow cooking to a glossy, dark purée that makes a lovely autumn curry alongside dhal, chapattis and spicy *brinjal* (aubergine) pickle.

Heat the oil in a heavy-bottomed saucepan. Add the spices and when they begin to snap and pop, add the ginger and then the pumpkin pieces. Stir well so that all the pumpkin pieces are coated in oil and spices. Add a good pinch of salt, cover and turn the heat down to low. Cook very gently for 45 minutes. Stir the pot from time to time and if it's catching add a tablespoon or so of water.

Mash the pumpkin with the back of a wooden spoon to get a good smooth paste. Stir in the amchoor powder or lemon juice, taste and add a little more salt if necessary before finishing off with a good grind of black pepper. Stir in the butter and serve.

Pumpkin and garlic purée

1 tbsp olive oil
a smallish knob of butter
(15g)
1 clove garlic, peeled and
crushed with the
flat side of a knife
1 shallot, peeled and
finely chopped
450g pumpkin peeled and
cubed, seeds and
fibres removed
6 stalks thyme
a good pinch of sea salt
pepper

A purée more Mediterranean in flavouring can be made using the same method of 'melting' through slow cooking. This purée can be made ahead of time and stored in the fridge before being thinned with chicken stock to make a simple soup, or mixed with grated Parmesan and crème fraîche to make a sauce for pasta, or stirred into a plain risotto (made with onions and chicken stock). Convenience cooking of the highest order.

Place the oil, butter, garlic and shallot in a heavy-bottomed pan over a medium heat. When the oil and butter are sizzling and there is a good garlicky aroma coming from the pan, add the pumpkin pieces, salt and thyme. Stir well, cover and turn down the heat to low. Cook for 45 minutes, checking from time to time and stirring vigorously to break down the pumpkin towards the end. Fish out the thyme stalks (the leaves will have detached, flecking the purée with tiny dots of dark green). Taste and add more salt if necessary before finishing with black pepper.

Use as required.

FIRST TAKE ONE ORCHARD

Apples and other autumn fruits

> *What fruit can compare with the Apple for its extended season,*
> *lasting from August to June, keeping alive for us in winter, in its*
> *sun-stained flush and rustic russet, the memory of golden autumnal*
> *days?…*
>
> *Is there any other edible, which is at once an insurance, a pleasure*
> *and an economy?*
>
> Edward A. Bunyard – *The Anatomy of Dessert*

Given the choice of an elaborate pudding or a perfect piece of fruit, I will always choose the fruit. If there isn't time for lunch then a good apple and a bit of cheese isn't such a hardship. For me, really fine soft fruits cannot be improved by cooking and need only a bowl of thick cream to elevate them into pudding. One of England's greatest epicures, Edward Bunyard (1878–1939), was moved to write an entire and very lyrical book, *The Anatomy of Dessert*, on the subject of fruit eaten unadulterated and at its best. Even if you love making puddings it's worth reading as a lesson in how to really taste fruit and as an inspiration to seek out and grow as many old varieties as you can.

Bunyard's title is a bit misleading; by dessert he meant a course of fresh fruit served after the pudding. He may well have eaten puddings too, but it is clear that fruit is his overwhelming passion. Bunyard writes about fruit like a lover, his *Anatomy* is an extraordinarily sensual book and at times he goes so far that one suspects his tongue of being firmly in his cheek. But reading Bunyard is a bittersweet pleasure, as many of the varieties he describes so evocatively have been lost. I can't pretend that the fruit trees I chose to plant were based on an exhaustive reading of the *Anatomy*. I got my hands on the book only after I'd planted my trees. But if you are inspired to seek out strange fruits you may find that the only way is to plant the trees for yourself – and Bunyard's book is an excellent guide. For once the weather is on your side as, in the case of apples in particular, he thinks England's temperate climate produces the finest fruits: 'slow ripening is the secret as it is of good wine'.

Standing in front of a supermarket fruit counter piled high with apples from other continents at the peak of our own apple-growing season is a dispiriting experience. Britain has an extraordinarily large number of apple varieties but the big stores have whittled them down to a reliable but uninspiring gang of five (Gala, Cox, Golden Delicious, Braeburn and Granny Smith). Even at the height of our apple-growing season it can be hard to get anything else. Farmers' markets are a different matter and I can buy a good variety at our local one. However, this year I finally decided to grow some fruit of my own. As apple trees can live for two hundred years, planting one feels like one green act that might actually have some longevity.

It's taken me a few years to get around to planting trees; somehow hastily sticking trees into ground I had only just begun to look after seemed presumptuous. Six years of digging, weeding, planting and harvesting felt like a decent apprenticeship, so last November I finally got round to buying two apples and two plums (a damson and a greengage). To give myself a head start I ordered half standards (three-year-old trees), which will only grow to about four metres. Choosing what to grow was hard but in the end I went for Spartan for the children and Russet for the adults. The plums I chose on more selfish grounds, I adore damsons but the season is so short that I often miss it, so growing my own supply seemed a good way of making sure this never happens again, and although I love greengages they are hard to buy ripe, and so I decided to apply Bunyard's words to the letter:

To have the best fruit you must grow it yourself for only then can we gather it at the moment of perfection.

The Spartan apple tree, I bought from Mark, the Suffolk farmer I buy apples and vegetables from at our local farmers' market, but due to poor planning on my part, the other three trees arrived four days before Christmas. Leaving a tree bare rooted for any length of time is a good way to kill it. I knew they had to go into the ground before we left for the holiday. A whole morning that should have been spent present-wrapping and dashing to the shops was instead spent hacking into very cold earth at the allotment. It will pay dividends.

Apple compote
Serves 4

2 or 3 large cooking apples,
peeled and cut into slices
a few shards of cinnamon
bark or half a stick
2 long slices of lemon peel
2–3 tbsps granulated sugar
(sugar kept in a jar with a
vanilla pod goes very well
with stewed apple)
4 tbsps water

There are times of the year when soft fruits are not at their best, and this is when one has to fall back on a little judicious poaching. Apple compote is a favourite cold weather standby of mine, eaten with muesli for breakfast or with cream or yoghurt as dessert. A bowl keeps well in the fridge for a week or so and makes a soothing end to any meal. One of my crankier friends lays great store by its digestive efficacy.

Place the sliced apple in a saucepan and scatter over the cinnamon, lemon peel and sugar. Add the water. Place the lid on the saucepan and simmer on a medium to gentle heat. After 5 minutes have a look. You want the fruit to fluff up but not catch on the bottom of the pan. You may like to mash the mixture up with a fork a bit to help it along. Taste and add a little more sugar or water if you think the mixture is not sweet enough or too dry. Remove the peel and cinnamon before decanting the apple into a bowl.

Variations
Any seasonal berries can be added, blackberries and raspberries make particularly good additions.

Plum compote

Serves 4

8 dark-red plums (if you feel strongly about stones, cut them out but they are much easier to fish out once the plums are cooked)
4 tbsps granulated sugar (or more to taste)
4 tbsps water
2 long strips of lemon peel

Greengrocers often have dark-skinned plums with very red flesh. They may not be very ripe but can be helped along with lemon and sugar to make a more than passable compote.

Place the plums in a pan with the sugar, water and lemon peel. Bring them very gently to the boil. You want the plums to retain their shape, not explode from too much heat. Poach very gently until soft and then remove from the heat and transfer to a china bowl. You can take the stones out at this stage quite easily but unless your guests are very young they should be able to do this for themselves. Remove the lemon peel. Be warned, if this compote is kept for more than a day or two in the fridge the peel will start to taste bitter and taint the plums.

Apricot compote

Serves 4

12–15 apricots, halved and stoned
4 tbsps water
4 tbsps granulated sugar (vanilla sugar is best)

When apricots are in season a compote made with vanilla sugar makes a very fine breakfast when eaten with yoghurt. Place the apricots in a saucepan with the water and the vanilla sugar (adjust to taste depending to how sweet your apricots are). Poach gently with the lid on until the fruit has disintegrated. If you have it, you will find the vanilla sugar (sugar stored with a vanilla pod) rounds out the acidity of the apricot beautifully.

Flat apple tart with wild apple jelly glaze
Serves 4

*1 x portion pâte sablée
pastry (see Basics, page 271)*
4 dessert apples
50g butter
1 egg
1 tbsp milk
3 tbsps vanilla sugar
*2–3 tbsps wild apple jelly
(see recipe on page 203)*

You need a tart, flavoursome dessert apple that will retain its shape for this tart, such as Cox's Orange Pippin or Reinette varieties or the excellent James Grieve, a wonderful apple with a flushed red appearance, which is equally good as a cooker or an eater.

Make up the pastry *(see Basics, page 271)* and leave it to rest in the fridge whilst you prepare the apples. Peel, quarter and core the apples. Slice into 5mm-thick crescents. In a small pan heat the butter and cook the apple slices very gently until they are soft and golden but not falling to bits. Place them in a bowl whilst you roll out the pastry, reserving the buttery juices.

Line a rectangular baking sheet (22cm x 33cm) with baking parchment. Roll out the pastry as thin as you dare (3mm if possible) and spread it out onto the sheet, folding in the edge 1cm all round. Brush the edges of the tart with an egg wash (the egg beaten with the tablespoon of milk) and sprinkle some of the sugar over the crust. Lay the apples out in neat circles. Sprinkle a little more sugar over the top. Bake for 30–40 minutes, pushing down the apples into the pastry with the back of a spatula half way through cooking to release some of its juices and stick them to the pastry. Reheat the apple butter and pour it over the apples at this point. If the top looks as if it is going to brown too much before the bottom is cooked, cover with tin foil. Remove the tart from the oven when the pastry is golden brown. Carefully holding either side of the parchment, lift the tart onto a wire cooling rack (this helps keep the bottom nice and crispy). Heat the jelly *(see recipe on page 203)* in a small saucepan. When it is liquid, use a pastry brush to glaze the top of the tart. Allow the tart to cool then transfer to a large platter and serve with plenty of thick cream and a bowl of freshly picked blackberries.

PICKLING AND PRESERVING

Pesto

Makes a small pot of pesto, enough for pasta for 4

1–2 cloves of garlic (10g)
50g basil
1 tsp sea salt
30g pine nuts
30g freshly grated Parmesan
100ml extra virgin olive oil
pepper

Pesto is the pride of the Italian province of Liguria. Freshly made, it is an aromatic, unctuous, glossy sauce flecked with shards of pine nuts, shreds of Parmesan and dark flecks of pounded basil. It will sleep happily under oil at the back of the fridge until awoken by the heat of freshly-cooked pasta, filling your kitchen with an alluring smell. Pesto is delicious at any time when basil is in season and, for those who have taken the time to grow their own, it's the perfect way to maximise the use of your carefully reared crop.

Jars of supermarket pesto have become so ubiquitous that it's often hard to remember that pesto came from a very specific place – Genoa, a busy sea port in the middle of the northern Italian coastal region of Liguria. Liguria stretches in a thin ribbon from the French border to La Spezia, the bay where Shelley drowned in his homemade boat, washed ashore with a copy of Sophocles in one pocket and Keats's poems in the other.

My first taste of pesto came when I was 11 (and it was a highpoint in the dark days of the 1970s and 101 Ways with Mince). I got my first hit in its most authentic form, made by a native. We were visiting my aunt who lived just south of Genoa in the village of Sant'Ambrogio, in a tall, grey-stone house perched high up on the mountain with a view that stretched out across the bay to Portofino. One morning, my sister and I were sent off down the vertiginous drive to buy pine nuts from the nearby grocery shop. I can't remember much about the shop, a roadside cave with shelves stacked high up to the ceiling, except that the 100g or so of nuts were wrapped in a twist of paper and the change, too small to be counted out as coins, came in the form of a sweet wrapped in gold paper. When we got back home, an old lady named Yola made the pesto; she then cooked an enormous cauldron of minestrone which she served with a fat dollop of the oily green pesto. I will never forget the taste. Later we ate it again but this time the pesto was mixed with spaghetti, green beans and new potatoes and I think this is still my favourite way to eat it.

Crush the garlic with the flat side of a large kitchen knife. Remove the leaves from the basil and discard the stalks. Roughly chop the leaves.

In a pestle, pound the garlic and sea salt. Add the nuts and cheese and keep mashing, adding the leaves a few at a time. Add a little of the oil and keep mashing: it takes time but the smell will keep you going. You can cheat and use a food processor but it won't taste so good.

Add the rest of the olive oil in a thin dribble, stirring all the time until you have a thick, unctuous paste.

Place in a small bowl and cover with a thin layer of olive oil, it will keep well in the fridge like this for a week or even two.

Pesto with green beans and new potatoes
see page 94

Damson vodka

1kg damsons
a couple of large Kilner jars,
sterilised in the oven – see
Basics, page 266 (Don't be
tempted to use big pickle or
mustard jars as the residual
smells will taint the vodka)
500ml vodka
caster or granulated sugar,
to taste

Wash the damsons and remove any that are mouldy or damaged. Pack them into the jars, stopping about 4 fingers width, from the top, and cover with vodka. Put them in a coolish cupboard and give them a shake now and again when you remember.

About 4 months later, get the jars out of the cupboard and strain the contents through a scalded jelly bag, wringing it to help squeeze as much juice out as possible. A few hours later, when all the juice has dripped through, add the sugar. Stir and taste often, stopping when it tastes good to you.

Put back in the cupboard for another month, shaking every other day for at least 2 weeks. It's ready when the liquid is clear and the sugar will have completely dissolved. Strain through muslin into sterilised bottles. It is worth saving up small, attractive, clear glass bottles that might have held brandy or other spirits. Corked and sealed with melted candle wax, they make a very special gift.

Spiced apple chutney with tamarind and home-grown chillies

Makes approx. 5 x medium/350ml jars

pickling spices
(see Basics, page 275)
1 x 5cm lump dried
tamarind
450g onions, finely chopped
(about 4 largish onions)
300ml white malt vinegar
900g cooking apples (weight
after they are peeled and
cored; about 4 large cookers
or 8 smaller ones)
100g raisins
350g soft light brown sugar
1 walnut-sized piece of
ginger, peeled and finely
grated
6 fresh red chillies, deseeded
and thinly sliced
1 tsp mustard seeds
sea salt and pepper

The sour pulp extracted from the bean of the tamarind tree is sold in cakes wrapped in thin cellophane by Indian grocers. It adds an extra note to this sweet and spicy apple chutney. I also add a teaspoon of mustard seeds into the mixture as I like the way they look in the jar. I make my jam and chutney labels out of the strips of gummed brown paper you can buy in art supply or stationery shops.

Put the pickling spices in a bag (*see page 275*) but leave out the mustard seeds. Put the dried tamarind in a teacup, pour in some boiling water and leave to soak.

Peel and slice the onions. Put them in the bottom of a large stainless steel saucepan with half the vinegar. Simmer gently for 10 minutes. Meanwhile peel, core and chop the apples into roughly 2cm cubes.

Keeping the heat low, add the apples to the pan along with the rest of the vinegar, the spices, raisins, sugar, ginger, chillies, mustard seeds and a little sea salt and pepper. Keep stirring the mixture until the sugar is fully dissolved. Then rub the tamarind mixture through a sieve with a wooden spoon, straight into the pan until you are left with nothing but a few dried seeds. Stir well. Cook for about 45 minutes at a gentle simmer, stirring from time to time. You are aiming for a thick jam-like texture. Take out the spice bag. Remove the chutney from the heat and spoon it into hot sterilised jars (*see Basics, page 266*). Seal and store in a dark cupboard for at least a month. This gives the flavours a chance to develop and mellow

End-of-season piccalilli

for the brine
75g sea salt
1 litre water

2kg mixed vegetables cut
into approx. 1cm pieces –
courgette or marrow, green
tomatoes, cucumber, green
beans or small runner beans,
small onions or shallots
(peeled but left whole; large
ones can be quartered),
cauliflower (broken into
small florets)

for the spiced vinegar
1 litre distilled malt vinegar
2 tbsps pickling spices
(see Basics, page 275)

for the mustard sauce
50g plain flour
1 tbsp spiced vinegar
2 tbsps dry mustard powder
2 tsps turmeric
1½ tsps ground ginger
1 tsp amchoor (double up
the ginger if you can't
find amchoor)
2 tsps whole black
mustard seeds
100g granulated sugar

It is very likely that however vigilant you are about picking your courgettes you will end up with one or two marrows. You could stuff them but I've never been fond of the watery, slightly bitter taste of marrow and a far tastier option is piccalilli. This sweet mustard pickle must have been invented by a market gardener – or at very least a cook really in tune with the seasons – so adept is it at using up those otherwise unpalatable vegetables such as marrows and green tomatoes. Marrow time on the allotment fortuitously coincides with the arrival of cauliflowers, whose creamy clenched heads seem designed for a crunchy pickle. Using up every last scrap of vegetable from your plot is a very gratifying and delicious way to round off the vegetable growing season.

Piccalilli is traditionally a mixture of vegetables, always including small onions and florets of cauliflower, soaked in salted water to give it crunch and then preserved in spiced vinegar blended with a mustard sauce. Homemade piccalilli is far superior to the starchy glop available in shops and will provide you with the means to throw together many good lunches when served with pork pies, cold ham, good Cheddar and crusty bread or crumbly pasties filled with a mixture of cheese, onions and leeks.

In a large bowl, mix the salt with the water and stir until the salt is dissolved. Add the vegetables and weigh them down with a plate. Leave for 24 hours.

The next day make the spiced vinegar by simmering the litre of vinegar and the pickling spices for 10 minutes. Strain and set aside. *(cont.)*

Sterilise some jam jars – 6 x medium/350ml jam jars or 2 x 1 litre Kilner jars (*see page 266*). Drain the vegetables and rinse them in cold water.

In a large bowl, blend together the flour, 1 tbsp of the spiced vinegar and the spices. Add the sugar. Whisk in the rest of the hot, spiced vinegar a little at a time until you have a smooth sauce.

In a pan large enough to hold all the vegetables, heat the mustard sauce over a medium heat. Stir continuously as the sauce continues to thicken, about 5 minutes. Whisk well to ensure a smooth consistency then add the vegetables and stir well (but gently) so that all the vegetables are well coated. Bring back up to the boil and simmer for 1 minute. Spoon the piccalilli into the hot, sterilised jars and screw on the lids.

Variation

For a sweeter piccalilli, add 200g (instead of 100g) granulated sugar to the mustard sauce.

Wild apple jelly

Makes approx. 6 x medium/350ml jam jars

Chestnuts in their spiky cases, squashy medlars, pink sorbs and tart tasting sorb apples – the autumn drives before it a profusion of modest fruits which one does not pick but which fall into one's hands, which wait patiently at the foot of the tree until man deigns to collect them.

Colette – Journal à rebours

as many crab apples as you have the energy to collect – 2kg makes a good amount granulated sugar (500g for each 500ml of juice you get) water jelly bag (see Basics, page 270) 6 x medium/350ml clean sterilised jam jars (see Basics, page 266)

If you are a novice jelly maker, wild apple jelly is a good one to start with. You will be left with jars and jars of deep rosy-pink-coloured jelly with a delicate sharp-sweet taste.

In autumn, thick carpets of small sour apples lying beneath wild apple trees are a common sight and, with a little trouble (but not too much), can be transformed into a very good jelly. Foraging for wild apples means that you are getting something for free that is actually better for your purposes than anything you could buy. Wild apples (commonly called crab apples) have a distinctive sour flavour that is quite unlike that of a cultivated apple; they are full of pectin which will give your jelly a good set. Keep your eyes open and you will be surprised how many wild plum and apple trees are growing within city limits. If not, a quick skirmish into the countryside should do the trick.

As jelly made from wild apples tastes better than normal apple jelly, there is no need to pep it up by adding other flavourings (some people add lemon, ginger or rose-flavoured geranium leaves to the latter).

You will need a very big saucepan or a preserving pan. It really is worth investing in one of these if you think you're going to become a committed preserver –

and who wouldn't want a cupboard full of chutneys, jams and jellies to gloat over? Once you have grasped the principles of jelly-making the possibilities are endless – try raspberry and redcurrant, gooseberry, sloe and apple, wortleberry, blackberry and elderberry or blackcurrant.

Jelly is excellent for breakfast or at teatime on crumpets or scones, but should not be preserved purely for sweet dishes. At The Sportsman, an excellent pub just outside Whitstable, I once ate a delicious starter of soda bread thickly spread with crab apple jelly and topped with a home-smoked mackerel fillet and some watercress.

The amount of jelly you make is entirely dependent on the amount of windfalls you collect. If you get carried away (as I do) you can always give it to your friends.

Fill your sink with water and pour in the crab apples. With a brush, make sure any dirt or leaves are dislodged. You don't need to peel them, but if there are bruised bits cut those off. Put into a large saucepan and just cover with cold water. If this rather inexact way of jelly-making frightens, measure 500ml of water for each 500g of fruit, but the really important measuring comes after you have extracted the juice from the cooked fruit.

Allow the fruit to simmer gently until it is soft. Using a wooden spoon or potato masher, crush the fruit so that the juice is extracted and you have a pulp.

The next part of the process requires a jelly bag (*see page 270*). Having placed a large bowl underneath the jelly bag pour the pulp in. The juice will run through very quickly at first and then slow to a dribble. After about an hour it should all be through. Don't be tempted to squeeze your jelly bag as this will make your jelly cloudy. Measure the juice and place in your cleaned saucepan.

Let your juice cool before you go on to the next stage. Some people think that heating the juice and sugar from cold gives you a better colour because it prolongs the cooking time. I do it this way and my apple jelly is always a lovely delicate shade of pink. But don't leave the cold juice for more than a day before you finish making the jelly.

In your cleaned saucepan bring the juice to the boil and add the sugar. Stir until the sugar has dissolved and then boil rapidly. The setting point should be reached within 10 minutes. You can use a sugar thermometer or do the flake test (*see Basics, page 270*). I do both tests because I am always paranoid about my jelly not setting. Remove the jelly from the heat and skim off any scum. Pour into hot sterilised jars (*see Basics page 266*).

Cut out little circles of greaseproof paper and put on top of the jelly before screwing the lids down tightly. Store in a coolish dark place. Keep it in the fridge after opening.

SOURDOUGH BAKING

Bread can of course be made at any time of year but, if you've never tried it, then autumn, when there is less to do in the garden and more warming food such as soup to mop up, seems as good a time to start as any.

To make a sourdough starter

To make a loaf of sourdough bread you must first catch your wild yeast. This is much easier than it sounds. Sourdough is simply bread made with a natural leaven (raising agent) rather than bought dried yeast. Once you've made your starter it's no different from baking ordinary bread and the result is considerably tastier.

A sourdough starter is a combination of natural yeast and bacteria, fed with flour and water. It is the bacteria that make the acids that 'sour' the starter. You can capture your yeast by fermenting just flour (the French way) but you'll probably find it far easier to use raisins or grapes and water. To maximise your chances of success use organic grapes or raisins which have the advantage of not having been chemically treated. It may sound tricky but once you have created your starter, it should live on for years, if cared for properly, improving in taste as it ages. Bread made with this natural leaven not only tastes great and has a wonderful springy, open texture but it also keeps very well and never falls apart, making it ideal for sandwiches.

In San Francisco they call it sourdough because of its distinctive vinegary taste. In

France they call it *le pain au levain naturel*. I first came across it in America so I used the starter recipe of a San Franciscan baker, Greg Tompkins of the Tassajara Bread Bakery, from *Fields of Greens* by Annie Somerville. However this bread recipe is my own refinement from eight years of sourdough bread baking.

Stage 1

225g organic raisins or grapes
(give yourself the best chance of success by using organic, untreated ones)
600ml water

Place the raisins or grapes and the water in a bowl and squeeze. It will look revolting but the purpose is to release the sugars within the raisins, which will then 'feed' your yeast over the next few days.

Cover the bowl loosely with a tea towel or foil and leave at room temperature for 2 or 3 days. You will notice the mixture fizzing a little when you shake the bowl. This is the yeast carbonating the water. Don't worry if there are patches of mould floating on the surface (yeast and mould like the same growing conditions). You can scoop them off with a teaspoon and any bits left behind will be removed when you drain the liquid. Strain the raisins or grapes through a sieve; discard the raisins keeping the raisin water.

Stage 2

500g unbleached white flour
400ml raisin water

Combine the flour and raisin water to make a sticky dough, beating well with a wooden spoon until it is fully amalgamated. Place in a container at least three times as big as the mixture and cover with a tea towel. Let it ferment for 24 hours in your kitchen and then put it in the fridge for 24 hours. The dough should be swelling and bubbling. If it looks like it's going to escape over the top of the bowl punch it down and let it keep on fermenting.

Stage 3

450g starter (discard the remainder or give to an idle friend)
500g unbleached flour
400ml water

In a bowl combine the starter, flour and water to make a sticky dough. Let it ferment in your kitchen for 24 hours before putting in the fridge for another 3 days. It is now ready to use. This is what I refer to as starter from now on.

Over the course of the next year your starter will gradually sour and become more vinegary, this is what you want; as the starter gets more sour, your bread will slowly achieve the distinctive sourdough flavour. After you've gone to all this trouble you want to take care of your starter, which is easy as long as you follow these simple rules.

Always keep your starter in the fridge.

Always let it come to room temperature before you use it (although I always cheat on this one by taking it straight from the fridge but using slightly hotter water to heat it up when I'm in a hurry in the morning).

Only use unrefreshed starter (starter in which the latest addition of flour has had time to ferment) to make your bread and always refresh your starter after you use it, or ideally at least once every 3 weeks (although mine has frequently been neglected for longer and survived).

Keep the starter at the same strength by always refreshing in these quantities by volume:

1 part starter, 1 part water, 1½ parts unbleached white flour.

When you've combined the ingredients let the starter ferment overnight or for 3 or 4 hours before refrigerating. You can change the nature of the starter by using different kinds of flour (rye, wholemeal) to refresh.

Sourdough loaf with seeds
Makes 2 x 2lb (900g) loaves

250ml sourdough starter (see pages 205-207)
600ml warm water
100g strong wholewheat organic bread flour (experiment with barley or rye for different flavours)
800g strong white organic bread flour
1½ tbsps sea salt, rubbed into fine crystals between your hands
a handful of sunflower seeds
a handful of pumpkin seeds (experiment with your own combinations: I've used poppy, rye, walnut and sesame).
olive oil

This bread takes a long time to rise. It either needs to be made first thing in the morning or last thing at night so that the initial proving can last for at least 10–11 hours. I used to knead my bread by hand but when I got a Kenwood I found that mixing it in the machine was almost as good; the resulting bread was just a little denser. The main advantage was that it was a lot less messy and was quicker to prepare, which meant I was baking far more regularly. When you get used to making the dough, the initial mixing should only take about 15 minutes and is very achievable before getting ready for work or school (especially if you leave the mixing bowl to soak and wash up later – with any luck someone else might do it for you).

I always make two loaves at a time and put one in the freezer. That way I only have to bake once a week. Perfecting your loaf and really understanding what makes it work is something that will take time, but once you've cracked it you will find there is nothing more satisfying than taking two enormous, well-risen sourdough loaves out of the oven and letting the smell of fresh bread fill your kitchen. Sometimes I use seeds and sometimes I don't, but I don't make the bread too heavy – it's healthy enough already without weighing it down too heavily with whole grains.

Above all, don't despair if your bread sometimes comes out flat (human error is one of the hazards of home baking and I always feel my bread is an emotional barometer of my mood). It always tastes great even if our sandwiches end up looking rather eccentric.

Combine the starter and water in the bowl of a Kenwood, KitchenAid or other food mixer. Combine the flours and add the flour to the bowl a teacupful at a time, stirring well each time you add more flour. After about 4 or 5 cupfuls add the salt and the seeds. Continue to add the flour and keep on stirring but stop if it looks as if it is getting too dry; you can always add a bit more later on. Put the dough hook in and mix for about 6 minutes on the lowest setting. Halfway through, stop and scrape down the sides and underneath the dough, making sure any dry flour gets incorporated. Add a little more flour as you go, if you have any left over and if the dough does not look too dry. The wetter the dough, the more the bread will rise. But be careful: if it's too wet, cracks will appear in the loaf. The optimum consistency is something you will learn over time. It should give a little but not be too sticky.

Oil a large mixing bowl with olive oil and turn the dough into the bowl. Rub the dough round the bowl as it is easier to handle when it's a bit oily. Give the dough a good stretch up and then double it over, folding in the air. Do this a few times before shaping into a ball and twisting the ends of the dough in underneath. Cover with cling film and leave somewhere warm. If you don't have an airing cupboard you can always put it on a chair beside a radiator with a towel covering it. In the summer it should be fine in your kitchen.

The next morning (or early evening, depending on whether you're a night owl or a lark), punch the dough down and divide into 2 pieces. Oil 2 x 2lb sandwich loaf tins. Take the dough and stretch it out and then into a ball, tucking the ends underneath, and then place the dough in the tins. Cover with cling film and leave to rise in a warm place (the kitchen counter is fine). After roughly 2½ hours the bread will have risen above the level of the tin (it will take longer if it is cooler in the kitchen, whereas on a hot day it will rise like magic). You want to get it in the oven whilst the dough is still rising and before it starts to flop over the side. As with all cooking, it's a matter of paying attention.

Before you turn on the oven, place a shallow cake tin filled with water in the bottom of the oven; the steam will help the bread to rise. Pre-heat the oven to 230°C/gas mark 8. Just before you put the bread into the hot oven, take a sharp knife and score each loaf about 1cm deep vertically along the length of the bread. Pour a tablespoon of warm water over the top of each loaf and bake at this temperature for 15 minutes. Turn the oven down to 190°C/gas mark 5 and bake for another 35–40 minutes. The loaves should have a good colour and sound hollow when tapped on the bottom. Leave to cool on a wire rack. Let it cool completely before attempting to slice it.

Going outside the tin

Once you've made your bread a few times and got a feel for it, try getting rid of the tins. At the second rising stage, simply divide your dough in half and shape into two tight spheres by pulling and squeezing the dough, sealing the join of the dough by pressing down with the heel of your hand. Place join-side down on a baking sheet lined with baking parchment. Mine usually fit side by side with room to grow. Before you bake the bread, slash the top diagonally three times with a razor blade or sharp knife and brush with warm water before proceeding as page 209. For a really round loaf, let the dough rise in a bowl lined with a floured tea towel, slide out onto a tray and cook as above.

COOKING WITH CRUSTS

The grandest place was the chimney, so high and deep I could walk into it, and the (fire) dogs (which were called landiers) were almost as high as I was. It was lovely to see a fat chicken or a row of partridges revolving slowing on the spit and becoming more and more golden. They were carefully basted and a subtle perfume filled the kitchen. Meanwhile a crisp salad was being prepared with a chapon rubbed in garlic.

X. Marcel Boulestin – *My Two Countries*

Sourdough bread goes stale very slowly. In the haste to make toast or sandwiches, crusts often get thrown back into the bread bin where they are discovered perhaps a week later. Never throw your crusts away for they have their own special place in the kitchen. In summer, they can be rubbed with garlic, sprinkled with olive oil and crisped up in the oven. Once treated in this way they can be used in any number of dishes – as the bottom of a *salade au chapon*, crumbled and broken up into croûtons or, perhaps best of all, as the basis for *pan con tomato* (or, more correctly, as it is a Catalan dish, *pa amb tomàquet*): crisp garlicky toast rubbed with the very freshest and juiciest of tomatoes *(see page 135)*.

Salade au chapon

Serves 2

1 clove garlic
enough slices or crusts of
sourdough bread to cover
the bottom of your
salad bowl
olive oil
sea salt
a handful each of several
varieties of salad leaves
perhaps catalogna, endive,
dandelion and Little Gem
3 tbsps roughly chopped
herb leaves (a mixture of 2
or more of mint, chives,
flat-leaf parsley, chervil)
vinaigrette (2 parts oil to one
part vinegar or lemon juice,
seasoned with sea salt and
pepper)

A *chapon* is nothing more exotic than a crust or slice of bread that is rubbed with garlic, sea salt and olive oil, toasted and put at the bottom of the salad bowl underneath the green leaves. It is humble and delicious and for Elizabeth David it was one of the very best of all salads. For those who find garlic overpowering it offers the flavour of the bulb without insisting too much upon it.

Preheat your oven to 180°C/gas mark 4.

Crush the garlic clove lightly with the flat side of your kitchen knife and rub all over the crusts. Sprinkle the bread with olive oil and a scattering of sea salt. Place on a baking tray to crisp up in the hot oven for 10–15 minutes. Remove from the oven and leave to cool for 5 minutes on a rack.

Place the *chapons* at the bottom of the salad bowl. Scatter the salad leaves and herbs over the top. You can do this about 20 minutes ahead of time to allow the flavours to mingle. Just before serving, dress the salad, but don't overdo it; there is nothing worse than a green salad swimming in oil. Toss the salad at the table.

Variations

In late summer the *chapon* can be topped with chopped fresh tomatoes and black olives over which a little olive oil can be poured.

A small amount of cold roast chicken or ham can be added to the salad to make it slightly more substantial.

A handful of thin green beans or broad beans can be added along with some smoky fried lardons.

Onion *panade*
Serves 4

4 chapons (see page 211)
2 small tbsp (30g) butter
2 large sweet Spanish onions
(about 500g), finely sliced
1 tbsp soy sauce
sea salt and pepper

to finish
freshly grated Parmesan
flat-leaf parsley or chives,
chopped

Onion *panade* is a simple version of onion soup, a nourishing mess of slowly caramelised onions served on top of a crust of stale bread. Onion soup can be a masterpiece of slow and careful cooking or a hastily thrown together bowl of thin, bitter, brown liquid topped with gluey cheese. For Richard Olney, even the worst offering had its charms, becoming 'a symbol recalling a fantastic and beautiful surrealist world in the heart of Paris through whose glorious mountainous landscape of vegetables and fruits wandered the most extraordinary collection of night denizens, each in search of a last drink and the obligatory bowl of onion soup'. This is a meal to soothe the finances and restore well-being.

Make the *chapons* as on page 211. Meanwhile take a heavy frying pan (using cast iron aids the caramelisation process). Melt the butter and then add the onions and a pinch of sea salt. Cook the onions very slowly over a low heat for about an hour, stirring now and again. They should colour and become sticky towards the end. Add the soy sauce and let it bubble and evaporate a little then pour over enough boiling water to just cover. Exact amounts are not important as it all depends on the kind of onions you've used, but what you are aiming for is a sloppy compote rather than a soup. You can always add a little more liquid later on. Cover and cook for another 15 minutes. Taste and season.

Place a *chapon* in the bottom of each bowl, spoon over the onion mixture and top with grated Parmesan and a little chopped parsley (or chives) if you have it.

WINTER

PLOTTING AND PIECING –
PLANNING FOR THE FUTURE

In the dog days of winter, it's hard to imagine ever enjoying my garden again; the ground is either sodden and waterlogged or hard as iron. Tender plants are frost blackened and decaying; twigs are bare; buds show, but with only a meagre hint of promise. The thought of visiting my allotment at this time of year makes me shudder. So in the darkest days, when hardly any life shows above ground and I despair of my real garden, I dream a new one. This year, prompted by Gerard Manley Hopkins' love of dappled nature, I sow imaginary rows of freckled lettuces, striped tomatoes and borlotti beans speckled pink and white.

Vegetable gardens, more than any other kind of garden, allow you the chance to start again each year. I think of my garden as something I can sew and unpick over and over again. Last year, emotional turmoil, work, illness or just plain lethargy may have held you back, rain may have brought ravenous slugs, blight and weeds in their thousands, drought may have withered your crops, rats may have gnawed holes in your gourds – but each year, whatever has happened, winter will come and lay a cold, cleansing hand on your garden. You can dig your soil back to black, empty and bare and then, in spring, unfurl a new patchwork quilt, piecing together bright squares of rainbow chard, feathery carrot tops, vivid salad greens and the pewter blue of globe artichokes. But for now all you have to do is sit inside, in the warm, and get out the coloured pencils.

Every year before I even think about buying a single seed, I make a plan on paper, just a simple hand-drawn rectangle for each bed – not to scale or on graph paper, just a scribbling of possibilities. I sit down with gardening books and seed lists and make profligate plans for a plot of unparalleled beauty and productivity. It doesn't matter if the reality can't match up to my imagined rows of brightly-coloured flowers and blemish-free vegetables; they have existed in my mind. Some part of the garden will live up to or even exceed my expectations but never all; things counted on will fail but self-seeding plants may provide unlooked for combinations. Last year it was a bed of glaucous pea plants straggling through a sea of bright orange pot marigolds, another year dark red nasturtiums romped through my beetroot. The joy of drawing up a plan comes with the knowledge that it can never reveal the unexpected wanton chaos of July.

Each year, I try and grow one or two completely new vegetables alongside old favourites and I try to make these things I wouldn't otherwise be able to get hold of: old varieties with odd names and even odder appearances. Over all I opt for taste rather than uniformity but I am not a masochist. I want to give myself as much of a chance of success as possible; so if I sow heirloom tomatoes with unique tastes, I make sure to plant them alongside one or two failsafe gardener's favourites that have more chance of surviving. This year's new varieties met with mixed success. Slugs ate my Minnesota Midget melons and my slender French aubergines but the Parisian pickling cucumber supplied me with many salad cucumbers and great warty fruits for pickling.

My choices are often impulsive. I am swayed by magazine articles and the descriptive powers of the seed merchant but one thing I make sure to do is go to the RHS's great autumn show every year and see what other far more experienced gardeners are growing. In this way I discovered winter purslane, blood-veined sorrel and dandelions and freckled lettuces. Whatever you decide to grow you'll find that once you've started ordering seeds it can be hard to stop; I always over-order. Now I split each of my seed packets with my dad. That way I can order twice as much without wasting seeds or money and make him grow things he would never otherwise try.

RECIPES FOR AN UNDER-THE-WEATHER WINTER WEEKEND

When skies are grey and heads are full of colds, bodies need foods that scour the palate with astringent, cleansing flavour – clear soups infused with ginger and sour, clean-flavoured puddings shot through with the warmth of spices. If you find that just when your taste buds need to be woken up, you are at your most sluggish then here are a series of connecting recipes designed to restore your wellbeing over a winter weekend.

MEAL 1
Poached chicken with tapenade, wilted greens and rice
Baked rhubarb with star anise and pomegranate juice

MEAL 2
Aromatic broth
Chicken, mushroom and ginger noodles with coriander and lime
Pomegranate jelly

Risotto with baked squash, sage and pancetta
Poached pears with cinnamon and lemon
Caraway seed biscuits with blue cheese

THE FIRST MEAL

Poached chicken with tapenade and wilted greens
Serves 4

1 chicken (1.5kg–2kg)
1 bunch parsley stalks
a few slices ginger
1 carrot
1 onion
2 sticks celery
6 whole black peppercorns
2 cloves garlic

for the Wilted greens
2 tbsps olive oil
1 clove garlic, peeled
1 colander of winter greens
(e.g spinach, chard, spring
greens, mustards, kale,
cavolo nero)
sea salt and pepper
juice and zest of ½ lemon

tapenade, bought or make
your own (see page 133)

Make sure you buy a decent free-range chicken; you will have to pay more but poaching it means that, with the resulting stock and meat, a good-sized chicken will do at least three meals. The salty bite of the tapenade is a good foil for the light flavour of the boiled chicken and stock.

Wash the chicken. Place the chicken on its side in a large saucepan (the chicken should have plenty of room to bathe). Add the other ingredients, except the tapenade and what you need for the greens, and just cover with water. Bring to the boil and simmer very gently with the lid half on for 45 minutes, turning the chicken onto its other breast after the first 20 minutes. While the chicken is poaching, you can make the tapenade, if you want homemade (*see page 133*).

Check the chicken is cooked by slipping a knife between the breast and thigh. If it is still looking a bit pink, give it another 10 minutes or so. Allow the chicken to rest off the heat but in the stock for 10 minutes before serving. Using tongs, place the chicken in a deep-sided dish. Strain the stock into a bowl and serve a jugful at the table. Serve the chicken with a little of the stock poured over.

You can use any winter greens here. If you are going to use a mixture of leaves, start cooking the tougher leaves earlier than quick-cooking leaves such as spinach. Tougher greens may need a couple more minutes with the lid on.

In a large heavy frying pan heat the olive oil with a clove of garlic (lightly crushed). When the oil is hot, add the greens and stir for a couple of minutes over a high heat until wilted. Remove from the heat and place in a bowl. Season with sea salt and pepper and a squeeze of lemon juice and a little of the zest (about 1 teaspoonful). Serve with the chicken and tapenade and the rice below.

Rice
Serves 4

200g rice
300ml water
½ tsp sea salt

Rice cooks perfectly when you add water at one and half times the volume of rice and cook it for 11 minutes. Weigh the rice, allowing 50g rice per person, then pour the rice into a measuring jug to see how much water you need.

Put the rice, water and salt in a medium-sized saucepan. If your lid is very close fitting, good; if not, you may have to place a piece of kitchen paper under the lid (try not to set fire to it). Bring to the boil and then turn down to the very lowest heat and simmer for 11 minutes. Remove from the heat, take the lid off and gently separate the grains with a fork. Allow the rice to steam for a couple of minutes before turning out into a serving bowl.

Roasted rhubarb with star anise and pomegranate juice

Serves 4

6-8 stalks of rhubarb
(depending how thick)
½ pomegranate
granulated sugar, to taste
(about 3 or 4 tbsps)
3 star anise

Dark days need bright colours and there is nothing brighter than pale pink sticks of forced rhubarb baked in the oven with the ruby juices of a pomegranate. This year I forced my own rhubarb by placing an old terracotta chimney pot over part of the plant. The resulting sticks were paler, sweeter and tastier than any I have ever had before. Unfortunately forcing exhausts the plant, making it less productive, so you really need two plants (so one can have a year off).

Roasting rhubarb instead of poaching it concentrates the flavour and keeps the pieces whole, surrounded by the clearest, most intense of juices. The star anise adds a subtle liquorice heat. For an instant rhubarb and custard effect, pour over some golden Jersey cream. You can eat any left-over rhubarb with your porridge or muesli at breakfast time.

Preheat the oven to 140°C/gas mark 1.

Wash, trim and cut the rhubarb into 4cm chunks. Put in the bottom of an ovenproof dish (an oval Le Creuset is perfect) or an enamel roasting dish. Take the seeds out of the pomegranate and squeeze them through a sieve, using your hands or the back of a wooden spoon.

Scatter over a couple of tablespoons of the sugar (you can always add more later), the star anise and a tablespoon or two of water. Cover and bake in the preheated oven for 50 minutes. Remove the star anise and serve straight from the oven or warm. Put a pot of sugar on the table to sprinkle on top; you'll find the crunch not unwelcome.

Variations

Bake your rhubarb with the zest of an orange and its juices and a walnut-sized knob of ginger finely grated.

Roasted rhubarb exudes a wonderful pink juice this can be used to make jelly *(see page 222).*

THE SECOND MEAL

Aromatic broth

500ml chicken stock
juice of 2 limes
1 tbsp soy sauce
1 tbsp fish sauce
2 slices ginger
1 clove garlic
1 stalk lemongrass (outer layer removed)
6 coriander roots
½ cinnamon stick
2 star anise

for the garnish
leaves from a small bunch of mint and coriander, finely chopped
2 chillis, deseeded and finely chopped
2 spring onions, cut into thin slivers

This is a teacup of light, ginger-scented stock with fresh herbs and spring onions designed to make the tastebuds sing. Serve either before or alongside the stir-fry. It can be used as a base for a more substantial dish by adding cooked vermicelli noodles, beansprouts and some fish or meat, most often chicken in our house but also prawns or beef, the latter seared and cut into slices.

Pour the chicken stock into a saucepan, add the lime juice, soy sauce and fish sauce. Bruise the ginger, garlic, lemongrass and coriander roots with the handle of a heavy knife. Add these, along with the cinnamon and star anise, to the stock. Bring to the boil and simmer for 20 minutes. Lift out the aromatics with a slotted spoon and serve the soup, garnishing each cup with a little chopped coriander, mint, chilli and spring onion (and some deseeded and chopped tomato, in season).

Chicken, mushroom and ginger noodles with coriander and lime

Serves 4

100g rice vermicelli noodles
2 flat field mushrooms or 8
button mushrooms, sliced
1 knob ginger, sliced into
very thin sticks
6 spring onions, sliced
lengthways into thin shreds
100g broccoli, each clump
quartered
2 cloves garlic, sliced
400g roast chicken meat,
shredded
1 stalk lemongrass, outer
layer removed, chopped
in half (or juice of 1 lemon
and 1 tsp of zest)
2 tbsps vegetable oil
2 tbsps soy sauce (plus more,
to serve)
1 tbsp fish sauce

for the garnish
1 tbsp toasted sesame seeds
(optional)
1 handful fresh coriander
1 fresh red chilli (optional)
1 lime, quartered

This stir-fry pleases both adults and children and is a good way of using up cold chicken in these post-fricassé years.

Bring a pan of salted water to the boil and cook the noodles until soft, as per the packet instructions. Drain, rinse them in cold water and leave in a sieve until needed.

Prepare the mushrooms, ginger, spring onions, broccoli, garlic and chicken. Arrange in dainty piles on your chopping board, reserving a tablespoon of spring onions for the garnish. Bruise the lemongrass with the handle of a kitchen knife. If you want, toast the sesame seeds for your garnish in a hot, dry pan. You're aiming for nutty and brown not burnt so keep your eye on them. Put them in a teacup until later.

Heat two tablespoons of oil in the wok, making sure it gets nice and hot (not hot enough and everything will stick). Put in the garlic, ginger, lemon grass and spring onions. Swirl around the wok for a minute before adding the mushrooms, broccoli and chicken. Keep moving the vegetables rapidly round the pan. Add the soy and fish sauces. Keep cooking for 3 more minutes then add the noodles. If you need to add a tablespoon of stock (or water) at this point to keep things from sticking that's fine.

Scatter the fresh coriander, spring onions, sliced chilli and sesame seeds on top and serve in the wok. Put the lime quarters on the table with a bottle of soy sauce. If you're cooking for adults and children you can always leave the chillies out and put them in a bowl on the table.

Pomegranate Jelly
Serves 4

3 pomegranates to make
450ml pomegranate juice
(any leftover seeds can be
scattered around the
edge of the plate)
1–2 tbsps of caster sugar
(optional)
4 leaves gelatine (9g total
weight)

There is something tremendously alluring about jelly. Children love it partly for its high sugar content but also because they are unquestionably silly, light-hearted and foolish. Jellies are the slapstick clowns of the pudding world and it takes a very serious-minded person not to be amused by them.

Freshly-squeezed berry juice gives you the best colours; using redcurrants, blackcurrants and blueberries results in a range of translucent jewel-tones. But don't save jelly for the summer months; pomegranate makes a wonderful garnet creation. A candlelit winter meal that ends with a plate of these wobbly treats will not fail to please your guests. My jellies are made in my sister's collection of antique moulds, a highly individual collection of swirling domes, absurdly small rabbits and crenellated castles.

If you don't have much time you could use commercially produced pomegranate juice. Your jelly will still look good, it just won't taste quite as delicious.

Cut the pomegranates in half across the middle. You should see a star shaped pattern in the fruit. Take one half and pull the two sides of the pomegranate apart along the line of the white pith – this is the easiest way to pick out the seeds. Place the seeds in a bowl. When you have finished, fill the bowl with cold water and any tiny bits of membrane should float to the top. Skim them off and then drain the seeds.

Put the seeds in a sieve and use the back of a wooden spoon and your hands to crush them. It's messy but effective. Taste the juice and if it's too tart for you add some sugar during the next stage.

When you have obtained 450ml of juice, pour 100ml into a pan and heat (but do not let it boil as this will impair the flavour). Now is the time to add the sugar should you want it. Give it a stir to help it dissolve.

In another bowl, soften the gelatine leaves in cold water for 2–3 minutes, squeeze them and then add to the warmed liquid, stirring well until they are dissolved. Stir this mixture into a jug with the rest of the juice. Pour into jelly moulds or a serving bowl. Cool.

Leave to set in the fridge for at least 4 hours and overnight is even better. If you are using moulds, dip them in a bowl of just-boiled water very briefly (prolonged contact with hot water will melt the outer jelly and ruin the shape) then run a knife around the top before tipping them out onto individual plates.

THE THIRD MEAL

Risotto with baked squash, sage and pancetta
Serves 4

1 butternut squash (or a wedge of orange pumpkin about 700–800g)
olive oil
2 cloves garlic, sliced
approx. 10 sage leaves or some sprigs of thyme
1 tbsp butter (20g), plus more for serving
1 litre chicken stock
1 onion
200g risotto rice
50g bacon or pancetta
125g freshly grated Parmesan
sea salt and pepper

At certain points during winter, sage and rosemary seem to be practically the only things available to cook with on the allotment. Finding recipes that use these strong herbs means I maintain a link with my garden right through the year.

Preheat the oven to 200°C/gas mark 6. Slice the squash into quarters and remove the seeds. On a baking sheet toss the squash with 2 tablespoons of olive oil, the garlic and about six sage leaves, season and bake, cut-side down, for 40 minutes. Remove from the oven and when it has cooled slightly, slice off the skin using a sharp knife then cut the flesh into chunks (don't worry if some of it disintegrates).

In a heavy-bottomed saucepan gently heat the butter and another tablespoon of olive oil. In another pan, heat the stock so that it is simmering but only just. Sweat the onion very gently until soft in the butter and oil (about 15 minutes). Add the rice and stir for a minute so that every grain is coated. Add a couple of ladlefuls of stock and stir well. After a couple of minutes the rice will have absorbed the stock, add more. Continue until you have used up the stock and the rice is cooked but retains some bite. If you run out of stock just-boiled water is perfectly acceptable too. Towards the end of the cooking process add a couple of tablespoons of the cooked squash and mix well.

Whilst you are cooking the rice, add a teaspoon of olive oil to a heavy frying pan and add the bacon or pancetta. Cook slowly until very crispy. At the very end add 4 sage leaves (1 for each serving) and fry for about a minute on each side. Remove the sage and drain on kitchen paper.

When the rice is cooked add the rest of the squash and stir gently until it is heated through. Add 2 tablespoons of the grated Parmesan, another knob of butter, stir through and season. Serve with the crispy bacon and a fried sage leaf on the top of each bowl. Have plenty more Parmesan on the table.

Poached pears with cinnamon and lemon
Serves 4

4 pears (under- rather than over-ripe)
2 long pieces of lemon peel
1 stick cinnamon
4 tbsps caster sugar
juice of 1 lemon

Using a potato peeler, peel the pears as carefully as you can, retaining a nice shape and the stalk. Slice off the bottom of the pears so they can stand up and, if you feel the need, remove the pips by hollowing out the bottom with a sharp knife (you can always leave this to your guests to do whilst they are eating).

Find a saucepan that will hold all your pears snugly. Place all the other ingredients into the pan (but not the pears yet). Add a litre of water and simmer until the sugar has dissolved. Add the pears and poach very gently for at least 15 minutes or until the pears are very tender. Remove from the heat and serve with a little of the poaching liquid and perhaps some vanilla ice cream or cream.

Caraway seed biscuits for blue cheese

Makes roughly 25–35 (depending on how thin you cut the dough)

50g rolled porridge oats
50g wholemeal flour
150g strong white flour
½ tsp baking powder
2 tsps caraway seeds
1 tsp sea salt
3 tbsps (60ml) olive oil
water, to mix (about 90ml)

to roll out
3 tbsps plain flour mixed
with 1 tsp sea salt (to give a
nice crusty finish)

Everyone knows about cinnamon toast – hot-buttered toast sprinkled with ground cinnamon and sugar. For many people it's a taste of childhood, but it also happened to be Elizabeth David's preferred fuel when engaged in long bouts of writing. Caraway toast (the same idea as cinnamon toast but with only a scrap of sugar) is less appreciated but makes an excellent accompaniment for blue cheese. This recipe for caraway seed cheese biscuits takes that idea and makes it just a touch daintier.

Place the porridge oats in a large bowl and sieve in the flours and the baking powder. Stir in the seeds and the salt.

Add the oil, using your fingertips to work the mixture until it resembles damp sand. Add water to mix until the dough starts to come together. Knead for a few minutes until it is smooth and holding together well. Roll the dough into two sausages, 4–5cm in diameter, wrap them in cling film and chill for 30 minutes. You can always speed things up by putting them in the freezer for 10 minutes if time is against you. If you only want a few biscuits, leave half the dough in the freezer for another day.

Preheat the oven to 190°C/gas mark 5. Line two baking sheets with baking parchment. Take the dough out and cut the cylinder into discs about ½ cm thick.

Spread a little of the salty flour out on a large board and roll the discs as thin as possible. Don't worry about the shape too much – they will look wonderfully artisanal if they come out slightly different.   *(cont.)*

Bake the crackers until they are crisp and brown (about 20–25 minutes). Cool on a baking rack for maximum crispiness and then store in a biscuit tin (they keep very well).

Variations

Start with caraway but go on and try fennel, sesame or poppy seeds or a tablespoon of Parmesan added at the beginning.

SLIM PICKINGS AT THE END OF JANUARY

When a patch of leggy, small-headed sunflowers sprang up at the edge of my first bed I was charmed. I picked the flowers and put them in a jug on the windowsill; spotting them there, a more knowledgeable friend kindly told me that they were Jerusalem artichokes, a North American relative of the sunflower. That first winter I harvested as many as I could but they kept on multiplying; Jerusalem artichokes are real bullies once they take hold. Two or three years later they were on the rampage, their shoots sprang up hydra-like whenever I pulled one up, threatening to engulf a patch of potatoes sown in the same bed. So I tore them up ruthlessly, perhaps too ruthlessly, and by January only a few brown sticks were showing, pointing to the tubers hidden in the cold soil. I didn't mind, as the sweet flavour of Jerusalem artichokes isn't really everyday food, more a taste you crave once or twice throughout the winter. (They cause some people terrible wind but I have always found that if you eat them the day you dig them up the effects are fairly mild.)

Jerusalem artichokes are knobbly – ugly, even – with a brown and white, striated skin; once peeled they have a smooth, creamy flesh with a waterchestnut-like crunch to it. Everyone knows about artichoke soup but there are several other things you can do with these vegetables. Use them in the same way you would use other root vegetables: they can be fried like chips, grated into salads raw or layered into a gratin with potatoes or other root vegetables, made into a purée half and half with potato, or steamed and then fried in butter, resulting in a lovely golden crust and a soft interior. On a rare sunny day in January, I went to hoe my garlic and found, to my joy, that the sodden winter had resulted in long lines of elegantly curved bright green garlic shoots. My hoeing done, I went to the other end of the allotment and dug up a small bagful of fearsome looking tubers and picked a very small bunch of flat leaved parsley that had survived from the summer before.

A Jerusalem artichoke does not come from Jerusalem nor does it share anything, apart from its taste, with a globe artichoke – no one quite knows how this vegetable got its name but it is most likely a corruption of the Italian for sunflower, *girasole*. *The Oxford Companion to Food* records that it was brought back from the New World to France in 1613 at the same time as six Brazilian Indians of the Topinambous tribe. The Brazilians were the talk of Paris and at some point a greengrocer with an ear for the zeitgeist decided to call the new tubers *topinambour* by which name they are still known in France.

Artichoke, parsley, ham and caper salad
Serves 2

12 small 'eggs' of peeled Jerusalem artichokes
2 large or 4 small slices of ham, chopped
1 small bunch of parsley, leaves chopped to get approx. 2 heaped tbsps
1 rounded tsp capers

for the oil and lemon vinaigrette
3 tbsps extra virgin olive oil
1 tbsp lemon juice
sea salt and pepper

Artichokes are extraordinarily knobbly and their weight before peeling doesn't bear much resemblance to what you end up with, but once you've peeled them to the size of a small egg, you probably need about six per person.

Peel the artichokes and place them in a pan of salted water, bring to the boil and simmer for about 10 minutes or until tender.

Whisk together the ingredients for the vinaigrette.

When the artichokes are cooked, drain and place in a bowl. Sprinkle over the ham, parsley and capers and pour over the vinaigrette. Toss lightly. Eat with a slice of bread and butter.

Root vegetable pasties
Serves 4-6

for the pastry
400g plain flour
½ tsp sea salt
200g butter, straight from
the fridge
very cold water

for the pasty filling
1kg peeled vegetables,
chopped into small cubes e.g.:
1 medium potato
2 large or 3 medium carrots
1 sweet potato (½ if large)
1 parsnip or 1 kolrabi
2 stalks of celery

for the pasties
1 tbsp olive oil
1 small or ½ large onion
2 cloves garlic, smashed
1 thumb of ginger, peeled
and chopped very finely
1 tbsp whole mustard seeds
1 tsp ground cumin
1 tsp ground coriander
juice of ½ lemon
1 tsp salt

for the egg wash
Beat together: 1 egg
and 1 tbsp milk

Winter always seems to go on longer than you want it to and finding something to do with the more venerable members of the vegetable family isn't always easy. This recipe uses up lots of different roots and tubers all in one go. Grown-ups can eat these pasties with lime pickle, or call them *empanadas* and children can have ketchup with this many vegetables. You can freeze whatever you don't eat or simply halve the recipe (makes about 18 medium-sized pasties). This is a good snack for winter walks, journeys and packed lunches, or a proper lunch when served with rice and *guasaca*, a South American relish of avocado and horseradish (see recipe below).

Weigh the flour and tip into the bowl of a food mixer with the salt. Chop the ice-cold butter into cubes and add to the flour. Mix until the flour and butter resemble fine breadcrumbs. Keeping the machine running, pour in cold water a little at a time (you may need a small glassful) until the pastry starts to come together. Knead together to form a ball then wrap in foil or cling film and put in the fridge whilst you prepare the vegetables for your pasties.

Bring a large pan of salted water to the boil, add the cubed root vegetables and boil for about 8 minutes or until cooked but not falling apart. (You could also use beetroot, swede, parsnip, celeriac, turnip or whatever you have at home or in the garden. Just make sure you have a fairly even mix of each vegetable.)

Drain and refresh the vegetables with cold water. Leave them to cool in a colander.

(cont.)

Heat the olive oil in a large pan and sweat the onion and the garlic. When the onion is well cooked (about 10 minutes) add the ginger and the spices and cook for 1–2 minutes. Add the lemon juice, stirring well to dislodge any spices that may have stuck to the bottom of the pan and then add the cooked vegetables. Add the salt and mix well. Cook for 3 minutes then remove from the heat and leave to cool in a large bowl.

Preheat the oven to 180°C/gas mark 4.

Flour a board and roll out the pastry to about 4mm thick. Using a saucer or a small bowl to draw round, cut out as many circles as you can. Paint a line of egg wash around the edge of the circles. Spoon a heaped tablespoon of mixture into the middle of each pastry circle. You want the pasty to be full but not bursting. Pick up each one gently and cradle it in one hand whilst using the other hand to pinch the edges of the pastry together. If it is all getting a bit slimy, dip you fingers in flour. Place each pasty on a baking tray lined with baking parchment (or a non-stick tray) and brush all over with the egg wash. With the end of a sharp knife make a tiny hole in each pasty, near the seam, to let out steam. Gather up any pastry scraps and roll them out again until you have used up all the pastry.

Bake in the preheated oven for 25–30 minutes or until golden brown. Remove and place on a cooling rack.

Guasaca relish (avocado with horseradish)
Serves 2

1 ripe avocado
juice of 2 limes
1 spring onion,
finely chopped
3 tbsps finely chopped
coriander leaves
1 tbsp creamed horseradish
1 tsp mustard
1 small fresh chilli, deseeded
and finely chopped
sea salt and pepper

Guasaca is a popular Venezuelan relish. It is more authentic with freshly-grated horseradish but using a good quality creamed horseradish is perfectly acceptable. It is very good with steak but I also think that the sweet potato in the pasties above calls out for the flavours of lime and avocado.

Blend all the ingredients, retaining 1 tbsp of the coriander leaves, together until smooth. You can use a pestle and mortar if you have a big enough one or a food processor. Serve with the remaining coriander on top.

Winter minestrone
Serves 4

1 stick celery
3 medium potatoes
200g butternut squash or
pumpkin
2 carrots
2 small or 1 medium onion
1 large leek (or 2 small ones)
100g cavolo nero
2 cloves garlic
2 tbsps olive oil
1 x 410g tin of borlotti
beans or 100g dried beans,
soaked overnight and
cooked until soft
1 piece of Parmesan rind
(always save your rind up for
soups but if you haven't any
just chop a bit off the
Parmesan you are still using)
Parmesan, freshly grated

for the bouquet garni:
Tie together with string
a bundle of parsley stalks
a few sprigs of thyme
1 fresh bay leaf

If you've ever helped bring in an olive harvest by hand then you'll know that picking olives is hard work. Nets are laid beneath the trees and then each branch is 'milked'. You pull downwards stripping the fruit (and the odd leaf) which cascade down onto the net. When the tree is stripped bare, you gather the net together and pour the olives into a box. The next 5 minutes are spent blissfully seated whilst you pick out leaves before going on to the next tree. I got my first and possibly only taste of olive picking when I went to pick the trees in my aunt's garden in Tuscany. The countryside was beautiful but it was slow work, the crop was particularly fruitful and the wind unseasonably cold. This soup helped restore the will to live (and, most importantly, the desire to go back out and pick more olives). At the end of four days we had picked enough fruit to make 15 litres of oil. We took our 17 boxes of olives to the *frantoio* (olive press) – a barn-like building roofed with curved terracotta slabs. As we watched the fruit go through the extracting machines they gave off a wonderful warm smell of olive oil and crushed skins. That night the cloudy green oil was dribbled onto bread and devoured by the hungry workers. This fresh new oil has a pungent taste that catches the back of the throat but is oddly moreish.

Root vegetables and cavolo nero make up the bulk of this soup which requires a much longer cooking time than its summer counterpart. With summer vegetables, longer cooking destroys their freshness but here the root vegetables combine with the Parmesan to create a real depth of flavour.

Peel and chop all the celery, potato, squash and carrot into 1cm cubes (or thereabouts) and reserve. Slice the onion and leek thinly (keep separate from each other). Strip the cavolo nero from is central stalk and chop the dark green leaves into ribbons.

Peel and crush the garlic cloves with the flat side of a knife. Add to the pan with the couple of tablespoons of olive oil. When this starts to sizzle add the onions and sweat until transparent, then add the leeks and when they soften add the root vegetables and the beans. Fill the pan with water so that it covers the vegetables by about 4cm. Add the Parmesan rind, the *bouquet garni* and the cavolo nero. Bring to the boil and simmer, covered, for about 40 minutes. Remove the bouquet garni. Serve with plenty of freshly grated Parmesan.

Mustard greens with soy sauce and sesame oil

As winter continues, the spicy mustard greens sown in September thrive, laughing off frosts and gales. Over time, the harsh weather conditions cause their leaves to toughen and their flavour to increase in heat, making them a bit less suitable as a salad component. You can still use them but just wilt them first as I do. When cooked with garlic and dressed with a little soy sauce and sesame oil they are the perfect foil for an omelette laced with ginger and chilli. You can eat this as a supper dish with steamed rice or a slice of bread and butter. Make sure you have your rice already cooked and standing by before you start cooking your omelette.

Pick a colander full of spicy mustard greens (I use a mizuna, mibuna, red and golden mustard mix but you can mix your own by buying separate packets of seed).

Wash the greens and leave to drain (a little bit of water on the leaves is fine).

In a large, heavy frying pan heat 2 tablespoons of olive oil and a clove of garlic. When the garlic starts to sizzle add the greens and keep moving them round the pan until they are wilted. Remove to a serving plate and dress very lightly with a tablespoon of soy sauce and a few drops of sesame oil. Keep warm whilst you make the following omelette.

Wok-fried omelette with coriander and spring onions

Serves 2

4 eggs
1 tbsp soy sauce
a few drops of Tabasco
2 tbsps vegetable oil
1 thumb of ginger (peeled and chopped into fine sticks)
4 spring onions (sliced into long, fine shreds)
1 red chilli, finely chopped
fresh coriander leaves, roughly chopped

dressing for omelette
1 tbsp oyster sauce
1 tbsp soy sauce
a few drops of sesame oil

Beat the eggs in a bowl and stir in the soy sauce and Tabasco. Whisk the dressing ingredients together and reserve.

Heat the oil in the wok and when it is nice and hot throw in half the ginger and half the spring onions and stir-fry rapidly for 1 minute.

Tip in half the egg mixture and tilt the pan so that the egg runs round. Cook for a minute or so (depending on how solid you like your omelette) then sprinkle on half the chilli and half the coriander and flip the omelette over onto a serving plate. If it sticks, turn it into a scramble and it will taste just as good. Wipe the pan clean and repeat. If you have a big wok you can make one big omelette instead.

Pour over the dressing and serve with the wilted mustard greens.

Pizza with chives, mustard leaves, rocket and goat's cheese
Makes 2 pizzas

a batch of pizza dough
(see Basics, page 274)

for the topping
100g mozzarella (1 ball)
150g goat's cheese
baking parchment or 2 tbsps
of semolina (the latter is
optional but gives a
wonderful grainy crunch to
the bottom)
25g freshly grated Parmesan
olive oil
a colanderful of mustard
leaves, rocket and radish-top
leaves, washed, dried and
sliced into ribbons
a small bunch chives,
chopped
4 spring onions, cut into thin
slivers
approx. 1 tbsp lemon zest
juice of ½ lemon
sea salt and pepper

On a bright day in February, my sister and I set out to repaint the parrots she had drawn on my shed door, now faded by six-summer's-worth of sun. Afterwards we picked a bag of mustard leaves, rocket, radish tops and chives and that night I made a pizza of peppery winter greens and goat's cheese.

Make up one batch of pizza dough *(see Basics, page 274)*.

Whilst the dough is rising, chop the mozzarella into small pieces and crumble the goat's cheese. Heat the oven to its highest setting (probably 250°C/gas mark 10).

Get 2 large baking trays and cover them with baking parchment or sprinkle with semolina.

Flour your work surface and, either using your hand or a rolling pin, flatten the dough out into 2 rectangles that will fit the baking sheets. Try and get the dough as thin as possible without tearing it. Gently flop the dough onto the sheets, pinching together any small holes that might have appeared. Don't worry if your first attempt goes wrong simply scoop the dough up and try again, this time using a rolling pin to lift it.

Dot the dough with the mozzarella, leaving a space around the edge and sprinkle on the Parmesan and the goat's cheese. Season with sea salt and pepper and zigzag a thin stream of olive oil over the surface of the pizzas. Put the pizzas nice and high up in the oven. They should take about 10 minutes depending on how crispy you like them and how efficient your oven is. You want golden cheese rather than burnt brown plastic.

Take the pizzas out of the oven and put the sheets on top of the stove. Put a large wooden board ready beside the stove top and slide the pizzas onto the board. If one sticks because it's too thin, push a thin metal fish slice underneath. Scatter over the leaves, the chopped chives, the spring onions and a few more drops of olive oil. Grate some lemon zest over the top, squeeze a few drops of lemon over each pizza and grind over some black pepper. Cut into slices and serve immediately.

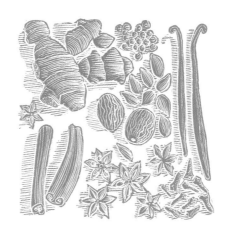

FAR FLUNG FOOD

From December to the middle of February, the allotment is bleak, windy and fairly unproductive. Without the stimulation of a constantly changing supply of vegetables coming into season, I find my cooking soon gets repetitive, so when the allotment is asleep, I look for inspiration from abroad. I try out ingredients previously unknown to me from the Vietnamese, Thai, Indian, Polish and Turkish shops in the neighbourhood. This winter I will cook with the frozen soft-shell crab and the ready-made dim sum pastry from the Vietnamese shop and I will try out the dried limes they sell at the Turkish. I will explore the smoky, spice-rich world of Polish food and teach myself more about Southern Indian flavours. I will try and cook a dish a week from a herring cookbook bought in Stockholm and in doing so call up the wide blue Swedish sky of our summer holidays. I love the excitement of discovering new tastes and introducing them to my family, but on top of this, cooking with flavours from round the world helps to curb the wanderlust that comes over me during short, grey days when I all I want is to be somewhere else, somewhere exotic.

When the weather's bad there is nothing better than pottering around a warm spice-filled kitchen, trying out new dishes or perfecting my bread-making. I can get my fix of allotment life from occasionally breaking off and sitting down with a cup of cardamom tea and marking up the seed catalogues that regularly pop through the letter box at this time of year. You will see that most of the dishes in this next section work better as part of a menu because there's a degree of preparation needed that is absent from more improvised summer cooking.

MALGUDI DAYS

He explained what basic ingredients were required for the special items in the menu, the right stores which supplied only clean grains and pulses imported from Tanjore, and Sholapur, honey and saffron from Kashmir, apples from Kulu valley, and rose water from Hyderabad to flavour sherbets to quench the afternoon thirst of guests, spices, cardamom, cinnamon and cloves from Kerala, and chillies and tamarind from Guntur. Swami not only knew where to get the best, but also how to process, dry, grind and pulverise them before cooking. He also knew how to make a variety of sun-dried fritters, wafers and chips. He arranged for sesamum from somewhere to extract the best frying oil and butter from somewhere else to melt and obtain fragrant ghee.

R. K. Narayan – *Salt and Sawdust, The Grandmother's Tale*

One happy day, years ago, I was idling away an office lunch-break in a dusty bookshop on Camden Parkway when my eye was caught by the bright pink spine of R. K. Narayan's, Malgudi Omnibus. The fattish paperback contained his first three novels, *Swami and Friends* (1935), *The Bachelor of Arts* (1937) and *The English Teacher* (1945). It was thanks to chance (and good cover design) that I came to know and love Malgudi, the fictional Southern Indian town where Narayan set almost all of his novels.

Through Narayan's eyes I first learnt of and longed for a *pyol* (a raised wooden platform on the side of the house for lounging on after dinner). With him I sat down on a dining plank and was served rice and curds from a banana leaf. I went to coffee houses and ate jaggery and then down to the palm-fringed banks of the river Suruyu to bathe. Through all this I developed a longing for India, one I still haven't satisfied. I will get there one day but for now I make do with kitchen travels.

A year or so after I discovered Malgudi, I regularly bought my takeaway lunch at the back of a bright pink Southern Indian restaurant in Charlotte Street in London. Here, for a very small amount of money one could buy a paper-thin rice pancake made to order and expertly cooked on what looked like a child's metal school desk, heated until smoking hot. The batter was poured and spread out with the back of a ladle to form a thin circle something like an enormous paper doily. The dosa was filled with a potato curry spiced with ginger and curry leaves and then rolled up to form a crisp shell and served with coconut chutney on the side. That revolutionarily tasty restaurant was Rasa, run by Das Shreedharan whose own dosa recipe inspired this one.

When I want to go to my imagined Southern India I make the potato filling but I don't make dosa batter the authentic way. I did this once but all the soaking and grinding of pulses was too much for me. For day-to-day cooking, the best way to get the crispy dosa-effect is to use filo pastry to make little samosas. You can also buy ready-made samosa pastry from an Indian supermarket. As this is quite a stodgy dish I always have it with a bowl of *rasam*, a thin tomato soup made with tamarind and chillies.

Samosa or Dosa-style parcels with potato curry and coconut chutney
Serves 4

600g potatoes, peeled and cut in half (or quarters if very large)
1 tbsp vegetable oil
1 tsp mustard seeds
25 curry leaves (I freeze the extra curry leaves I buy – they come in enormous bundles – so that I always have some on hand)
3 green chillies, deseeded and finely sliced
200g onions, finely chopped
a thumb-sized piece of ginger, peeled and finely chopped
1 tomato, chopped
100g peas
½ tsp turmeric
1 tsp sea salt
1 x 200g packet filo pastry (or ready-made samosa pastry). If you're feeling authentic, use the batter recipe (see page 106) but you'll need to start it half a day ahead of time
vegetable oil, for brushing

Place the potatoes in a pan of salted water, bring to the boil and simmer until done but not disintegrating. Drain and put back in the hot pan to steam off some of the moisture.

Heat the oil in a heavy-bottomed pan and add the mustard seeds. When they start to pop add the curry leaves and the chillies, and then a few seconds later add the onions. Fry over medium heat until the onions are soft (about 10 minutes). Add the ginger, tomato, peas, turmeric and salt. Stir well. Then remove from the heat whilst you crush the potatoes roughly with the back of a spoon or a masher to break them up a little, but not too much. Add to the onion mixture and return to the heat, mixing well, and cook for about 5 minutes more, stirring constantly. You can do all this part of the recipe in advance.

Preheat the oven to 180°C/gas mark 4. Line 2 baking sheets with non-stick parchment.

Take a sheet of the pastry (returning the rest to the packet so it doesn't dry out) and brush with vegetable oil. If you are using filo rather than the slightly thicker pastry available in Turkish shops then lay another sheet on top. Ready-made samosa pastry should be used in a single layer.

Cut the pastry either with scissors or by scoring it with a knife into long strips, roughly 25cm x 10cm.

Place about a good rounded tablespoon of mixture into the bottom right-hand corner of the rectangle. Take the bottom right-hand corner and fold it across to the opposite edge. You should now be looking at a right angle triangle, with the diagonal side nearest to you. Keep going until you have reached the penultimate fold. Give the final flap a good brushing with oil (this is the glue for your parcel) and place on a lined baking sheet.

Bake in the preheated oven for about 20 minutes (or until the pastry is crispy and the mixture is hot right through the middle.

Serve each dosa with a little pile of chutney on the side and a bowl of *rasam* (*see opposite*).

Coconut chutney
Serves 4 as a side-dish

150g fresh coconut (1 coconut should do it)
4 green chillies, deseeded and finely sliced
4cm piece of ginger, peeled and cut into chunks
3 tbsp chopped fresh coriander leaves
juice of 1 lime
sea salt
2 tbsp Greek yoghurt

Patak's hot lime pickle is a good stand-by and something I can't seem to do without, but when you've got the time this coconut chutney really is worth the effort. You can keep it for a couple of days in the fridge.

You can use pre-grated (desiccated) coconut but fresh is so much tastier. When buying your coconut make sure it has no mould on it. When you shake it there should be liquid inside. I usually crack one open by whacking the middle against the edge of a heavy chopping board and if you're lucky it should break evenly along a natural seam. If it doesn't, give it a few more whacks on the board and that should do it (or use a hammer). Prise out the flesh then peel off the skin. This is hard work but any coconut flesh you don't use can be frozen, making next time much easier.

Put the coconut into a food processor and grind quite small. Add the chillies and the ginger and grind. Then whizz in the chopped coriander, lime juice and yoghurt. Taste and season with salt according to your taste. If it seems too dry, add a small amount of water. You want a smooth green paste.

Rasam

Serves 4 as a side-dish, or 2 with rice

4cm square of dried tamarind (25g)
4 ripe and juicy tomatoes
2 cloves garlic, peeled
1 thumb-sized piece of ginger, peeled and finely grated
½ tsp freshly ground black peppercorns
1 tsp freshly ground cumin
1 tbsp vegetable oil
1 tsp mustard seeds
1 medium onion, finely sliced
3 dried red chillies, crumbled
½ tsp turmeric
water to thin (about 200ml)
leaves from a small bunch of coriander, finely chopped
sea salt

Rasam, or pepper water, comes in many forms across South East Asia, where it is used as a liquid accompaniment for dry curries, but it is always made with tamarind and lots of spices. You can also serve it with plain rice for a simple, clean tasting lunch.

Place the tamarind in a teacup and pour in enough boiling water to cover. After at least 10 minutes, and preferably 30, push it through a sieve with a wooden spoon, reserving the drained tamarind water (this should make about ½ cupful/100ml tamarind pulp). Scrape the bottom of the sieve with a knife to get as much of the creamy paste as possible.

In a food processor or using a blending wand, combine the tomatoes, garlic and ginger. Grind the pepper and cumin together in a pestle and mortar. In a saucepan, heat the oil and put in the mustard seeds. When they start to pop, add the onion, chillies, cumin and black pepper and turmeric. When the onions have browned, add the tamarind water and the tomato and ginger mixture. Add the water (you should end up with a thin, watery-looking soup) and cook for about 10–15 minutes. Add salt to taste. Just before you are about to serve, stir in the chopped coriander.

Staying in Indian

Indian food occupies an unusual place in British hearts; an alien cuisine that has somehow become a national comfort food. Staying in for an Indian takeaway is something we do when we are tired and in need of a treat that requires absolutely no effort to arrange. In their way, takeaways are a fine stand-by but they vary wildly in quality, tend to get repetitious fast and can often be very oily. To satisfy your cravings for spicy food it's a good idea to have a few reliable, relatively easy curry recipes to fall back on. One of the delights of living in the city is not having to look too hard for the raw materials. In fact the easy availability of exotic ingredients is one of the things that keeps me here even as I hear the siren call of nature.

I may toy with the idea of turning myself into a latter-day Dorothy Wordsworth but a quick trip to the spice-free shires is enough to cure me of any sentimental longing for nature. I usually race back desperate for food from far away places, especially India. I want spices, sour hot lime pickles, tiny poppadums flecked with cumin, packets of cardamom-spiced tea, boxes of sweet Alphonse mangos and plates of chick peas soured with tamarind and garnished with crunchy yellow bhel puri. As I live only a short bicycle ride from London's famous Brick Lane, I buy my Indian groceries either at the Taj, a very comprehensive supermarket halfway up Brick Lane, or the Saver Plus supermarket on Bethnal Green Road.

There is always something new to try at the Taj (chat powder, nutty brown chick peas or cracked black lentils). I am forever discovering and being shamed by the number of vegetables they stock, so many still unknown to me. When I'm in the mood for a mid-week Indian meal that is tasty without being too taxing I usually make a chick pea curry soured with tamarind and a very basic dhal, to which I add spinach wilted with chilli and garlic or sorrel. We eat these with chapattis, lime pickle, mango chutney and a blob of yoghurt. If I have time, I make a relish of fresh coriander, tomato, onion and cumin; if not, I just chop up a bit of cucumber, sprinkle over some chat powder and squeeze a lime over it. If you're feeling a bit poor but need a treat this kind of supper is perfect. Indian cooking has always seemed straightforward and unthreatening to me thanks to Madhur Jaffrey and her extremely down to earth, encouraging cookbooks.

Sour chick peas with tamarind
Serves 4

5cm square of dried tamarind
vegetable oil, for frying
1 medium yellow or white onion
a thumb-sized piece of ginger, peeled and finely grated
1 x 400g tin plum tomatoes drained of their juice or 4 fresh tomatoes (skinned)
1 heaped tsp coriander seeds, freshly ground
1 heaped tsp cumin, freshly ground
½ tsp turmeric
2 x 410g tins chick peas drained (or 200g of dried chick peas soaked and boiled, see page 246)
½ tsp salt
a good pinch of cayenne pepper
1 heaped tsp garam masala (see page 245)
1 fresh green chilli, finely sliced (optional) 3 spring onions, finely sliced
1 tbsp chopped fresh coriander leaves
1 lime, quartered, to serve

Put the tamarind in a teacup and cover with boiling water. Leave for at least 10 minutes but 30 minutes is better really.

Heat the oil in a large heavy-bottomed pan over a medium heat and fry the onions until they begin to colour. Add the ginger and then the tomatoes and cook for about 5 minutes. Place a sieve over the pan and tip the tamarind water in, rubbing the pulp with a wooden spoon to get as much purée through as you can (use a knife to clean all the sticky tamarind purée off the underside of the sieve). Add the coriander, cumin and turmeric. Fry quickly for 30 seconds then add the drained chick peas along with a tinful of tap water. Add the salt, cayenne and garam masala. Also add the chilli, if the dish is for adults. Children might not like it. Cook for about 30 minutes, half covered.

Taste, adjust the seasoning if necessary, then add the spring onions and fresh coriander. Serve with lime quarters for those with a taste for really sour pulses.

Chapattis

Serves 4

300g chapatti flour
200ml warm water

Once, on an impulse, strolling down a superstore's otherwise uninspiring aisles, I bought an enormous bag of chapatti flour. Of course then I had to use it up – luckily it had a chapatti recipe printed on the back and once I'd got into the habit of making them it was hard to stop. Now whenever I make a simple curry supper I try to make chapattis too. I cook all of them in my heavy black frying pan (the authentic implement would be a *tava*, a circular cast-iron griddle). Although you can do it on your own, chapatti-making works best as a two-person job, one of you to work the frying pan and the other to do the puffing up. Any chapattis we don't eat go into the freezer – they take only a few minutes to reheat from frozen and are perfect for gobbling up small amounts of left-over curry a few days later.

The amount of water is more of a guide than an exact measurement. You want the dough to be soft and fairly sticky (you can use lots of flour to help you handle it).

Put the flour in a bowl and add the water a little at a time, mixing it with a spoon. When it has come together, gather it up and start kneading it on a well-floured work surface.

Knead for about 8 minutes, until the dough is pliable and elastic. Place in a clean bowl, cover with cling film and leave for at least 10 minutes.

When you are almost ready to eat, start heating a heavy frying pan. While the pan is heating, divide the dough into balls, each one about the size of a walnut.

Roll out each dough ball with a rolling pin into a flat circle like a pancake. Slap the chapatti to get rid of any excess flour and place in the hot frying pan. Keep the heat medium hot. After 15 seconds or so turn it over (tongs help) and give it another 15 seconds. Repeat. The next step is to puff up the chapattis. Do this by placing each one directly, and carefully, over a gas flame for about 30 seconds a side. As the chapatti puffs up, move it around a little (the odd charred spot doesn't matter). If you don't have a gas flame, you can experiment with putting them directly on the hob or back into the pan, but it works best over gas. Line a plate with a clean tea towel and stack up the chapattis as they are cooked, keeping them covered all the time. (Madhur Jaffrey suggests puffing up the chapattis by 'blasting them' in a microwave for 30 seconds but I have never tried this). If you want to freeze your chapattis, just let them cool and wrap them in tin foil.

Chana dhal with spinach
(see page 120)

Garam masala

1 tsp cardamom seeds (crush the pale green pods and remove the seeds)
1 tsp cinnamon bark or 2cm of cinnamon stick
½ tsp cumin (black or normal)
½ tsp cloves
½ tsp black peppercorns
¼ tsp nutmeg (slice off thick chunks)

This recipe doesn't make much but you only ever really need a pinch (it's more of a garnish and a last minute flavour enhancer) and it is much nicer fresh.

Put into a coffee grinder or pestle and grind to a fine powder. Store in a clean jam jar.

Brown chick peas with tamarind and bhel puri

Serves 4

200g dried brown chick peas, soaked overnight (2 x 410g tins of chick peas will do at a pinch)
2 medium potatoes, peeled and chopped into 1cm-ish cubes
juice of 2 limes (reserve some for thinning yoghurt)
2 green chillies, deseeded and thinly sliced (optional)
2 shallots, sliced into thin shards
1 tbsp chopped coriander
1 tbsp chopped mint
a pinch of chat masala or garam masala (see page 245)
sea salt, to taste

to serve
bhel and sev puri (2 tbsps per serving)
tamarind chutney (see recipe on page 247)
yoghurt dressing (4 tbsps of plain yoghurt thinned until runny with lime juice or water)
sprigs of chopped coriander

Most Southern Indian restaurants will serve up variations on this delicious starter, a combination of boiled chick peas, tamarind chutney and cracked and puffed rice and wheat. My own particular favourite, Ravi Shankar, has a faded charm all its own. I always order the same thing: bhel puri followed by an enormous paper dosa shaped like a fan of coral all washed down with a long, cool glass of foaming lassi or a Cobra beer.

I had never thought about making bhel puri at home until I came across a big 'ready to eat bhel puri meal kit' at my local Indian supermarket. Bhel puri is puffed dried rice and the sev puri (like bright-yellow crumbled shredded wheat) is made from gram (chick pea) flour. Both are mixed with spices and turmeric which gives them their slightly lurid appearance. The puffs and wiggles of sev and bhel puri are usually served on top of a bowl of boiled chick peas and potatoes, layered with sliced shallots, fresh coriander and tamarind chutney. To confuse matters, this whole dish is called bhel puri in Southern Indian restaurants. The meal kit comes in a box with sachets of very salty, overly glutinous prepared sauces. Throw these out and tip the puris into a Kilner jar ready for whenever you get a craving for bhel puri. Brown chick peas (*kala chana*) have a wizened appearance but once cooked they are strangely beautiful shiny little kernels with a delicious nutty texture. Ordinary chick peas will do if you can't get hold of the brown ones.

Drain the chick peas and place in a large pan with a good three fingers-depth of fresh water above the level of the pulses. Do not add salt as adding salt before the chick peas are cooked hardens them. Depending on the age of your pulses (newer pulses cook quicker) they could be ready in about an hour but you should test them – undercooked pulses are not pleasant. After about 50 minutes, or when the chick peas are well on their way, add the cubed potatoes. By the time the potatoes are soft, the water should have reduced but you can always drain off a little of the liquid if it looks too runny.

If using tinned chick peas simply boil the potatoes and add to the drained chick peas with a little of the potato water. This will still be tasty, just not quite as flavoursome.

Dress the chick peas and potatoes with the lime juice, green chilli, shallots, coriander and mint and a sprinkling of chat masala (a ready-made sour and hot mix of spices) or some garam masala (*see page 245*). Taste, season with salt and adjust the flavourings (you may like more lime or a bit more chat).

Place a serving of chick peas in each bowl, top with sev and bhel puri, drizzle about a tablespoon of each dressing (tamarind chutney (*see below*) and yoghurt) over the top and add a sprig or two of coriander.

Tamarind chutney
Serves 4

50g dried tamarind (roughly 8 x 8 cm)	Put the tamarind in a cup, cover with boiling water and leave for at least 2 hours and preferably more; the longer you leave it the more the dried pods will swell and rehydrate. Take the tamarind and pour it into a sieve and rub the tamarind through the sieve, making sure you scrape as much as you can off the bottom. When you feel it has all gone through, season the tamarind with sugar to taste, salt, chilli powder and cumin. Mix well. You can keep this for a week or so in the fridge.
1–2 tablepooons caster sugar	
½ tsp sea salt	
½ tsp chilli powder	
1 tsp freshly toasted and ground cumin	

Food from Poland

A Polish winter lunch with sweet and sour red cabbage, sausages and cwikla (beetroot purée)
Serves 4

4 hard-boiled eggs
an assortment of smoked sausages, sliced
gherkins
pumpernickel bread
a jar of beetroot and horseradish purée
a jar of creamed horseradish

When I think of Polish food I think of colour: dark brown pumpernickel bread, bright pinky-red beetroot purée (*cwikla*), shiny ribbed gherkins, smoky blood-red sausages and the creamy white of horseradish. There are Polish delis popping up all over the place, all filled with intriguing unpronounceable ingredients. But foreign cuisines can be hard to crack. It's one thing gazing longingly at exotic unknown goods, quite another to put a tasty meal together from alien shelves – sometimes one needs a helpful introduction. Mine came via lunch at a local café cum grocery shop. At Leila's, breakfast starts at ten o'clock with eggs fried with sage and thick glasses of frothy coffee served alongside platters of smoked sausage, boiled egg and dark bread.

A few days later I craved another Polish lunch so I popped into Kryzo, an Eastern European deli in the neighbourhood, for the raw materials. Kryzo's shelves are lined with colourful preserves, fruit cordials and stacks of rye bread and there are freezers full of *pierogi*. At the cold counter there is a large range of *kielbasa* – smoked sausages in a variety of sizes from long batons to Punch-and-Judy-show strings to bundles of thin cigar-sized ones. I bought several of each as well as a jar of beetroot purée, some crunchy gherkins and a packet of pumpernickel bread. They don't get that many English visitors and, as my Polish is minimal, I'm reduced to pointing at things, but this works fine. I went home and made a pan of sweet-and-sour red cabbage cooked with port. I boiled some eggs and spread out my Polish platter.

Shell and quarter the eggs and arrange with the sliced sausage, gherkins and pumpernickel bread on a big platter and serve with the beetroot and horseradish purée and creamed horseradish.

If it's really cold or your guests look hungry serve up a big pan of mashed potato (*see page 124*) alongside the cabbage (below) and the cold platter.

Red cabbage and apple with port
Serves 4 or 6 as a side-dish

1 small red cabbage
3 sharp apples (cookers or Granny Smith), peeled and cored
300ml port (or 300ml red wine and 1 tsp granulated sugar)
100ml wild apple or redcurrant jelly (see page 203)
2 tbsps lemon juice
1 tsp orange zest
1 tsp sea salt
pepper

Raw red cabbage keeps for ages in the bottom of the fridge and for about a week after you've cooked it. This is one dish that really benefits from being made a day in advance.

Finely slice the cabbage and the apples. In a heavy bottomed pan or casserole dish combine the apples, port or sweetened wine, jelly, lemon juice, orange zest and salt. Bring the mixture up to the boil, cover, lower the heat and cook for 1½ hours. Check occasionally to stir and see if the mixture has dried out, adding a little water if it looks as if it's going to stick. Season with pepper and more salt if necessary and serve.

Smoked eel, beetroot and horseradish purée and watercress toasts with damson vodka
Serves 4

6 thin slices of sourdough bread, toasted and cut into quarters
4 tbsps beetroot and horseradish purée
1 small bunch (50g) watercress, washed and dried
100g smoked eel fillet sliced into rough 1 cm chunks (if you find smoked eel hard to get hold of then smoked mackerel makes a respectable substitute)
50ml thick sour cream or crème fraîche
pepper

A couple of months later, out Christmas shopping, I found myself near Leila's shop again. I was tempted inside by a colourful display: branches of pale lemons with shiny dark green leaves, sheaves of Cavolo Nero, piles of blood oranges flushed with crimson and bunches of emerald green watercress. My bags were already heavy, so instead of the glazed terracotta cooking vessels I craved, I made do with a bunch of watercress and another jar of horseradish and beetroot purée, which Leila told me the Poles eat with smoked fish. I had friends coming over for a drink so I made up a new canapé: tiny toasts with a sprig of watercress, a blob of purée and a sliver of smoked eel. The emerald green of the watercress is the perfect foil to the bright purple of the purée and the strong colours are nicely set off by the cream. It was a cold crisp winter night, perfect for eating food with an eastern European flavour so I broke out the damson vodka I'd laid down in the autumn (*see page 199*).

Take a square of toast and add ½ teaspoon of the purée. Use the purée to glue on a sprig of watercress and a little bit of eel. Top the lot with the daintiest blob of cream you can manage. Arrange as many as you can on a large platter and grind a little black pepper over the top. Arrange a little more watercress around the edge of the plate as a garnish. Serve with tiny frosted glasses of vodka, preferably damson.

Scandinavian Food

As well as being deeply peaceful and restorative, several dreamy summer holidays on the pine-fringed, golden coast of Southern Sweden turned out to be a revelation in terms of taste. Swedish food, with its reliance on berries, very fresh fish and shellfish and the clean taste of dill, has an unusual lightness to it that leaves you feeling refreshed and bursting with health without any compromise in taste. Added to which, Scandinavian food is surprisingly spice-rich: anise, fennel, cardamom, caraway and dill flavour pastries, roasts, breads and salt-cures in ways that can be very uplifting for a jaded palate, especially in winter when warming spices are most welcome.

Prawn Skagen
Serves 4 as a starter

300g peeled, cooked prawns or shrimps
3 tbsps mayonnaise
3 tbsps of sour cream or crème fraîche
2 tbsp freshly chopped dill
2 tbsp freshly chopped chives
1 tsp Dijon mustard
1 tbsp lemon juice
black pepper

to serve
3 or 4 slices of toast, crusts removed and cut into quarters
1 x 100g pot salmon or golden caviar
dill sprigs
lemon quarters

In Sweden, prawn skagen is a popular party appetiser, generally served with a sprig of dill waving jauntily on top. It's a really delightful combination of sweet pink prawns, a creamy dill dressing and the pop and crunch of golden caviar. I came across it first via Swedish restaurateur Anna Mosesson, and soon afterwards in a Swedish supermarket in rather more downmarket form, where it was sold ready-made in big plastic tubs. Even the less posh versions are impossible not to eat all in one go. I like buying a pot and wolfing it down with a packet of giant round rye crispbread. Made at home, it is a good starter served with lemon quarters and on small slices of toast.

You can buy Swedish food online from Totally Swedish and Ikea is another good place to pick up Swedish ingredients, especially the slightly sweeter matjes anchovies that are perfect for making the cream and potato gratin Jansson's Temptation.

If you have bought them raw (or been lucky enough to catch them yourself) cook the shrimps briefly in boiling water and shell them, remembering to keep your shells for a bisque. If the prawns are very large then chop them up into bite-sized morsels.

Combine all the ingredients except the shrimps, the lemon juice and pepper and whisk to a smooth paste. Add the lemon juice and stir in the shrimps. Season with black pepper but no salt as the caviar is quite salty.

Pile the prawn mixture up on the toasts and top with a small teaspoonful of salmon caviar and a sprig of dill. Golden caviar, made from whitefish roe, is very, very good but harder to source than salmon caviar. You can omit the caviar altogether on more homely occasions. Serve with the lemon quarters.

Gravadlax
Serves 10–12

1 salmon, weighing very roughly 3kg (for everyday dining divide the following recipe by 4 and use a smaller piece weighing around 750g)

for the cure
2 large bunches fresh dill (100g)
40g black pepper
240g sea salt

480g caster sugar
dill sprigs and lemon quarters, to serve

Gravadlax is simply salmon cured in salt, pepper, dill and sugar. It is an extremely straightforward process, resulting in a deep orange slab of dense, dark, sweet, cured fish. Eaten with freshly-pickled cucumbers, rye bread and mustard dressing it is a treat whose superlative tastiness is out of all proportion to the ease of its preparation. I cure mine in the fridge but my friend Frank has cured three or four fish at a time and then buried them in the garden for a few days (well wrapped up, of course).

A whole salmon can be cured in this way for special occasions but for everyday dining a smaller piece cut from the middle of the fish works very well. There is no cooking involved, making it a good recipe for those not confident with fish – only a little forethought is required (you must start this recipe at least five days but even better seven days before you need to eat it). Salmon cured this way keeps for about seven days but any left-overs will freeze very successfully if you are unable to eat it all in one go.

Slice the salmon or fillet into two halves lengthways and if using a whole fish remove the back-bone. I always get the fishmonger to do this for me. If you're lucky they'll take the pin bones out for you too, but if they don't then, before you start, lay the salmon on a board, silver-side down, gently run your hand over the top and you will feel the odd prickle of bone. These are the pin bones and are easily removed with tweezers. Wipe the fish clean with damp paper towel and pat dry.

Chop the dill roughly and coarsely grind the pepper (you might want to use a spice grinder or pestle for this amount of pepper). Mix together in a bowl with the sea salt and sugar.

Take a very large piece of tin foil and spread about one third of this mixture on it. Place one fillet on top of this, silver-side down, spread the next third of the salt and herb mixture on top of this fillet and top with the other piece of fish, silver-side up. Top with the remaining mix and wrap the foil around the fish, tucking the ends in to get a good seal. Place in a deep gratin dish or roasting tray with a board on top of the whole lot and weigh it down (I use the weights from an old fashioned pair of scales but a brick would do equally well). Leave in the fridge to cure, turning the fish over every day. Don't worry if the fish seems to be swimming in syrupy juices, this is to be expected.

After at least 5 days, preferably 7, take the salmon out and wipe off the salt, pepper and dill. You can wash it very gently if you prefer but I like the look of the specks of dill adhering to the fish. Lay your hand flat on the salmon and with a sharp knife cut away from you to get thin slices of fish cut diagonally and leaving the skin behind. Arrange on a platter with a few sprigs of dill and some lemon quarters. Serve with dill cucumbers and mustard dressing (*see page 254*), and with rye bread and boiled potatoes.

Dill cucumbers

Divide this recipe by four as above, if you are making the smaller amount of salmon.

8 tbsps caster sugar
1 rounded tsp sea salt
400ml Japanese rice vinegar
or white wine vinegar
4 small cucumbers (if I
haven't grown the cucumbers
I buy the short, crunchy ones
from my local Turkish shop,
which are about 10cm long)
4–6 tbsps freshly chopped
dill

A few hours before you are going to eat the salmon, prepare the cucumbers. The day before is fine if you feel like getting ahead. The cucumbers will keep for a few days but gradually lose their crunch.

Mix the sugar, salt and vinegar together in a pan and heat gently until the sugar has dissolved.

Slice the cucumbers thinly on the diagonal and layer them in a pottery dish with the chopped dill. The cucumbers should fit snugly. Halfway up, pour in half the vinegar mixture. Continue with the dill and cucumbers then pour over the rest of the liquid when you reach the top. Put a saucer or small plate on top and weigh down. Leave in the fridge until you are ready to serve.

Mustard dressing

1 tbsp caster sugar
2 tbsps Japanese rice vinegar
or white wine vinegar
4 tbsps freshly chopped dill
2 tbsps Dijon mustard
enough olive oil to make a
smooth dressing (4–6 tbsps)

In a small pan, stir the sugar and vinegar together over a gentle heat until all the sugar has dissolved. Allow to cool. Whisk the dill, Dijon mustard and the vinegar and sugar together. Slowly pour the oil in, whisking all the time until you have a fine smooth, glossy sauce.

Serve with the cucumbers and salmon with rye bread and boiled potatoes.

Fennel and dill salad
Serves 2

for the dressing
3 tbsps crème fraîche
1 tbsp mayonnaise
3 tbsps lemon juice
sea salt and pepper

1 handful fresh dill, chopped
(keep a little back to
sprinkle on top)
1 crisp pear or apple
1 bulb of fennel, tough outer-
leaves removed
1 small shallot, peeled and
sliced into fine rings
chopped dill, to garnish

Gravadlax, rye toast and this crisp salad make an extremely refreshing meal.

Before you start slicing the fruit, make the dressing, so you can immediately coat the fruit and stop it going brown.

In a small bowl mix the crème fraîche, mayonnaise and lemon juice, season with salt and pepper and add a little more lemon juice if you like your dressing tangy. Add the dill and set aside.

Using a mandolin if you have one, cut the peeled and cored fruit and the fennel into delicate thin slices. Dress immediately and sprinkle the shallot rings and a little more dill on top. Taste and season once more if needed. Refrigerate until you are ready to use it.

Dry roasted chicken with spices
Serves 4

½ tsp ground turmeric
½ tsp cayenne pepper
1 tsp freshly ground cumin
½ tsp ground cinnamon
2 cardamom pods (seeds
removed and ground)
sea salt and pepper
1 medium free-range chicken
(1.5–2kg)

This recipe got its inspiration from Swedish chef, Marcus Samuelsson's cookbook, *Aquavit*. In it, he recalls how his grandmother dry-roasted a chicken rubbed with a mixture of cinnamon, cloves and star anise every Sunday night. Over time, my own mixture has evolved, slightly more Indian in flavour and a special favourite of my children.

Mix the spices and seasoning in a bowl. Rub into the chicken skin. Do this over a plate so you can scoop up any spices that slide off and rub them in. *(cont.)*

Preheat the oven to 230°C/gas mark 8.

Place the chicken on a rack over a roasting tray. Pour a cup of water into the bottom of the tray. Cook for 15 minutes at this top temperature and then turn down to 180°C/ gas mark 4 and cook for a further 45 minutes. Pierce the thigh with a skewer and if the juices run clear the chicken is ready; if not, give it a few more minutes. Serve with a green salad (maybe watercress in winter) and creamy dauphinoise potatoes (*see page 123*) or mash (*see page 124*).

Rhubarb cordial

Sour-sweet cordials made from berries and rosehips are popular in Sweden. You can buy them in cartons in Swedish speciality shops or try making your own with home-grown rhubarb (*see page 67*).

Homecooked ham

1 half leg of good free-range ham, about 4.5kg
1 onion studded with 5 cloves
4 carrots
2 bay leaves
a few sprigs of thyme
a nice big bunch of parsley
3 tbsps dark molasses or black treacle or brown sugar or 200ml good cider or ale (what you use is something you can experiment with and find out for yourself what suits you best)

for the glaze
3 tbsps Dijon mustard
2 tbsps brown sugar or honey
juice of 1 orange, or a little of the cooking liquor (or use 2–3 tbsps of BBQ sauce)

Once a week I go to Westbourne Grove, a world away from Hackney, but where I work at *The Week* magazine. I get my lunch from Tavola, ace chef Alistair Little's cook shop. Mr Little himself can be seen whisking around behind the counter, gruffly turning out London's best takeaway lunch, an air of slightly irascible efficiency hanging over him.

On top of the cold counter there is usually a most appetising pink ham, with creamy white fat and a dark-red glaze, and with a bone sticking jauntily out of one end. This superlative ham was the inspiration behind my own. The few words of advice given to me by Mr Little over the counter one lunchtime, worked like a charm and my ham, though maybe not quite as juicy as his, was still very tasty. It fed a houseful for a week and half before ending its days as the ham bone in a restorative early January pot of *pasta fagioli*.

A good sticky glaze that hardens without burning and doesn't slide off can be hard to pull off. Alastair Little suggests using a bought barbeque sauce and in his own words 'painting it on like creosote'. It certainly gives the ham a lovely dark, sticky exterior with minimum bother.

Soak the ham for 24 hours, changing the water 3 times.

Place the ham in the largest saucepan you have. I use the big pan I make preserves in. Bring the water to the boil and taste it. If it's far too salty, throw away the water and start again, bringing the pot back to the boil with fresh water. Add all the other ingredients and mix well. Bring to the boil once more and simmer (very gently – the odd burp rather than a constant bubbling) until cooked. You want the ham to cook for 40 minutes per 450g, minus 10 minutes for the initial boil-up (or minus 20 if you replaced the liquid and brought it up to the boil twice), and minus 30 minutes for the glaze cooking that you will do at the end. Hams over 5kg should be calculated at 20 minutes per 450kg/1lb. Leave to rest in the liquid in a cool place or squeezed into the fridge for no less than 6 and up to 12 hours.

The next day remove the ham from the water, reserving a little of the ham water for the glazing part. Meanwhile preheat the oven to 180°C/gas mark 4 and mix all the ingredients for the glaze or open your bottle of sauce.

Take the ham and place on a rack in a roasting tray. Pour two cups of the ham water into the bottom of the tray. Peel off the skin, score the fat in a diamond pattern by cutting diagonal lines first one way and then the other and then paint on the glaze. Bake for 30 minutes, watching carefully to see that the glaze doesn't burn.

Allow to cool completely before wrapping up well in cling film and refrigerating.

Ham hocks

An economical way of making your own ham is to use ham hocks. A ham hock is the end of the pig's leg, the bit in between the ham and the foot. It is a muscly piece of meat but very tasty. It won't look as pretty as a big ham but is great for sandwiches, pies, quiches and so on. You will be pleasantly surprised by how little a butcher charges you for this cut. There are also smoked hocks, which fill the house with a lovely frankfurtery smell when they are cooking.

Soak your hock in water for 24 hours, changing the water three times. If using a smoked hock, you may not need to soak it as much, or at all – ask your butcher whether it is necessary.

Put the soaked hock in a pan with the same herbs, vegetables, molasses/treacle/sugar or ale or cider, as page 257. Cover with water and simmer very gently for 1 hour. Leave in the liquor for a couple of hours. Take the ham out and press it into the best shape you can. You can put it under a weighted board for a couple of hours, before removing it and glazing it in a hot oven as above.

It's not always easy to get a good shape to your ham hock but don't worry – if the ham collapses, simply shred the meat and you can still use it in salads, soups and sandwiches.

One of the best ways of using the meat is to shred it and fry with boiled and crushed potatoes to make ham hock hash. Serve with a fried duck egg on top and a sprinkling of parsley.

Cold ham hocks can be used in a variety of ways. Here are few of my favourites.

Slices served with:

a dish of puy lentils, parsley and beetroot

a potato salad and a celeriac rémoulade

hot red cabbage and boiled potatoes – a very colourful lunch,
    that is a treat for the eye as well as the stomach

Shredded and used in:

thick vegetable or bean soups

egg and potato tortilla

simple pea risotto

pasta fagioli – a borlotti or kidney bean stew cooked with a ham bone and pasta –
    very good for feeding lots of people

or with sautéed leeks as a filling for pasties

Dry five-spice belly pork with sticky rice and steamed pak choi

Serves 4

1kg piece of belly pork, scored into lines 2cm apart (ask your butcher to do this, or many sell pork belly already done this way)
2 tbsps five-spice powder

homemade five-spice mixture
4 star anise
2 tsps fennel seeds
2 tsps Sichuan pepper (substitute 1 tsp peppercorns and 1 tsp chilli flakes if stuck)
1 tsp cloves
1 tsp cinnamon

Although thought of as a cheap cut in Britain, pork belly is highly prized by Chinese cooks because it delivers three different textures: crisp outer skin, creamy fat and tender meat. Five-spice powder can be bought in Chinese, Vietnamese and Thai supermarkets. It's a mixture of at least five spices – star anise, cinnamon, cloves, fennel seeds and Sichuan pepper – supposed to exemplify the five basic tastes: sweet, sour, bitter, hot and salty. Making your own is very easy and makes for an even spicier marinade.

If you are making your own five-spice mixture, grind all the spices together in a spice grinder to a fine powder and keep in a jar to use as required.

The night before you are going to eat, take the belly pork out of the fridge and lay it skin-up on a rack (I use a cake-cooling rack) over the sink. Scald the skin with just-boiled water from the kettle – the skin should open up along the scores nicely – then pat with kitchen towel to dry the meat off. Place the meat on a plate, skin-side down and rub the spices into the flesh.

Put the belly pork back on the rack, flesh-side down and rub sea salt into the skin. Put a plate under the rack and cover the whole thing loosely with foil (you want air but not flies) and leave overnight. A meat-safe would be perfect here but the only person I know who still has one of those is my 95-year-old great aunt in Berwick-upon-Tweed.

The next day preheat the oven to 230°C/gas mark 9. Brush a little of the salt off the and put the meat in a very lightly oiled roasting tray, skin-side down. Place the meat in the oven and cook for 20 minutes. Turn the heat down to 180°C/gas mark 4 and cook for 30 minutes. Meanwhile, start preparing the rice (*see below*).

Take the meat out and turn it over using a spatula. Try to get the skin off in one piece without tearing it, return the skin and the meat side-by-side to the oven and cook for another 30 minutes. The meat should rest for about 10 minutes before you serve it. When the rice is cooked, cut the meat into long thin slices. You may need to use scissors to cut the crackling. Arrange on a plate with the pak choi and rice.

Sticky rice and pak choi
Serves 4

50g jasmine rice per adult and 25g per child
2 heads pak choi (approx.200g), washed and separated into leaves

Start cooking the rice about 45 minutes before you want to eat. Measure out the rice and wash it in a sieve until the water runs clear. Pour into the bottom of a large heavy bottomed saucepan and cover with fresh cold water to the level of one finger joint (about 2cm) above the rice. Place on the heat, cover and bring to the boil. Put the lid on slightly ajar and turn down the heat. Boil for about 10 minutes until all the water is absorbed (you should be able to see little steam holes in the rice). Now put the lid on very tightly – you may need to put a cloth under the rim to stop steam escaping – and turn down to a very, very low heat. Let it steam for another 10 minutes.

About 10 minutes before the pork is ready, place the pak choi on top of the rice and put the lid back on tightly, wrap the pan up in a tea towel and leave undisturbed on the worktop. There will be enough steam from the rice to wilt the pak choi.

MADELEINES FOR ANAÏS NIN

*One morning, when Henry was staying with us, after all his
starvation, sloppy meals, café-counter slobbery, I tried to give him a
beautiful breakfast. I came down and lit the fire in the fireplace.
Emilia brought, on a green tray, hot coffee, steaming milk, soft boiled
eggs, good bread and biscuits, and the freshest butter. Henry sat by
the fire at the lacquered table. All he could say was that he longed for
the bistro round the corner, the zinc counter, the dull greenish coffee
and milk full of skin.*

*I was not offended. I thought that he lacked a certain capacity for
enjoying the uncommon, that is all. I might be down in the dumps a
hundred times, but each time I would clamber out again to good
coffee on a lacquered tray beside an open fire. Each time I would
clamber out to silk stockings and perfume. Luxury is not a necessity
to me, but beautiful and good things are.*

Anaïs Nin - *Henry and June*

It seems apt that having started with the clink of Colette's wine bottles I should end
with something from Anaïs Ninn whose love of good things inspired this recipe.
Homemade madeleines must surely qualify as an 'uncommon' pleasure and I like to
imagine that Anaïs would have enjoyed carefully arranging a tray with a plateful of
these small scallop-shaped cakes, a juicy orange and some good coffee.

Henry Miller, silk stockings, and lacquered tables may seem worlds away from an
allotment in winter but there is something in the spirit with which Anaïs approaches her
breakfast that keeps me going when it is cold and bleak outside. There is no glamour
and very little beauty to be found on my plot in deep mid-winter. But on a dark day in
January I am cheered by the elegant scribble of a few withered brown sunflowers rattling
in the wind and a silvery cloud of seagulls whirling above the dump. This time of year
is known as the hungry gap, a month or so when little home-grown produce is available
and apart from a few vibrant green mustard leaves there is nothing for me to pick. But
there are still jobs I can do. As well as tidying up the shrivelled remains of last year's
crops, I can spread manure and in doing so look forward to bigger and better crops next

year. A giant mountain of muck has been dumped on the road beside the gate for plot-holders to help themselves to. As I fork a load onto my wheelbarrow and trundle it down to my plot I can see the skeleton of the site revealed; repeating rectangles of brown earth split down the middle by a winding muddy track.

I heap up manure around the fruit trees and notice shiny, tightly-closed dark brown buds on the greengage and one wrinkled rhubarb leaf just showing above ground; both hold out the promise of spring days. My hands are chapped and rough from digging, my knuckles pink from the cold. It is desolate here now but in just a few months these plots will be covered with new growth, bright poppies, tall speckled beans and the intermittent splash of egg-yolk yellow gourd flowers. Until then there is nothing to do but feed the soil, kick the sticky mud off my boots and head home for sweet and delicious morsels.

Madeleines
Makes 20–24

100g unsalted butter (plus a little soft butter for greasing the tin)
1 tbsp runny honey
3 eggs
75g caster sugar
1 tsp grated lemon zest
100g plain flour
1 tsp baking powder
1 tbsp ground almonds (optional)

A good kitchen shop should sell you a madeleine tray (a tin tray with a double row of scallop-shaped indentations). As well as a breakfast-time treat, madeleines make a lovely pudding served with compotes or a comforting treat on their own with a cup of coffee or tea.

Grease a madeleine tray or two (you will probably have enough batter to make nearly 2 tray-loads). Put the butter in a small pan over a low heat with the honey, letting it bubble gently until it is melted.

In a large mixing bowl (or the bowl of your food mixer), break the eggs and whisk with the sugar and lemon zest until light, thick and doubled in volume (this takes longer than you think).

Into another large mixing bowl, sift the flour and baking powder and add the almonds if you are using them. Fold the flour into the egg and sugar gently, keeping as much air in as possible. Pour the honey and butter mixture in from the side and gently fold that in too. Allow to rest, with cling film on top, until you are ready to make the madeleines (at least 20 minutes and not more than 3 hours).

Preheat the oven to 190°C/gas mark 5.

Spoon the batter into the moulds – about halfway up – and cook for 8–12 minutes (the madeleines should be a nice golden colour, not pale and anaemic, and springy when you prod them).

Allow the madeleines to cool slightly and harden before using a knife to pop them out onto a plate (make sure it's a pretty one).

The second batch, to be eaten later on (unless you are exceptionally greedy or have a houseful) can be dusted with icing sugar when cool. Madeleines keep well and look nice in a tall jar.

BASICS

STERILISING

Sterilising jam jars or glass bottles

Put your scrupulously clean, washed and dried jam jars or bottles into a cold oven without the lids. Turn the oven on to 170°C/gas mark 3 and put the timer on for 20 minutes. When the bell goes, turn off the oven leaving the jars inside. When ready, pour in the jam, jelly, chutney or syrup while the jars are still hot.

If you are making chutney or pickles with vinegar make sure you use jars with glass or plastic coated lids as vinegar corrodes metal. I never buy special preserving jars but use up empty jam and pickle jars, most of which have vinegar-proof lids. If not, just place a disc of greaseproof paper on top of the pickle or chutney.

Sterilising bottled sauce or whole tomatoes

Have ready your sterilised and filled Kilner jars or preserving jars. Kilner jars must be fastened securely before being put in the sterilising saucepan (the clip lifts up as the vacuum is formed). Screw-band jar lids should be screwed on loosely during processing and then fastened tightly after the 40-minute boiling period. Kilner jars can be re-used provided you always use new orange sealing rings each time.

Place the jars in a large saucepan. The jars should not touch each other or the bottom of the pan – you can stand them on a trivet (a wire frame with little legs) but if you don't have one then a couple of folded tea towels will do. Wrap the jars in tea towels to stop them knocking together. The jars should be covered with water. Make sure you put the pan lid on firmly with a cloth underneath to stop steam escaping. Heat very gently to the boil and simmer for 40 minutes. Turn off the heat and use a cup to bail out the water so that you can remove the bottles with an oven glove or cloth. Place on a wooden board (any contact with a cold surface may cause the glass to crack). If using screw-band jars, tighten them up immediately. Leave until the next day before putting away in a cool, dark cupboard.

MARMALADE AND JELLY

Lemon and ugly lime marmalade

6 lemons
1 ugly lime
2 round juicy Indian limes
2 yellow grapefruit
3 litres water
approx. 2.5 kg unbleached granulated sugar

One summer we spent two sun-dazzled weeks in a hamlet right on the edge of the Aegean. Three doors down lived an old lady who spent her days peacefully sitting out on the terrace of her small stone house. In her yard grew a lime tree; one afternoon as we walked past on our way for a swim she handed me one of its fruits and motioned for me to scratch the peel with my thumbnail and then sniff. When I inhaled, the aromatic burst of citrus oil had an instantly stimulating effect. Months later, while shopping for mangoes in my local Indian supermarket I came across some very large, very ugly knobbly-looking limes and decided to perform the same trick. The unprepossessing fruit gave off an incredible citrus zing and inspired me to make this marmalade, which has an almost sherbet-like kick.

Working on a tip from the checkout clerk (who had observed me buying limes over a couple of years), I now also add the big, sweet, juicy limes used all over India to make the ubiquitous lime and soda drink. Their sweet flavour nicely rounds out the bitterness of the ugly limes (more commonly called kaffir limes). This marmalade makes a good Christmas present for anyone who loves eating homemade marmalade. They will usually have run out by Christmas and be suffering marmalade withdrawal, waiting desperately for the new season Sevilles to arrive in mid January.

Scrub the lemons and limes and cut in half. Squeeze out the juice and pips (the ugly lime will not be very juicy). Put the juice in a jug and save the pips for later.

Meanwhile, cut the lemon and Indian lime halves into very thin julienne strips (or to your own preference). Place in the preserving pan.

The ugly lime and the grapefruit will have a lot of pith so peel off their skin with a potato peeler. Cut the pith from the flesh of the grapefruit, remove any pips, chop the flesh of the grapefruit roughly and add the flesh to the pan. Place the peeled ugly limes, the grapefruit pith and all the pips into a muslin jelly bag and tie it up with string. Chop the ugly lime and grapefruit peel into very fine strips and add to the pan.

Add the water to the pan, along with the jelly bag. Bring to the boil and simmer gently for 1–1½ hours, or until the peel is soft enough to be rubbed apart very easily with your fingernail. Make sure the peel is really well cooked because, once you add the sugar, the peel will never get any softer. When the peel is soft, take the jelly bag out and place in a sieve over the pan, squeezing the bag with tongs to get as much juice out as you can (there is lots of pectin in the pith and pips which will help to make your marmalade set well).

Remove the pan from the heat and pour the mixture into a bowl. Put the mixture back into the pan using a measuring jug, counting as you go. For every 500ml of marmalade mixture add 450g sugar. Add the juice you reserved earlier and put on a low heat. Bring to a simmer, stirring occasionally, until the sugar is fully dissolved. Turn up the heat and bring to a fast boil, then boil rapidly for 15–25 minutes. Start testing sooner rather than later as marmalade reaches its setting point early. You can test either with a sugar thermometer or by using the wrinkle test (*see page 270*). Whilst you are boiling up the marmalade, sterilise your jam jars (*see page 266*).

Let the marmalade cool (skimming off any impurities) for 30 minutes, stirring occasionally so the peel is evenly distributed before pouring into your warm jam jars and sealing down. Store in a cool, dark place. I don't bother using a wax paper seal – these days most jam jar lids seem to have a plastic coating – but I do make sure I never use a jar that's had pickles in it as you can never completely get the taste out.

Zested Seville jelly
Makes 3 jars

3 Seville oranges
(about 400g)
1.5 litres water
juice of 1 lemon
approx. 750g unbleached
granulated sugar

Making a small amount of anything is far less daunting in terms of time (and cost, too, if it turns out to be a complete disaster). The relatively small amounts involved in this recipe mean it will set much more easily, and there is no tedious chopping which makes it a good recipe for marmalade virgins and those who like their marmalade very fine. Jellies are useful things to have in the cupboard as they can always be melted and used as glazes for fruit tarts.

Zest the oranges anyway you like. If your kitchen is anything like mine it probably contains a variety of different grating implements. I do mine on a Microplane grater. Reserve the zest. An alternative for those who like a small amount of peel is to peel and finely cut the rind of one of the oranges and simply squeeze the other two without zesting.

Halve the denuded fruit and squeeze the juice out of them. Reserve the juice, straining out the pips. Cut the fruit into quarters and place in a jelly bag with the pips. Add the zest, water and the jelly bag to the pan, boil for 1 hour or so or until the zest is soft. Remove the jelly bag with tongs and squeeze it over the pan; the pectin is in the pips and pith so this will help it set.

Remove the pan from the heat and pour the mixture into a bowl. Add the reserved orange juice and the lemon juice. Put the mixture back into the pan with a jug, measuring as you go. For every 500ml of marmalade mixture add 450g sugar. Turn up the heat and simmer gently, stirring all the time until the sugar has completely dissolved. Boil fast until the setting point is reached. You can use a sugar thermometer or do the flake test (*see below*). Pour into sterilised jam jars and seal (*see page 266*).

Testing your jelly or marmalade

The flake test (for jelly)

Collect some jelly with a wooden spoon and then, holding it horizontally over the sink, let the jelly cool a little before tipping the spoon. If the jelly hangs down slightly pendulously and hesitates for a few seconds before dropping off, it is ready.

The wrinkle test (for marmalade)

Put a couple of saucers in the freezer when you start boiling up your marmalade. After about 10 minutes take a saucer out of the freezer. Put a teaspoon of marmalade on the saucer. Give it a minute then push the jelly with your finger. If it wrinkles you have reached the setting point.

If this all sounds too subjective for you, buy a sugar thermometer and heat the mixture up to the point where it says 'jam'.

Jelly bags

You can buy an actual jelly bag from a kitchen shop or just make one yourself out of a square of muslin or cotton. I once made such an enormous quantity of apple jelly (6kg) that I ended up using a cotton laundry bag – the pillowcase-shaped kind you get from hotels. Scald your jelly bag by pouring boiling water through it before you use it.

What you are aiming for is to suspend your jelly bag above a bowl so that the juice can drip through. If you have a stool then turn it upside down and tie a corner of your cotton square to each leg. If you don't have a stool you could put two dining room chairs back to back, or do as I do which is to suspend it from the bottom of my wall-mounted plate rack. If you want a clear jelly never squeeze your jelly bag. (This doesn't apply to marmalade jellies where the bag is boiled with the fruit.)

PASTRIES AND DOUGH

Pâte sablée or flaky pastry for tarts
Makes enough pastry for 2 tarts (1 for today, 1 to freeze)

250g plain flour
a pinch of sea salt
1 tbsp icing sugar (for sweet tarts)
175g butter (slightly soft, i.e. 10 minutes out of the fridge), cut into small pieces
60ml very cold water

This crispy, buttery pastry is adapted from Alice Waters' galette dough given in the *Chez Panisse Menu Cookbook*. It is easy to make and is great rolled out flat on a baking sheet and strewn with fruit or vegetables to make the simplest of tarts. You can also use it more conventionally in a tart tin, blind-baked and filled with either a savoury or sweet custard.

In a bowl combine the flour, salt, icing sugar (if making a sweet tart) and half the butter cut into small pieces. Use your fingertips to work it to fine breadcrumbs. Use a fork to work the rest of the butter quickly into the breadcrumb mixture, leaving large marble-sized blobs of butter (this will make the pastry much flakier).

Add the water and draw the mixture together. It doesn't matter if it's quite sticky. Pull the mixture apart into 2 balls and then use a large square of cling film to scoop up one of the balls. Make sure everything is safely inside the plastic, then knead the dough lightly through the plastic for a minute or two. Do the same with the other ball. Let the dough rest for 30 minutes in the fridge (you can make it a day ahead) or put it in the freezer and use it another time. This recipe makes enough for two tarts which is very handy for when you suddenly feel the urge for an impossibly buttery crumbly treat but haven't got time to make pastry.

Grease a 20cm quiche tin and place in the fridge (keeping everything cool stops the pastry shrinking).

Preheat the oven to 200°C/gas mark 6 and place a baking sheet in the oven.

Roll out the pastry very thin on a lightly floured worksurface and use a rolling pin to lift it into your quiche tin. Slide a large flat knife underneath the pastry if it's sticking. Don't worry if it rips a bit – you can always squish it back together again. You may have a small amount of raw pastry left over. Don't eat it; you may need this to repair holes. Wrap it up in a bit of cling film for later.

Cover the tart with baking parchment and fill with baking beans or dried pulses. Bake for 15 minutes with the parchment on and another 15 with it off (check after 10 minutes to make sure it is not browning too much).

When the case is crisp and an appealing golden-brown, take it out and fill it with whatever you like and bake it again – perhaps a savoury tart of allotment greens, or apple cooked with cinnamon and glistening with a syrup made from the apple peelings. If it is rhubarb time, I can never resist the chance to end a meal with the bright pink and yellow of a rhubarb-and-custard tart.

Yeasted tart dough

1 tbsp dried yeast (5g)
a pinch of caster sugar
50ml warm water
125g plain flour
1 egg
½ tsp sea salt
1 tsp of grated lemon zest
3 tbsps softened butter (60g),
plus more to grease the tin

When I can't be bothered with a real pastry shell, I make this crunchy hybrid of pastry and dough instead. Yeasted pastries take all the pain out of tart making. There is no need for tedious rolling out and prebaking. The dough is elastic, so no holes ever appear in the bottom of the tart and you never get a soggy bottom. I can't claim to have thought up yeasted pastry myself; I first read about it in Annie Somerville's *Fields of Greens*, where she freely admits to discovering it in Elizabeth David. Good ideas are meant to be passed around.

In a teacup, mix the dried yeast with the sugar and warm water. Put a saucer on top and let it froth up, in this way you can be sure the yeast is still active. This will avoid disappointment when your dough fails to rise because of geriatric yeast.

Place the flour in a bowl and make a well in the centre. Crack the egg into this hole. Pour in the yeast mixture. Add the salt and lemon zest and then the butter. Draw the dough together with a fork and form into a ball with a little extra flour. Put a plate on top of the bowl and leave it double in size (this takes about an hour). The kitchen is usually a warm enough place to do this.

Grease a 20cm tart tin with butter and put it in the fridge until you are ready to use it.

After an hour's rising, take the pastry ball (you may have to scrape it out of the bowl with a spatula) and put it in the centre of the buttered tart tin. Start pushing it down into the pastry tin with the heel of your hand using a little extra flour if it gets a bit sticky. It might look like there isn't going to be enough but gradually the dough will thin out from the centre and you will have enough to push well up the sides of the tin.

Fill with whatever vegetables are freshest and tastiest from the garden (*for recipes see the sections on sorrel, garlic, wild leaves and courgettes*). Cook in an oven preheated to 180°C/gas mark 4 for about 40–45 minutes or until risen and golden-brown.

Basic half-fat-to-flour pastry for pies, pasties and tarts (shortcrust pastry)

400g plain flour
200g cold unsalted butter
a pinch of sea salt
very cold water

You can vary the amount of pastry depending on what you are making; just make sure you always stick to half fat to flour.

Make sure the butter has come straight from the fridge and is very cold. Place the flour, butter and salt in the bowl of the food processor or Kenwood. Use a sharp knife to cut the butter into 2cm cubes. I find it easier to cut the butter when it's a bit floury. Turn on the mixer and blend until the flour and butter resembles fine breadcrumbs. Add a little very cold water until the pastry just starts to come together. Wrap up in cling film and place in the fridge until you are ready to use. The pastry will keep for a day or two in the fridge or can be wrapped in foil or cling film and frozen. Take it out of the freezer a good 4 hours before you want to use it.

Variations

If you want to make sweet pastry, take out a heaped tablespoon of flour and add the same amount of icing sugar.

If you are making a savoury tart with green vegetables such as courgettes or spinach a little finely grated lemon zest is always welcome. Grate it straight in with the flour at the beginning. My grandmother added a tablespoon of grated Parmesan to her pastry.

Pizza dough
Makes 2 medium-sized pizzas

*250g Italian OO pasta flour
or strong white bread flour
1 tsp salt
1 tbsp dried yeast
160ml lukewarm water
1 pinch of sugar*

In a mixing bowl, combine the flour and the salt.

In a jug dissolve the yeast and the water. Add the sugar, put a saucer on top and let it froth up (about 5 minutes).

Add the yeast liquid to the flour, mixing well to obtain a dough. If it's a bit too wet to handle, use a little more flour to shape the dough into a ball, cover the bowl with cling film and let it rest for 5 minutes. Either using the dough attachment on a Kenwood, KitchenAid or other food mixer knead the dough for 6 minutes, or knead it by hand for 8 minutes. You want to end up with a smooth, pliable ball. Divide the dough and shape into 2 round balls. Flour a chopping board and put the balls on the board with plenty of space between them and cover with a floured tea towel. Leave to rise for 30 minutes. It is then ready to use.

SPICES AND STOCK

Pickling Spices

2 star anise
1 tsp black mustard seeds
1 tsp cumin seeds
4 dried red chillies or 1 tsp
chilli flakes
8 black peppercorns
3 cardamom pods, cracked
open
1 tsp coriander seeds
3 cloves
a few shards or
½ stick cinnamon
2 slices of whole nutmeg

These can vary a bit according to what's in your cupboard; just be wary of using too much of any one spice, particularly something strong like cloves.

Mix all the spices together and put about 1 tablespoon of them into a cup, saving the rest for another day. Take a little square of cotton, about 10x10cm (a clean cut-up tea towel or T-shirt would do). Scald the cloth with boiling water from the kettle and lay the spices in the centre. Tie up firmly with string (you don't want them to escape).

Homemade chicken stock

*1 whole chicken carcass
(or 2 carcasses without leg
and thigh bones
from the butcher)
the green parts of 1 leek
1 carrot
1 onion
1 celery heart or
2 celery sticks
6 whole black peppercorns
1 clove garlic*

*bouquet garni (a bunch of
parsley stalks tied together
with a few herbs such as 1
stalk lovage, a sprig – but no
more – of rosemary, 1 sage
leaf, a few chives or onion
tops, 1 bay leaf)*

If you can get into the habit of converting old roast chicken carcasses into stock you will always have a good supply of stock in the freezer – an essential tool for the home cook. Good butchers should sell you stripped carcasses (ones without the leg and thigh bones) for next to nothing, which is another good way of making stock. What you put into your stock depends a little on what you have in the fridge – just avoid potatoes (they will make your stock cloudy) and over-boiling which will ruin the flavour. For aromatic Asian broths simply switch parsley stalks and English herbs for coriander roots, lemongrass, ginger, cinnamon and star anise.

Put all ingredients in a large pan and just cover with water. Bring to the boil and simmer very gently for one hour (you may like to do it for longer but I like a lighter, fresher-tasting stock). Let the carcass sit in the stock for another 40 minutes. Strain the stock through a fine meshed sieve, allow to cool completely and then refrigerate. If you are not going to use the stock immediately then freeze it. Homemade stock goes off after 3 days but only takes minutes to defrost. Don't leave in a warm kitchen for hours; stock is a wonderful medium for growing bacteria.

BIBLIOGRAPHY

Battiscombe, Georgina, *English Picnics*, Harvill, London 1949

Bedford, Sybille, *A Visit to Don Otavio*, Eland, London 2002

Boulestin, X. Marcel,

— *Recipes of Boulestin*, Heinemann, London 1971

— *Myself, My Two Countries*, Heinemann, London 1933

Brillat-Savarin, Jean Anthelme, *Physiologie du Goût*, Chatto & Windus, London 1889

Brissenden, Rosemary, *South East Asian Food*, Grub Street, London 2003

Bunyard, Edward, *The Anatomy of Dessert*, Chatto & Windus, London 1933

Colette –

— *Break of Day*, Secker & Warburg, London 1961

— *Earthly Paradise*, Secker & Warburg, London 1966

— *Cheri*, Secker & Warburg, London 1951

— *Flowers and Fruit*, Secker & Warburg, London 1986

David, Elizabeth –

— *French Country Cooking*, John Lehman, London 1951

— *Italian Food*, Penguin, London 1989

— *Spices, Salts and Aromatics in the English Kitchen*, Grub Street, London 2000

Davidson, Alan, *Penguin Companion to Food*, Penguin, London 2002

Dowding, Charles, *Salad Leaves For All Seasons*, Green Books, Totnes, Devon, 2007

Fisher, M.F.K., *With Bold Knife and Fork*, Vintage Classics, London 2001

Grahame, Kenneth, *The Wind In The Willows*, Methuen, London 1988

Gray, Patience –

— *The Centaur's Kitchen*, Prospect Books, Devon 2005

— *Honey From a Weed*, Prospect Books, Devon 2001

— *Work, Adventure, Childhood, Dreams*, Edizione Leucasia, 1999

Grigson, Geoffrey –

— *An Englishman's Flora*, Aldeine Press, London 1955

— *A Herbal of All Sorts*, Phoenix House, London 1959

Grigson, Jane –

— *Vegetable Book*, Penguin, London 1979

— *English Food*, Penguin, London 1974

Henderson, Fergus & Gellatly, Justin Piers, *Beyond Nose to Tail Eating*, Bloomsbury, London 2007

Hopkinson, Simon, *Roast Chicken and Other Stories Part 2*, Macmillan, London 2002

Jaffrey, Madhur, *Indian Cookery*, BBC Books, London 1982

Larkcom, Joy, *The Organic Salad Garden*, Frances Lincoln, London 2001

Lloyd, Christopher, *Gardener Cook*, Frances Lincoln, London 1997

M.A.F.F. – *Domestic Preservation of Fruit and Food*, Bulletin 21, 1962

Narayan, R.K., *A Malgudi Omnibus*, Vintage, London 1999

Nin, Anaïs, *Henry and June*, Penguin, London 1992

Olney, Richard –
— *Simple French Food*, Grub Street, London 2003
— *Reflexions*, Brick Tower Press, New York 1999

Pallister, Minnie, *A Cabbage for a Year*, Blackie & Son, Glasgow, 1934

Patten, Marguerite, *Jams, Preserves and Chutneys*, Grub Street, London 2001

Pomiane, Edouard, *Cooking with Pomiane*, Cookery Book Club, London 1969

Roden, Claudia, *Mediterranean Cookery*, BBC Books, London 1987

Samuelsson, Marcus, *Aquavit and the new Scandinavian Cuisine*, Houghton Mifflin, New York 2003

Shwarz, Oded, *Preserving*, Dorling Kindersley, London 1997

Shephard, Sue, *Pickled, Potted & Canned*, Headline, London 2000

Somerville, Annie, *Fields of Greens*, Bantam Press, London 1993

Spry, Constance –
— *The Constance Spry Cookery Book*, Dent, London 1956
— *Come into The Garden Cook*, Dent, London 1942

Stein, Rick, *English Seafood Cookery*, Penguin, London 1988

Toklas, Alice B., *The Alice B. Toklas Cookbook*, Penguin, London 1954

Waters, Alice –
— *Chez Panisse Menu Cookbook*, Random House, New York 1982
— *Chez Panisse Vegetables*, Harper Collins, New York 1996

Wifstrand, Selma, *Favourite Swedish Recipes*, Dover, London 1995

Wordsworth, Dorothy, *Journals of Dorothy Wordsworth*, OUP, Oxford 1958

SEEDS

Seed Merchants

Edwin Tucker & Sons Ltd
www.edwintucker.com
tel 01364 652233

The Real Seed Catalogue
www.realseeds.co.uk
tel 01239821107

Thompson & Morgan
www.thompson-morgan.com
tel 01473 695225

Chiltern Seeds
www.chilternseeds.co.uk
tel 01229 581137

Jennifer Birch (supplier of seed garlic)
Garfield Villa, Belle Vue Road, Stroud, Gloucs GL5 1JP
tel/fax 01453 750 371

ACKNOWLEDGEMENTS

This book could not exist without my vegetable garden. I am very grateful to the London Borough of Waltham Forest for providing me with a plot and I will always be in debt to Frank Ronan, for his very wise suggestion that I get an allotment. For their various kindnesses and support while I was writing this book I would also like to thank most sincerely: Stephen, Beatrice, Hannah and Matilda Brierley, Tim Barnes, Katherine Tulloh, Jemima Lewis, Claire Ptak, Kate Leys, Sharon Duckworth, Hattie Ellis and Michaela De Mori. I also owe thanks to Ronan Bennett for encouraging me and for introducing me to David Godwin, whose enthusiasm for this book was so important. My editors at Chatto & Windus, Alison Samuel and Poppy Hampson, have granted me everything I asked for and given most helpful criticism. Final thanks go to the three people who have made this book beautiful: Jason Lowe, Andy English and Will Webb.

I would like to thank Random House for their permission to quote from P.G. Wodehouse's *Uneasy Money*, Colette's *Flowers and Fruit*, *Cheri*, *Break of Day* and *Earthly Paradise*, and R.K Narayan's *The Grandmother's Tale*; Oxford University Press for the extracts from Dorothy Wordsworth's *Grasmere Journals*; Bricktower Press for the various quotes from Richard Olney's *Reflexions*; Eland Press (www.travelbooks.co.uk) for the general inspiration provided by their superb list but in particular the permission to use the paragraph from Sybille Bedford's *A Visit to Don Otavio*; Prospect Books for the lines from John Evelyn's *Acetaria*; Grub Street for their permission to use lines from Richard Olney's *Simple French Food*; and Penguin for permission to use lines both from the *Alice B. Toklas Cookbook* by Alice B. Toklas and from *Henry and June* by Anaïs Nin; and Miranda and Nicholas Gray for permission to quote from *Work, Adventure, Childhood Dreams* by Patience Gray.

INDEX